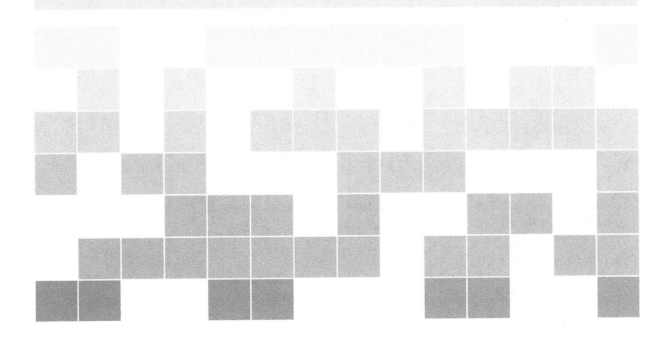

Machine Learning Handbook

Using R and Python

Dr. Karen Mazidi

Contents

Part Two: Linear Models

Part Three: Modern R

V   Part Five: Kernel Methods and Ensemble Methods

VII Part Seven: Neural Networks

VIII Part Eight: Modeling the World

IX   Part Nine: Supplementary Material

Preface to the First Edition

I accidentally started writing this book during Spring Break 2018. I was driving down a long Texas road out in the country, thinking about a problem with the undergraduate machine learning class I had been teaching. Chiefly, there was no book suitable for my course. There are several excellent machine learning books for graduate students, but most are too heavy on the math and too light on practical issues for undergraduate students. There are a few books for undergraduate students, but they didn't cover all the topics I was required to teach for my course at The University of Texas at Dallas. The solution I came up with was to format my own notes in latex. I scribbled an outline on a piece of paper as I drove down the road. When I came home I started looking for a suitable latex template and found this one which I really liked. It was designed for a book and I thought, why not just make this a book? And so the book began.

Many years ago I authored several textbooks on microprocessors and microcontrollers with my husband. These books were quite successful and provided a nice second income for our family. I was able to write the books at home while taking care of our two rambunctious sons. However, the days when one can write textbooks as a job are gone. As soon as a book is published, it is pirated, and the pdf is available for free to anyone in the world. That is not entirely a bad thing in my opinion. Yes it is stealing intellectual property from the owner but on the other hand it makes information available to people who want to learn but perhaps can't pay the exhorbitant price that publishing companies charge for textbooks. And so my goals are not monetary. The pdf of this book will remain free for my students, although there is a print version available on Amazon for those who prefer to read from paper. The Amazon print book is printed in grayscale to keep the cost low.

My goals in writing this book are the following:
- To create an undergraduate book that covers the most popular machine learning algorithms in a hands-on approach that reinforces understanding of the algorithms.
- To provide an accessible introduction to the field to professionals who want to get started with machine learning.
- To increase the number of practitioners in the field. I believe that machine learning is to the present and future what computer programming was in the 1970s when I started: a revolutionary new way of solving problems.
- To help people enhance their skill set. If I can introduce people to these skills it will help them in their career goals.

I hope you enjoy the book. The book covers what I teach in a one-semester undergraduate Introduction to Machine Learning course, and it is a work in progress.

Preface to the Second Edition

I always tell my students to learn both R and Python, since both look great on your resume. The primary motivation for this 2nd edition was to facilitate this advice.

The goals for the second edition of the book are the following:
- To provide an accessible introduction to both R and Python for machine learning.
- To augment the base R code with an introduction to modern R tidyverse code so that students are comfortable writing code with either syntax.
- To increase the variety of data sets and code examples.

The book was designed along with the following external resources:
- A companion GitHub site for code samples: `https://github.com/kjmazidi/Machine_Learning_2nd_edition/`
- Companion videos are available here: `https://www.youtube.com/c/JaniceMazidi`

Part One: Introduction to Machine Learning

1. The Craft of Machine Learning

This handbook provides an introduction to machine learning using R and Python. No prior experience with machine learning, R, or Python is necessary to learn from this book. The target audience is upper-level undergraduate or postgraduate students in computer science, as well as other disciplines, since machine learning has found application in a wide variety of fields from the social sciences, biological sciences, economics, and more. The handbook will also be a good resource for professionals wanting to get started with machine learning. Prior courses in linear algebra, probability and statistics are assumed; however, the book attempts to fill in as much detail as needed for the subject at hand. This is a handbook[1], not a textbook. A few practice problems are provided with the assumption that more problems will be provided by your instructor. In these days where solutions to textbook problems are found online, for a price, there is not much educational value to be had in end-of-chapter problems.

The aim of this handbook is to provide an introduction to the craft of machine learning through conceptual explanations of the algorithms and small examples of running the algorithms in R and Python. Sample notebooks are provided on the author's github at: `https://github.com/kjmazidi/Machine_Learning_2nd_edition`.

Figure 1.1 shows fields related to machine learning. Machine learning would not be possible without the fields surrounding it in the figure. Statistics and probability form the mathematical foundations of many of the algorithms described in this book. AI and computer science pushed the frontiers of what computers could do which made machine learning possible.

---

[1]A reference work providing guidance for a technical application or art.

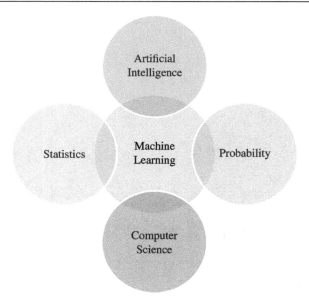

Figure 1.1: Fields Related to Machine Learning

1.1 Machine Learning

The term *machine learning* is an umbrella term for many closely related fields. Some statisticians call machine learning *statistical learning*. The field of *data science* and the task of *data mining* often involve machine learning techniques, coupled with more data exploration and analysis.

Machine learning has received varied definitions as the field developed. This book proposes the following definition:

Definition 1.1.1 — Machine Learning. Machine learning trains computers to accurately recognize patterns in data for purposes of data analysis, prediction, and/or action selection by autonomous agents.

The key words in this definition are: data, patterns, predictions, and actions, along with the caveat: accurate. Let's examine these in detail.

1.1.1 Data

Nothing can be learned without data. The data and what we wish to learn from the data go hand in hand. For many learning scenarios, data takes the form of a table of values where each row represents one data example, and columns represent attributes or features of the examples. One learning scenario, clustering, seeks to group like instances. Another learning scenario, supervised learning, seeks to learn about one feature based on combinations of the other features. Data can take other forms besides tables, such as a set of actions weighted by features that represent the current environment.

The data used in this handbook is small and neat compared to data you will encounter in real-world machine learning problems. This is by design, so that focus can be placed on the algorithms and how they learn from data. Just be aware that in real-world scenarios, more of your time will be spent in data gathering and data cleaning than in the actual machine learning.

When gathering data or using data from other sources, ethical considerations must always guide our actions. Who owns the data? Who are the subjects of the data? Has the data been anonymized? Did the subjects give consent for the use of the data? How will the analysis of this data be used? How might it impact the subjects in the data as well as the larger community?

1.1.2 Patterns

The best *general* pattern recognition machine is the human mind, but computers can in many cases beat human performance on narrowly defined tasks. The ability to recognize patterns in data enables algorithms to learn things like whether someone is a good credit risk, whether two people might be compatible, whether the object outlined in sensors is a human or a dark spot on the pavement.

When beginning a real-world machine learning project, how do you know what to look for? From raw data, organized data must be built. Once the data is organized, decisions must be made about what could be learned and what is important to learn from the data. These decisions often need to be in concert with domain experts and/or the owners and users of the data who wish to learn from it.

1.1.3 Predictions from Data

Learning patterns in data enables us to predict outcomes on future data – data the algorithm has never before seen. Predictions may simply involve finding similar instances in the data, or predicting a target value which may be quantitative or qualitative.

In the examples in this book, generally we train algorithms on a portion of the data and use the remaining data to test and evaluate how well the trained model can perform on previously unseen data. This is a common situation in machine learning, sometimes called batch learning because the data is fed into the algorithm in one batch. There are other approaches, however, such as online learning in which the algorithm is continually learning from newly available data and being evaluated in real time. Online learning techniques can also be used when the available data is too large to be stored in memory. An alternate approach to handle big data is to do parallel distributed machine learning, often in the cloud with specialized software.

1.1.4 Accuracy

Predictions must be accurate or they are not predictions but random guesses. Typically, predictions should beat some predetermined baseline approach. For example if 99% of the observations in a credit data set did not default on their loans, the goal is to beat a simple baseline that always guesses "not default" and has 99% accuracy. Machine learning makes use of many measurement techniques to gauge accuracy and evaluate performance of the algorithms. Many of these metrics are used to evaluate the training model itself and others will be used to evaluate performance on a held-out test set.

1.1.5   Actions

Every day more autonomous agents enter our lives, from smart thermostats, to automated assistants, to self-driving vehicles. These agents take actions based on what they have learned, and most continue to learn over time, usually by uploading data to a central learning repository. Some actions taken by autonomous agents will be controversial in the coming decades as ethical and legal issues evolve in response to humans co-existing with autonomous agents. The big players in AI are at the forefront of autonomous agents because they have the resources, expertise, and data to pursue big projects. In the future, we expect the development of autonomous agents to be available to more developers.

1.2   Machine Learning Scenarios

There are scores of machine learning algorithms with countless variations each. This book describes the most common algorithms, while providing a foundation for students to learn more algorithms on their own. There are many ways to classify machine learning algorithms, and not all algorithms fit neatly into categories but the following is a general overview.

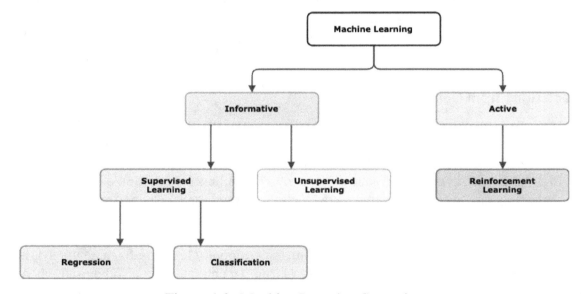

Figure 1.2: Machine Learning Scenarios

1.2.1   Informative v. Active

Most machine learning algorithms covered in this book are **informative** algorithms used for data analysis or prediction. These informative algorithms input data observations and output a model of the data that can then be used to predict outcomes for new data fed into the model. In contrast, the field of Reinforcement Learning teaches **active** agents to identify optimal actions given the current environment and what has been learned in past experience. The input to these algorithms for initial training comes in the form of data but some agents may continue to learn with sensors and other input methods that let them learn from the environment.

1.2.2 Supervised v. unsupervised learning

Informative algorithms are of two main types. The term **supervised learning** refers to scenarios where each data instance has a label. This label is used to train the algorithm so that labels can be predicted for future data items. The term **unsupervised learning** refers to scenarios where data does not have labels and the goal is simply to learn more about the data.

1.2.3 Regression v. classification

Supervised learning algorithms fall into two major groups. In **regression**, the target (or label) is a real-numbered **quantitative** value, like trying to predict the market value of a home given its square footage and other data. In **classification**, the target is **qualitative**, a class, like predicting if a borrower is a good credit risk or not, given their income, outstanding credit balance, and other predictors.

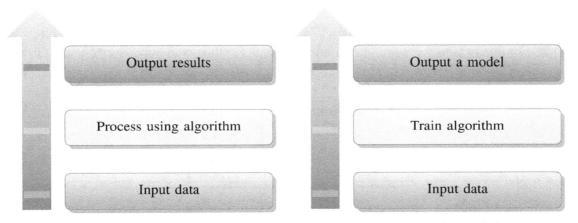

Figure 1.3: Traditional Programming (Left) v. Machine Learning (Right)

1.3 Machine learning v. traditional algorithms

Machine learning algorithms are different from traditional algorithms encountered in computer programming. Figure 1.3 shows the traditional computer programming paradigm on the left: data is fed into code that processes it and outputs the results of the processing. In the same figure, the machine learning paradigm is on the right: data is fed into an algorithm which builds and outputs a model of the data. In traditional programming, all knowledge is explicitly encoded in the algorithm by programmers using code statements, loops, and conditional statements. Therefore, knowledge must be known beforehand. In machine learning, knowledge is inferred from data. Knowledge is discovered.

Why do we need machine learning? Can't we just explicitly code algorithms for problems? There are two typical situations in which traditional programming cannot be used to solve problems. The first type is when it is not possible to encode all the rules needed to solve a problem. How would you encode rules for recognizing faces in photos? We don't even know the rules we use in our minds to recognize faces so it would not be possible to encode rules. However, we can train computers to recognize key edges and regions of photos that are likely to be faces. The second type of situation in which traditional programming cannot be used to solve a problem is when the scale of the problem is too large. If a company has huge amounts of customer data it would take millions of human hours to find useful patterns in the data that could be then extracted programmatically. Machine learning algorithms can find patterns quickly in large amounts of data.

As we go through the material in this handbook you will learn several machine learning algorithms. These algorithms typically have statistical and probabilistic foundations which we will explore. However, beyond the theory and technique, machine learning is also a craft as well as a science. Each major Part of the book devotes a chapter pointing out some innovations, ideas, and techniques from this evolving craft.

1.4 Terminology

Machine learning grew out of statistics and probability, computer science, as well as other fields. For this reason there are often multiple terms for the same thing. Let's start with names for data. The table below contains a sample data set (with headings).

GPA	Hours	SAT	Class
3.2	15	1450	Junior
3.8	21	1420	Sophomore
2.5	9	1367	Freshman

Table 1.1: Student GPA, Average Hours Studied/Week, SAT, Class

The table has 3 rows of data. Each row is a sample data point, also called an **example**, **instance**, or an **observation**. Each column in the table is an **attribute**, also called a **feature** or a **predictor**. The data has 4 features: GPA, average number of hours studied per week, SAT score, and classification. The first 3 are **quantitative**, or numeric, features while Class is a **qualitative** feature because it can only take on one of a finite set of values. Qualitative features are also called **factors** or **categorical data**.

If we want to learn GPA as a function of the other 3 features, we say that GPA is our **target**, or **response**, variable while the other 3 are **features** or **predictors**. If we want to predict SAT then SAT would be our target and all other columns our predictors.

1.5 **Notation**

This book uses the following notation conventions for data:

- x_i subscript i indexes observations in a data set; i ranges from 1 to N, the number of observations (rows) in the data set
- $x_{i,j}$ subscript j indexes predictors in a data set; j ranges from 1 to P, the number of predictors (columns) in the data set. Here we are referencing predictor j from observation i.
- In matrix notation, lower case letters like x represent scalars, bold face lower case letters like **x** represent vectors, and upper case bold face letters like **X** represent matrices.

2. Learning Base R

The goal of the book is to learn how to use both R and Python for machine learning. So why start with R? The main reason is that the early algorithms explored in the book have been used by statisticians for decades in R, and consequently the output of functions are more explanatory than the corresponding functions in Python. R is simple enough for programming novices to learn and a breeze for computer scientists. Everything in R is built in. You can switch seamlessly from data cleaning, to data analysis, to creating plots, to running machine learning algorithms, to performing statistical analysis on your results.

R is open source, supported by a core group of contributors. There is substantial online help from many sites. R gives us the ability to get work done quickly with minimal learning curves. R is the *lingua franca* in academia among data scientists, statisticians, and machine learning specialists. R is also used widely in industry by companies with a lot of data like Google, Microsoft, Amazon, as well as traditional industries. R also gives you great tools for easily sharing and communicating your results with html or pdf reports as well as interactive web sites.

In the next few sections you will learn:
- Where to find R and RStudio installation links and instructions
- R data structures and how to manipulate them in R syntax
- R data exploration functions and techniques
- R data visualization functions and techniques
- How to install and use R packages
- How to use R notebooks which combine text and code
- R control structures for more complex code
- Recommendations for R style

2.1   Installing R, RStudio

You will need to first install R and then install RStudio, a beautiful and powerful IDE for R. Both are available for Windows, Mac and linux.

Link to download and install R: `https://www.r-project.org/`

Link to download and install RStudio: `https://www.rstudio.com/`

Choose RStudio's free community edition. While you are on the site take a look around at some demos and tutorials.

2.1.1   Getting Started in R

If you open up RStudio you will see a couple of panes on the right, and one large pane on the left, similar to Figure 2.1. This pane on the left is the console. At the top of the console screen you will see some information about your version of R, then the interactive prompt > waiting for you to do something. In the figure, we've typed in a simple expression: 3+4.

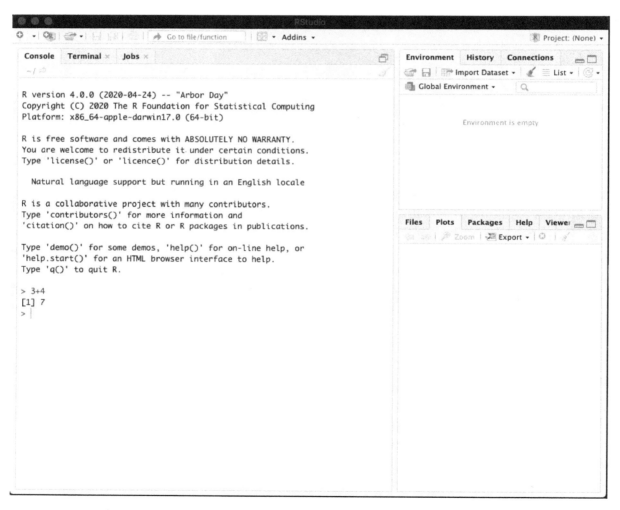

Figure 2.1: RStudio IDE

R is an interpreted language which makes it easy to experiment with ideas at the console. You can also save your code in notebooks or scripts, to run again and again. Although R is an interpreted language, most of the code is in C/C++ so it is fast. For now we will get to know R at the console.

Type along with these examples in the console window as we go. Below, we typed an arithmetic expression at the prompt, hit enter and we see the results on the next line. There should be no surprises here, it's the usual operators with the usual order of operations.

```
> 3 + 4 - 1 * 8 / 2
[1] 3
```

But what is that [1] doing there in front of the output 3? That's just telling you that your result is a one-dimensional object. It's actually a vector of length 1. In R, pretty much everything is an object. Let's type in the same expression as above but this time save it to variable x. By the way, the up arrow displays the previous command, just like in a unix console. The less-than-dash, < −, is the assignment operator in R. We did not have to declare variable x. R figured out what type it is by what was stored in it. R has dynamic typing; if we change what type of object is in x later, R will not complain.

```
> x <- 3 + 4 - 1 * 8 / 2
> x
[1] 3
```

Now when we type in x at the console, R echoes back its contents. What is x? Let's ask R about it. There are many functions we can use to inquire about an object:

```
> is.numeric(x)
[1] TRUE
> class(x)
[1] "numeric"
> typeof(x)
[1] "double"
```

Note that numbers are stored as doubles by default. If we specifically want to store an integer we use the L indicator:

```
> x <- c(1L, 2L, 3L)
> typeof(x)
[1] "integer"
```

The c() function combines elements into a vector. A vector is a sequence of objects of the same type. The c() function will coerce its arguments to a common type, the most inclusive type in the vector:

```
> x <- c(1L, 1.2, "hi")
> typeof(x)
[1] "character"
```

2.2 R Data

We have seen in the examples above that data in R can be logical, numeric (integer or floating point), or character. Data is organized into objects of varying types. In this section we learn more about R objects that hold and organize data. The following table organizes the R data structures by their dimensions and whether or not all elements have to be of the same type.

Dimension	Homogeneous	Heterogeneous
1d	atomic vector	list
2d	matrix	data frame
nd	array	

Table 2.1: R Data Structures

2.2.1 Vector

A vector is a sequential structure with one or more elements of the same type. There isn't really a scalar in R, it's just a vector of length 1. Follow along with this code:

```
> x <- 1:10
> x*5
 [1]  5 10 15 20 25 30 35 40 45 50
>length(x)
[1] 10
>sum(x)  # try mean(), median(), range(), max(), min()
[1] 55
```

In the first line, x is assigned to be a vector from 1 to 10 with the sequence operator ":". In the second line we multiply each element by 5. In most programming languages you would need a loop to do this but note the simple syntax that allows us to do this in one line. There are many built-in functions in R. The next line shows length(). The last line returns the sum of each element of x. You may be wondering why it is 55 since we multiplied each element by 5 above. The reason is that we did not assign it back to x as in x <- x*5.

The vector x is numeric but we can have other types of vectors such as character or logical. When we type "x > 5" at the console, a logical vector returns with TRUE or FALSE for each element.

```
> x
 [1]  1  2  3  4  5  6  7  8  9 10
> x > 5
 [1] FALSE FALSE FALSE FALSE FALSE  TRUE  TRUE  TRUE  TRUE  TRUE
```

If we sum(x>5), the TRUE values count as 1 and the FALSE values as 0 so we get a count of how many elements are greater than 5. Notice in the last line below that we can select those instances greater than 5 and replace only those with 0. Such power with such simple syntax!

```
> sum(x>5)
[1] 5
> x[x>5] <- 0
> x
 [1]  1 2 3 4 5 0 0 0 0 0
```

Subsetting vectors requires first learning one strange thing about R. It starts indexing at 1, not 0 like other programming languages. If you type x[0] at the console you won't get an error but some information about the vector, so it looks like that space is put to good use. Here are some indexing examples (anything after # is a comment):

```
> x <- 1:10
> x[0]
integer(0)
> x[2:4]       # use : for a range of elements
[1] 2 3 4
> x[c(2:4,8)] # use c() for noncontiguous elements
[1] 2 3 4 8
> x[11]
[1] NA
```

Notice above that we did not get an error when we had an index out of bounds, it just gave us an NA, for "not available".

To check the type of a vector you can use:

- typeof(x) – returns type
- is.integer(x) – returns boolean
- is.double(x) – returns boolean
- is.numeric(x) – returns TRUE for integer or double
- is.character(x) – returns boolean
- is.logical(x) – returns boolean

2.2.2 Lists

A list is an ordered collection of objects not necessarily of the same type. Lists can contain other lists as elements. Lists are often used as holders for things returned from functions. List elements are selected with double square brackets:

```
z <- list(1,2,3)  # create a list
z[[1]]
[1] 1
```

```
y <- list('a', TRUE, z)
> typeof(y)
[1] "list"
> length(y)        # y is a list of length 3
[1] 3
> length(y[[3]])   # the 3rd element is also a list of length 3
[1] 3
```

> ⓡ **Lists v. Vectors.** A list is a generic vector where elements do not have to be of the same
> type. For this reason, to check if an object is a vector, don't use `is.vector()` but the
> following:
>
> ```
> x <- 1:5       # create a vector
> is.atomic(x)   # check if x is a vector
> [1] TRUE
> ```

You can check if a list has lists as elements with the `is.recursive()` function. The
`unlist()` function converts a list into a 1-dimensional atomic vector, coercing all elements
into the most general type.

```
> w <- unlist(y)
> w
[1] "a"     "TRUE" "1"     "2"     "3"
> typeof(w)
[1] "character"
```

2.2.3 Matrix

A matrix is a 2-dimensional object with elements of the same type. The code below creates a
sequence from 1:10 and stores it in a matrix of 2 rows.

```
> m <- matrix(1:10, nrow=2)
> m
     [,1] [,2] [,3] [,4] [,5]
[1,]   1    3    5    7    9
[2,]   2    4    6    8   10
```

Notice the handy reminders showing how to index at the top of the columns and the left of
the rows. Practice indexing matrix m. Indices are [row, col].

We will mainly use vectors and data frames (discussed below) in machine learning but we
will use matrices from time to time.

2.2.4 Arrays

Arrays are similar to matrices but can have more than 2 dimensions. Like matrices, all elements
must be of the same type.

2.2.5   Data Frames

A data frame is a 2-dimensional structure where each column can be of a different type. Most of the time we will load a data frame from disk but we can create one manually by creating 3 vectors that we combine with cbind (column bind):

```
> x <- c(1,2,3)
> y <- c(1.1, 2.2, 3.3)
> z <- c('a','b','c')
> df <- data.frame(cbind(x,y,z))
> df
  x   y z
1 1 1.1 a
2 2 2.2 b
3 3 3.3 c
```

In a data frame, each column is a vector of a specific type. All the columns are of the same length. Observe in the code below that we can access these column vectors with the dollar operator and that we can also change the column names.

```
> df$x
[1] 1 2 3
Levels: 1 2 3
> colnames(df) <- c('Ticket', 'Discount', "Section")
> df
  Ticket Discount Section
1      1      1.1       a
2      2      2.2       b
3      3      3.3       c
```

We can read in a text file or csv file from disk as shown below. If you want to know more about the options for read.csv use the command at the bottom of the following code example. The str() functions tells you about the structure of the data frame, its columns, and what type of data it contains, as well as how many observations and variables.

```
> df <- read.csv("titanic.csv")
> str(df)
'data.frame': 1309 obs. of  14 variables:
 $ pclass   : int  1 1 1 1 1 1 1 1 1 1 ...
 $ survived : int  1 1 0 0 0 1 1 0 1 0 ...
 $ name     : chr  "Allen, Miss. Elisabeth Walton"  ...
 $ sex      : chr  "female" "male" "female" "male" ...
 $ age      : num  29 0.917 2 30 25 ...
 . . . and more . . .
```

There are also many built-in data sets in R. You can find out about them by typing data() at the console.

2.3 Data Exploration

You can load a built-in data set with the data() function and then look at a few rows with head() or tail(). Comments start with # so you don't need to type those in when you are working at the console.

```
> data(airquality)
> head(airquality, n=2) # see the first two rows
  Ozone Solar.R Wind Temp Month Day
1    41     190  7.4   67     5   1
2    36     118  8.0   72     5   2
```

Here are several data exploration functions you should explore at the console, replacing "df" with the name of your data frame, such as "airquality":
  * names(df) lists the column names
  * dim(df) gives the row, col dimensions
  * summary(df) gives summary statistics for each column
  * str(df) gives row and column counts, information for each column
  * head(df) and tail(df) give the first and last 6 rows by default

Missing items in a data frame are typically encoded as NA. This can cause some problems for built-in functions as shown below. Notice the mean() function returned NA until the na.rm=TRUE parameter was added.

```
> sum(is.na(airquality$Ozone))  # count the NAs
[1] 37
> mean(airquality$Ozone)
[1] NA
> mean(airquality$Ozone, na.rm=TRUE)
[1] 42.12931
```

A trickier problem is deciding what to do with NAs before we run data sets through machine learning algorithms. Some algorithms may not work and others may give less than optimal results with NAs. One option is to delete rows that have NAs but this could be a problem if your data set is already small. Another option is to replace NAs with a mean or median value as shown next. First we copy the data set to another variable so we won't alter the original.

```
> df <- airquality[]
> df$Ozone[is.na(df$Ozone)] <- mean(df$Ozone, na.rm=TRUE)
> mean(df$Ozone)
[1] 42.12931
```

R syntax can be quite compact and nested; it takes a little getting used to. The syntax df$Ozone[is.na(df$Ozone)] above selects only those rows in df in which Ozone is NA. Only these will be replaced by the mean of the column.

2.4 **Visual Data Exploration**

In addition to exploring data with the R commands described in the last section, and exploring the data with built-in statistical functions, we can also explore data with graphs. Type `demo(graphics)` at the console to see the variety of graphs you can create in R. The next chapter gives a concise overview of basic graph functionality in R. Next we continue looking at airquality with R graphical functions.

The plot() function is most often used to plot points as in `plot(x, y)`, where the first argument is plotted on the x axis and the second on the y axis. If only one argument is given, as in `plot(y)`, the x axis will be a numbering vector. Type the following at the console to see the graphs:

```
hist(airquality$Temp)
plot(airquality$Temp)
plot(airquality$Temp, airquality$Ozone)
```

Here are some useful arguments for modifying graphs:
- pch - specifies the symbol to use for points; 1 is the default
- cex - specifies symbol size, 1 is the default, 1.5 is larger, 0.5 is smaller
- lty - specifies line type, default is 1
- lwd - specifies line width, default is 1
- col - color of graph element; colors can be specified by name, number, hex; col=2 and col="red" are the same
- xlab - label for x axis
- ylab - label for y axis
- main - main label

We will learn more about graphs in R as we go. The following link provides a good overview of R graph parameters: `https://www.statmethods.net/advgraphs/parameters.html`

Below is an example of using some of these parameters in code. Figure 2.2 shows the resulting plot. The plot() code says to plot Ozone on the x axis and Temp on the y axis. These plot points are shown with pch=16 (see the statmethods link above for other options), color blue, and 1.5 times the regular size. We also specified a main label as well as x and y axis labels.

```
plot(airquality$Ozone, airquality$Temp, pch=16, col="blue", cex=1.5,
    main="Airquality", xlab="Ozone", ylab="Temperature")
```

Often we want to know if columns are correlated with other columns. A high positive correlation between x and y would look like a line of slope 1. A high negative correlation would look like a line of slope -1. Correlation is quantified on a scale of -1 to $+1$, with values closer to the 1s indicating strong positive or negative correlation and values closer to 0 indicating weak or no correlation. The code below shows how to generate a correlation matrix with the cor() function, and how to create a graph with the pairs() function. See if you can identify correlations in the graphs.

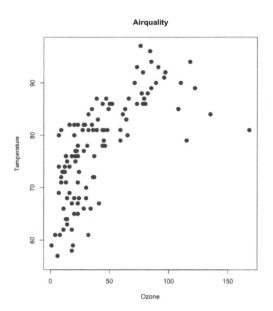

Figure 2.2: Airquality

```
> cor(airquality[1:4], use="complete")
            Ozone    Solar.R      Wind      Temp
Ozone   1.0000000  0.3483417 -0.6124966  0.6985414
Solar.R 0.3483417  1.0000000 -0.1271835  0.2940876
Wind   -0.6124966 -0.1271835  1.0000000 -0.4971897
Temp    0.6985414  0.2940876 -0.4971897  1.0000000
> pairs(airquality[1:4])
```

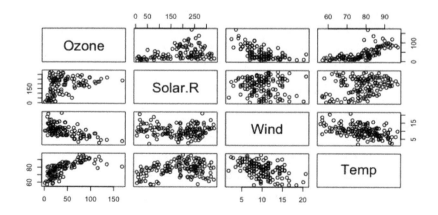

Figure 2.3: Correlation Pairs for Airquality

Machine Learning Handbook with R and Python © Karen Mazidi 2020

The cor() code above ignores NAs because of the use= parameter. Remove that extra parameter and compare your results to the output above. The pairs() command requested to look at only columns 1:4. The highest positive correlation we see in the cor() output is between Temp and Ozone. The graph confirms this correlation: the higher the temp, the higher the Ozone. The largest negative correlation is between Temp and Wind. Looking at its plot we see a definite downward trend. Solar.R and Wind have a correlation much closer to 0 and we see in the plot that there really is not much of a discernible pattern there.

2.5 Factors

We have seen vectors of various types: integer, numeric, character, and logical. There is one more type of vector that will be important to us. Factors are used to encode qualitative data. A factor vector is a vector of integers with an associated vector of labels. Internally it is stored as integers but for our benefit they display as labels. Look at the Titanic data.

```
> df <- read.csv("data/titanic.csv", na.strings="NA", header=TRUE)
> str(df)
'data.frame': 1309 obs. of  14 variables:
 $ pclass   : int  1 1 1 1 1 1 1 1 1 1 ...
 $ survived : int  1 1 0 0 0 1 1 0 1 0 ...
 $ name     : chr  "Allen, Miss. Elisabeth Walton"  ...
 $ sex      : chr  "female" "male" "female" "male" ...
 $ age      : num  29 0.917 2 30 25 ...
 . . .
```

The above code assumes that you have the data/csv file in the same directory you are working in. We used the parameter na.strings="NA" to tell R to fill missing cells with NA. This data is a bit messy because some things that should be factors, like pclass or survived, are not. Since R 4.0, strings are not read as factors. If you want strings read as factors use the stringsAsFactors=TRUE parameter. We can convert to another data type as shown below. Notice we can tell R about the factor levels we want if we use factor() instead of as.factor().

```
df$pclass <- as.factor(df$pclass)
df$sex <- factor(df$sex, levels=c("male", "female"))
```

If you rerun the str() function on the data you will see that pclass and sex are now factors. We can see how many levels a factor has with the levels() function, and see the encoding with the contrasts() function as shown below.

```
contrasts(df$sex)
       female
male        0
female      1
```

```
> contrasts(df$pclass)
  2 3
1 0 0
2 1 0
3 0 1
```

For sex we only need one variable to encode the two genders in the data. The contrasts for pclass shows that we need 2 variables to encode 3 classes. The base case will be class 1. R will create 2 *dummy variables* for classes 2 and 3. We will see the importance of these when we get to machine learning.

2.5.1 Adding a Factor Column to a Data Frame

The following code adds a new column to our data frame for airquality. First it makes all items = FALSE, then makes those with a temperature over 80 to be TRUE. Finally we coerce it to be a factor. The first line copies the data frame.

```
> df <- airquality[]  # copy the data set
> df$Hot <- FALSE
> df$Hot[df$Temp>89] <- TRUE
> df$Hot <- factor(df$Hot)
> df$Hot[40:46]
[1] TRUE  FALSE TRUE  TRUE  FALSE FALSE FALSE
Levels: FALSE TRUE
>plot(df$Hot)
```

Here are some plots of the Hot column, arranged in a 1x3 grid with the par() function. Plotting the column by itself just gives us a visual of the distribution of Hot and not Hot. The cdplot() gives a conditional density of Hot (light grey) and not (black) across the x axis which represents temperature. The third plot is a box plot in which the heavy middle line in the box denotes the median, the box itself indicates the IQR and the horizontal lines at either end of the dashed line indicate min and max, excluding suspected outliers which are dots beyond that line.

```
> par(mfrow=c(1,3))
> plot(df$Hot)
> cdplot(df$Temp, df$Hot)
> plot(df$Hot, df$Temp)
```

The graphs shown in this chapter are rather plain. We can add headings, labels, color and more. Read more about graphical parameters here: https://www.statmethods.net/advgraphs/parameters.html

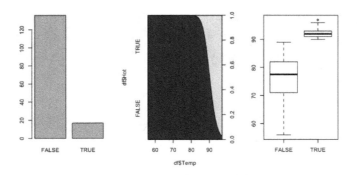

Figure 2.4: Airquality

2.6 R Notebooks

Here are a few things to keep in mind about R:

- R is case sensitive
- The period has no special meaning unlike many other languages
- The dollar sign acts somewhat like the period in other languages
- The hashtag starts comments
- White space is ignored
- The R workspace stores all the objects you create in a session. You can save it, but for now you should always choose No when it asks you to save the workspace upon exiting RStudio.

If you end up with items in your workspace that you don't want, you can list them with ls() and remove things with rm(). The second command below shows how to remove everything from the workspace environment.

```
> ls()
[1] "airquality"
> rm(list=ls())
```

R is a powerful language in its own right. However it becomes truly awesome when we load packages built for specific purposes. These packages are available on CRAN, the Comprehensive R Archival Network. We install packages at the console with the install.packages() command. You only have to install once. We load packages into our working environment only once per script with either the library() or require() functions.

In RStudio, go to File, New File, then R Notebook. Save your file. I recommend creating a folder to keep all your notebooks in, then always loading from that folder by double-clicking on it.

Before we get started, we should note that you can also create a simple R script. These are text files that end in .R and can be run from the console or from within RStudio. We are going to focus on R notebooks which intersperse text commentary and code.

Once you create the R notebook you will see some YAML code at the top. You can also add an author line, and you should change the title. YAML is a recursive acronym for YAML Ain't Markup Language. This YAML tells RStudio to what kind of output to create, in this case it will make an html notebook that you can upload to your website or github.

```
title: "R Notebook"
output: html_notebook
```

You'll notice white portions for text and grey portions for code in the boiler plate notebook that is created for you. Read through the standard text which provides some useful tips on things like how to add new code chunks and get started with markdown text. You can type regular text in the white portions but markdown is worth learning because you will encounter it in many situations beyond R. There is a nice cheat sheet for markdown in RStudio's web site. The really nice thing about markdown is that you can format as you type without taking your hands off the keyboard. In the figure below, the three hashtags denote a level-3 heading. When you create a pdf or html file from this notebook, you won't see the hashtags, just the text rendered as a level-3 heading.

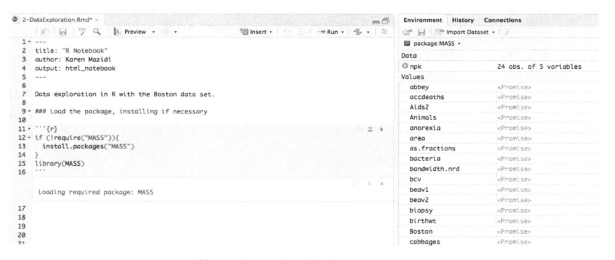

Figure 2.5: RStudio Environment

Figure 2.5 shows the RStudio environment with the white portions for text markdown and the grey portions for code. The full notebook is available on the github site for this book. You should practice making your own notebook similar to the sample. Let's point out a couple of things before we move on. First, once the MASS package was loaded, you can see it in the environment in the upper right. This environment is a great way to see your variables as you go. It is a great help in debugging. Second, notice the Preview button above the notebook. You can use this to "knit" or render your file into html or pdf or other formats. This option is also available under the File menu.

2.7 Control structures

We have seen earlier that a lot of things we might use a loop for in other languages can be done in simple R syntax. However there will be times when we want to code loops, conditionals, and functions. We describe those in this section, in an example getting you started using an R notebook.

This section uses more advanced R code so it is fine to skim through this section and come back to it when you need to use loops, conditionals, or functions. This code will become second nature only with practice. The notebook is in the github site so you can refer to it as you need it.

If you wish to go through this section now, open RStudio and go to File->New File->R Notebook. Get rid of the text in the white areas. Change the title at the top of the file. In the grey code box, remove the code that is there and type the following:

```
if (!require("mlbench"){
    install.packages("mlbench")
}
data(PimaIndiansDiabetes2)
str(PimaIndiansDiabetes2)
```

You can run this chunk of code with the green arrow on the right side of the box. The package mlbench contains several benchmark ML data sets. This code first checks if package "mlbench" is installed. If it is already installed, the package will be loaded into memory. If the package is not installed, it will execute the install.packages() function to install it. Installing a package should just take a minute. If R asks you for a mirror site in a pop-up, just pick one. Once the package is installed, from then on you just load the package into memory in future notebooks with library() or require().

In the upper right pane of RStudio, click on Environment then Global Environment. You should see that the data has been loaded into memory. You should see that it has 768 observations and 9 variables. The str() command you ran above will output information about each variable. You can learn more about this data set by typing ?PimaIndiansDiabetes2 at the console.

From the str() function above, you can see that there are a lot of missing values denoted by NA. Create a new code chunk at the botton of your notebook by clicking on Insert->R at the top of the notebook window. Type in the following code and see the results. The sapply function applies a function to data. Here we have an anonymous function coded on the fly to sum NAs. The sapply() function will apply this to each column. We have a few NAs for glucose, mass, and pressure, but a lot for triceps and insulin. If we just omit all rows with NAs that will cut our data in half. An alternative to just deleting them is to fill them with either the mean or the median of the column. In the code section 2.7.1 shown below, we use an if-else to either calculate the mean or median of a vector. Then we write a function to fill NAs of a vector with either the mean or the median. Whether or not it is a good idea to fill missing values in this way may depend on how you are using the data. Always document any changes you made to your data.

```
> sapply(PimaIndiansDiabetes2, function(x) sum(is.na(x)))
pregnant  glucose pressure  triceps  insulin     ...
       0        5       35      227      374     ...
```

Figure 2.6: Second Code Chunk and Results

2.7.1 if-else

Within the function is an if statement. The if statement in R has this form:

```
if (condition) {statements if true} else {statements if false}
```

The ( ) around the condition is required, as are curly braces around the statements. Statements should occur on individual lines for readability, although R will allow multiple statements separated by a semicolon. We will discuss R style preferences below, but note that the opening { is at the end of a line and the closing } is on a line by itself. The if-else statement below lets us use either mean or median, depending on the choice sent to the function.

We will see examples of the ifelse shortcut throughout the book. Here is the format:

```
ifelse(cond, true, false)
```

2.7.2 Defining and Calling Functions

The code below shows a user-defined function. The definition format is:

```
name <- function(args) {statements}
```

Code 2.7.1 — Function Example. Third Code Chunk

```
fill_NA <- function(mean_med, v){
  # fill missing values with either 1=mean or 2=median
  if (mean_med == 1){
    m <- mean(v, na.rm=TRUE)
  } else {
    m <- median(v, na.rm=TRUE)
  }
  v[is.na(v)] <- m
  v
}
# make a new data set with NA's filled
df <- PimaIndiansDiabetes2
df$triceps <- fill_NA(1, df$triceps)
df$insulin <- fill_NA(1, df$insulin)
df <- df[complete.cases(df),]  # omit rows with NAs
```

The next-to-last line of our function replaced all NAs in the vector with the mean (or median). Notice that there is no "return" statement. The result of the last statement in the function is what is returned, which in this case is our updated vector. Notice again that the opening curly brace for the function is at the end of the line and the closing curly brace is on a line by itself.

Statements to call a function simply have the name of the function and the arguments. The result of the function replaces the original values of those vectors. The last line of the third code chunk handles the remaining missing value which are few. The data set df will have 724 observations.

For an additional example of a function in R, let's look at a recursive function for the familiar Finonacci sequence: 1, 1, 2, 3, 5, 8, 13, 21, ...

Code 2.7.2 — A Recursive Function. Fibonacci Sequence

```r
fib <- function(n){
  if (n <= 1){
    return(n)
  } else {
    return (fib(n-1) + fib(n-2))
  }
}

# print a sequence
for (i in 1:8)
    print(fib(i))
```

Try this out on your computer. Note in the above code that we used return(). However, the function would work correctly without the surrounding return(). For example, instead of return(n) just n.

2.7.3 Loops

R has for-loops and while-loops. The formats are:

```r
for (condition) {statements}
while (condition) {statements}
```

Figure 2.7 shows an example for-loop. The loop creates 3 linear models with function lm(). We will learn more about this in the chapter on linear regression. The 3 iterations of the for loop will use formula "glucose~df[,cols[i]]" to build 3 models: glucose as a function of mass, glucose as a function of age, and glucose as a function of the number of pregnancies, because these are the columns selected in variable cols. These three models are stored in a list.

First we plot mass on the x axis and glucose on the y axis. Then we plot 3 ablines, one for each stored model. The abline function can be used to plot the regression line as we are doing here, but can also be used to plot straight lines. We make each line a different color by just letting color =i, our index. Finally we add a legend using the same color codes as the ablines.

```{r}
cols <- c(6,8,1)
plot(df$mass, df$glucose, main="PimaIndianDiabetes2")
for (i in 1:3){
    model <- lm(glucose~df[,cols[i]], data=df)[1]
    abline(model, col=i)
}
legend("topright", title="Predictors", c("Mass", "Age", "Pregnant"), fill=c(1,2,3))
```

Figure 2.7: Fourth Code Chunk

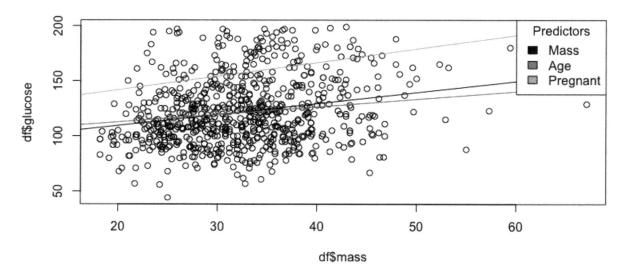

Figure 2.8: Graph with Regression Lines

Next, we demonstrate the ifelse() shortcut. The ifelse() in Figure 2.9 checks if insulin is greater than 155. If this is true, the element will be 1 otherwise it will be 0. The ifelse(df$insulin>155,1,0) creates an integer vector of 1s and 0s. This is then converted to a factor vector by surrounding it with the factor() function.

In the first line of the 5th code chunk we are adding a new column to the data frame. In the second line, we plot the observations again, this time color coding those with high insulin as red, and those that do not have high insulin as blue. The bg= argument indicates what fill color is used for the points. We have a vector of "blue" and "red". How these colors are selected is controlled by the unclass() function which converts the "large" column factors to 1 or 2. So observations with large insulin values display as red and those with low values display as blue.

```r
```{r}
df$large <- factor(ifelse(df$insulin>155,1,0))
plot(df$mass, df$glucose, pch=21, bg=c("blue","red")[unclass(df$large)])
```
```

Figure 2.9: Fifth Code Chunk

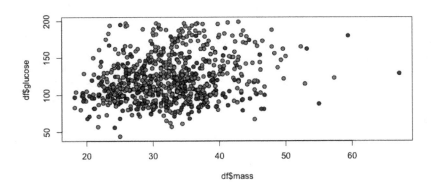

Figure 2.10: Graph with Color Coding

2.8 R Style

Google has its own R style guide available here:

`https://google.github.io/styleguide/Rguide.xml`

Another style guide, written by Hadley Wickham, is available here: `http://adv-r.had.co.nz/Style.html`. Hadley Wickham is the Chief Scientist at RStudio, and an influential R developer, having created several amazing open-source packages such as ggplot2, dplyr and more. The point is not to follow one style guide rather than the other, but to be consistent in your code. It makes it easier to read, even for you.

Here are a few recommendations from Hadley Wickham's style guide:

- variable and function names should be lowercase, using underscore to separate names
- variable names generally should be nouns and function names should be verbs
- try to use names that are concise but meaningful
- don't use names of existing functions; R will let you override them
- put a space around operators, except :
- otherwise don't add unnecessary spaces
- opening curly braces should not be on their own lines
- closing curly braces should go on a new line unless followed by else
- indent with 2 spaces, exception: function arguments

2.9   Summary

This chapter provided a fast-paced introduction to R. Don't expect to retain everything in the chapter right now, you can refer back to it as you need it. You will learn more R as we go, but now you already know enough to get started with machine learning in the next part of the book.

In the github are full notebooks of the data exploration and R control structure examples in this chapter. Make sure you understand the R code in these notebooks. Link: `https://github.com/kjmazidi/Machine_Learning_2nd_edition`. I have also created short video tutorials on my youtube channel which will provide a good review of what you should know from this chapter: `https://www.youtube.com/c/JaniceMazidi`

The RStudio website has a page full of useful cheat sheets: `https://rstudio.com/resources/cheatsheets/`. The Base R cheat sheet summarizes many aspects of R that have been covered in this chapter. The following Quick Reference supplements the cheat sheet with some additional code covered in this chapter.

This chapter showed several built-in functions for data exploration of a data frame:

- str(df) - gives an overview of the structure of the data
- dim(df) - gives the dimensions of the data frame
- summary(df) - gives summary statistics for each column; summary(df$col) gives summary statistics for just column 'col'
- head(df) and tail(df) - look at the first or last few rows
- names(df) - list column names
- cor(df) - print a table of correlations
- pairs(df) - display a table of graphical representations of correlations

Other functions are typically used to provide information about a column: mean(), median(), sum(), max(), min(), and range().

2.9.1   Quick Reference

Dealing with NAs

Reference 2.9.1 Count the number of NAs
```
sum(is.na(df$col))
```

Reference 2.9.2 Count NAs by column
```
sapply(df, function(x) sum(is.na(x)))
```

Reference 2.9.3 Run stat functions ignoring NAs
```
mean(df$col, na.rm=TRUE)
# works with sum(), min(), max(), and more
```

Reference 2.9.4 Replace NAs with the mean
```
df$col[is.na(df$col)] <- mean(df$col, na.rm=TRUE)
```

2.9.2 **Factors**

Reference 2.9.5 Check the factor encoding
```
# using levels
v <- factor(c(1, 0, 1, 0))
levels(v)  # output levels
[1] "0" "1"
```

Reference 2.9.6 Change the factor encoding
```
# change factor encoding
levels(v) <- c("male", "female")
```

Reference 2.9.7 Using contrasts()
```
# contrasts gives integer and char encoding
contrasts(v)
           female
male       0
female     1
```

3. Data Visualization in R

R has great data visualization functions that are quite simple to use. Modern R has extended the visualization capacities of R with the `ggplot2` package, discussed in Chapter 10. Here we give an overview of the types of graphs you can create using standard R. To get a feel for the R's graphic capabilities, type `demo(graphics)` at the console. The purpose of this chapter is to get readers familiar with how data can be visualized in R. You might want to skim over this chapter to get the big picture, then refer back to it as you make your own graphs in the context of machine learning solutions later in the book.

In this chapter we first discuss data visualization techniques for a single column of a data frame. Then we discuss data visualization for two columns, two dimensional visualization. Throughout the chapter we use the Titanic data for the sample graphs. As usual, you can find the code for all the graphs and full-color figures on the github. Additionally, there are two good resources that you should bookmark:

- An overview of graphical parameters from the stat methods site [1]
- Color names for colors in R provided by Professor Tian Zheng at Columbia [2]

You can display graphs individually, or display them in grids. The par() function is used to set up a grid. The following code shows how to save the original parameter settings in a variable called opar, then plot graphs in a 1x2 grid, and finally restore the original parameter settings. The par() function can be used to set up any grid pattern you like, such as 3x2, etc. The graphs will be placed left-to-right, top-to-bottom, in the grid.

---

[1] https://www.statmethods.net/advgraphs/parameters.html
[2] http://www.stat.columbia.edu/~tzheng/files/Rcolor.pdf

```
opar <- par()        # copy original settings
par(mfrow=c(1,2))    # set up 1x2 grid
hist(...             # make a plot
plot(...             # make another plot
par(opar)            # restore parameter settings
```

3.1   Data Visualization of One Variable

In the online notebook, we first load the Titanic data and do a little clean-up. A given column in a data frame is just a vector. We first look at ways to plot quantitative vectors and then look at visualizing qualitative vectors.

3.1.1   Quantitative Vectors

The most common graph type for one quantitative variable is the histogram. You can specify the bins, but in the graph below, using the default settings worked out well. Type ?hist() at the console to see all the parameters you can modify. Another plot type that is appropriate for quantitative data is a simple scatterplot. Since we only have one variable, R will supply row index numbers for the x axis. The code and graphs are shown below. Not that the plots are displayed side-by-side using par(), the original parameter setters were store at the top of the code block and restored at the end or the block.

Code 3.1.1 — **Titanic data.** Histogram and Scatterplot.

```
opar <- par()      # copy original settings
par(mfrow=c(1,2))

hist(df$age, col="slategray", main="Age of Titanic Passengers",
    xlab="Age")
plot(df$age, pch=21, cex=0.75,
    bg=c("snow", "slategray")[unclass(df$survived)], ylab="Age",
    main="Age (White Deceased)")

par(opar)
```

You can create the histogram with code as simple as hist(df$age) to get the visualization you need for the data. Later you can add the colors, titles, etc. For the scatter plot we added color, conditioned on the survival status of the passengers. The unclass() function converts the survived 0s and 1s into 1s and 2s, respectively. These values then index into the snow/slategray vector to select a color. We could accomplish the same thing by adding 1 to df$survived:

```
plot(df$age, pch=21, cex=0.75,
    bg=c("snow", "slategray")[df$survived+1], ylab="Age",
    main="Age (White Deceased)")
```

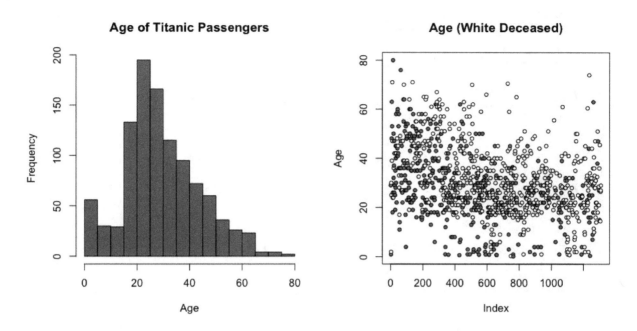

Figure 3.1: Plotting a Quantitative Vector

Another option for a quantitative vector is the kernel density plot. This plot gives you similar information as the histogram, but smoothing has been applied. In the code below, we first create the density vector, then use it for the plot() function. The last line of code below fills in the curve with a polygon.

Code 3.1.2 — **Titanic data.** Kernel Density Plot.

```
d <- density(df$age, na.rm = TRUE)
plot(d, main="Kernel Density Plot for Age", xlab="Age")
polygon(d, col="wheat", border="slategrey")
```

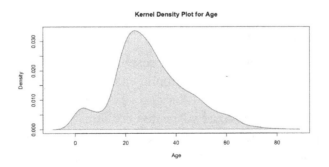

Figure 3.2: Kernel Density Plot

We can overlay several kernel density plots using package sm. First we subset the data frame to the two columns of interest so that we can use complete.cases() to get rid of NAs.

Code 3.1.3 — **Age by Class.** Overlaying Kernel Density Plots.

```
library(sm)
# subset the data and remove NAs
df_subset <- df[,c(1,5)]
df_subset <- df_subset[complete.cases(df_subset),]
# create the plots
sm.density.compare(df_subset$age, df_subset$pclass,
    col=c("seagreen", "wheat", "sienna3"), lwd=2)
title(main="Age by Passenger Class")
legend("topright", inset=0.05, legend=c(1:3),
    fill=c("seagreen", "wheat", "sienna3"))
```

Figure 3.3: Kernel Density Plots

A boxplot is another graph type that can represent quantitative data. A box plot is more commonly vertical but below we show a horizontal example. The box shows the 2nd and 3rd quartiles of the data. The "whiskers" at either end of the dashed lines show the 1st and 4th quartiles. Dots beyond a whisker indicate suspected outliers. The outliner dots seem to be for ages greater than around 65. We know that these really aren't suspect data, since we have the human knowledge that people in the time of Titanic often lived at least until their 80s. The bold line through the box indicates the median. In this data, the median age appears to be in the late 20s.

Code 3.1.4 — **Age Data.** Horizontal Box Plot.

```
boxplot(df$age, col="slategray", horizontal=TRUE, xlab="Age",
    main="Age of Titanic Passengers")
```

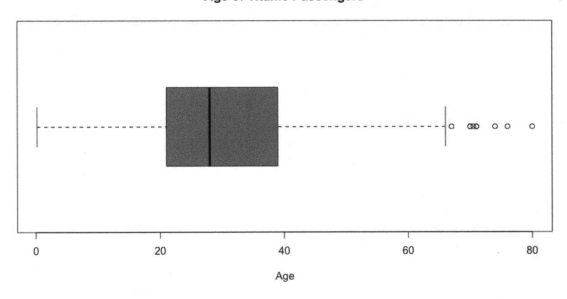

Figure 3.4: Box Plot

3.1.2 Plotting Qualitative Vectors

Barplots are often used for qualitative vectors. They can be vertical or horizontal. In the code below, adding parameter `horiz=TRUE` will cause the bars to be displayed horizontally instead of vertically. First, we make counts from the passenger class vector, then use those to create the bar plot.

Code 3.1.5 — **Passenger Class Data.** Bar Plot.

```
counts <- table(df$pclass)
barplot(counts, xlab="Passenger Class", ylab="Frequency",
    col=c("seagreen","wheat","sienna3"))
```

The table() function in the code block returns the following:

```
  1   2   3
323 277 709
```

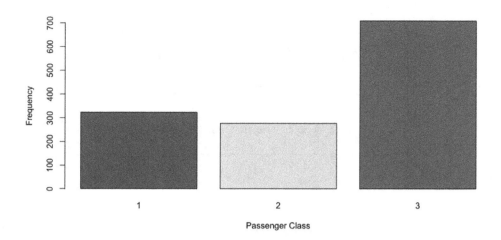

Figure 3.5: Bar Plot

A pie chart can be made with relative frequencies of a qualitative variable. First we specify frequencies for each of the 3 classes, then supply labels. With slices and labels defined, we can make a pie chart.

```
Code 3.1.6 — Passenger Class Data. Pie Chart.

slices <- c(sum(df$pclass==1, na.rm = TRUE), sum(df$pclass==2,
    na.rm = TRUE), sum(df$pclass==3, na.rm = TRUE))
lbls <- c("Class 1", "Class 2", "Class 3")
pie(slices, labels=lbls, main="Passenger Classes",
    col=c("seagreen","wheat","sienna3"))
```

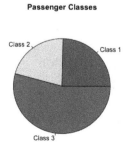

Figure 3.6: Pie Chart

3.2 **Data Visualization of Two Vectors**

If we have two vectors, X and Y, then there are four possible combinations of quantitative and qualitative vectors, listed below. In this section we look at graphs that are appropriate for each combination.

- both X and Y are qualitative
- X is qualitative, Y is quantitative
- X is quantitative, Y is qualitative
- X and Y are quantitative

3.2.1 **Both X and Y are Qualitative**

When both variables are qualitative, mosaic plots are the most common type of graph used. A related type is the association graph, which gives additional visual information about the deviation of the data from a uniform distribution. Both types of plots can be created with the vcd package, visualizing categorical data. First, we look at a mosaic example plotting the survived and pclass columns. The mosaic() function wants the first argument to be a table or formula, so we surround the subsetted data frame with table(). SHADE=TRUE gives you a color graph, FALSE gives you a grayscale graph. The mosaic plot shows each group in tiles. The area of the tiles is proportional to its counts in the data.

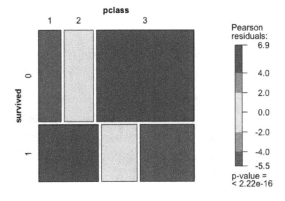

Figure 3.7: Mosaic Plot

The legend indicates the Pearson residuals. The "null" model would consider an even distribution into the cells but clearly we don't have that case here. The blue indicates we have more observations than expected, the red indicates fewer than expected, and gray is about what is expected given a null hypothesis. We didn't have to specify legend=TRUE because that is the default.

Code 3.2.1 — **Passenger Class and Survived.** Mosaic and Association Plots.

```
library(vcd)
mosaic(table(df[,c(2,1)]),  shade=TRUE, legend=TRUE)
assoc(table(df[,c(1,2)]), shade=TRUE)
```

What would happen if we reversed the order of columns 2 and 1? We would get the same information, but with the graph flipped around.

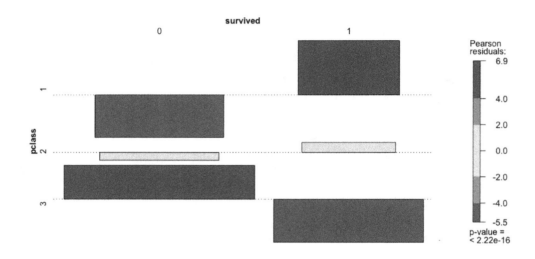

Figure 3.8: Association Plot

An association plot visualizes the residuals of an independence model. Each tile has an area that is proportional to the difference in observed and expected frequencies. The dotted line is the baseline. Tiles above the line have a frequency greater than what was expected, those below have a frequency below what was expected. In the plot above, pclass 1 survived more than expected, pclass 3 less than expected.

3.2.2 X is Qualitative, Y is Quantitative

When X is qualitative (a factor), and Y is quantitative, box plots are good choices. Notches at the median can be added with the notch=TRUE parameter.

Code 3.2.2 — **Passenger Class and Age.** Box Plot.

```
plot(df$survived, df$age, varwidth=TRUE, notch=TRUE,
    main="Survival and Age", xlab="Survived", ylab="Age")
# the following would create an identical plot
boxplot(df$age~df$survived, varwidth=TRUE, notch=TRUE,
    main="Survival and Age", xlab="Survived", ylab="Age")
```

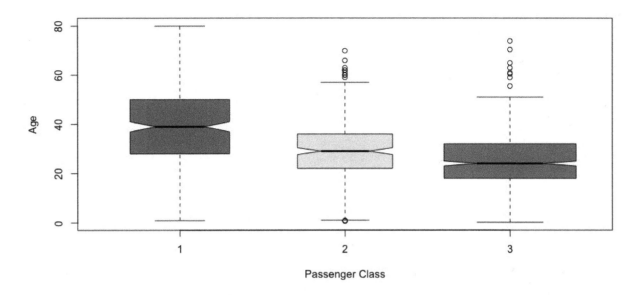

Figure 3.9: Box Plot

You can create violin plots with package vioplot. Violin plots are a combination of a boxplot and a kernel density plot. This plot does not like NAs so we remove them. This means that we will have less data and the plot may not be as informative.

```
Code 3.2.3 — Passenger Class and Age. Violin Plot.

library(vioplot)

# just look at columns 1, 2, 5
df_subset <- df[,c(1,2,5)]
# subset to remove NAs
df_subset <- df_subset[complete.cases(df_subset),]

x1 <- df_subset$age[df_subset$pclass==1]
x2 <- df_subset$age[df_subset$pclass==2]
x3 <- df_subset$age[df_subset$pclass==3]

# make the plot
vioplot(x1, x2, x3, col="wheat",
    names=c("Class 1", "Class 2", "Class 3"))
```

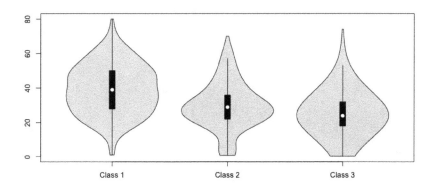

Figure 3.10: Violin Plot

3.2.3   X is Quantitative, Y is Qualitative

When X is quantitative and Y is qualitative, a conditional density plot can be used. The following plot shows how survived changes over the various ages. Note that if we switched the order of age and survived, we would get a row of dots at the top of the graph for one class and a row of dots at the bottom of the graph for the other class, not terribly informative.

Code 3.2.4 — **Passenger Class and Age.** Conditional Density Plot.

```
cdplot(df_subset$age, df_subset$survived, col=c("snow", "gray"))
```

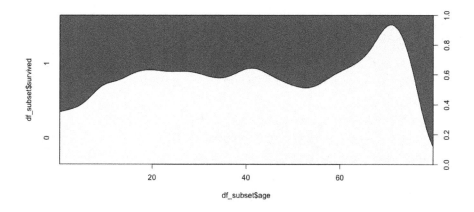

Figure 3.11: Conditional Density Plot

3.2.4 X and Y are both Quantitative

If X and Y are both quantitative, scatter plots are recommended. Here we have crosses for the points in blue, 75% of the usual size (by parameter cex). We would have to dig further into the Titanic data to understand this chart. Why do so many passengers seem to have a fare of 0? And why did a few passengers pay 500? Perhaps the 500 fares paid for several people and the 0 fares reflect passengers whose fares were paid by a spouse or parent or adult child? Further investigation is required to understand this.

Code 3.2.5 — **Fare and Age.** Scatter Plot.

```
plot(df$age, df$fare, pch='+', cex=0.75, col="blue",
    xlab="Age", ylab="Fare")
```

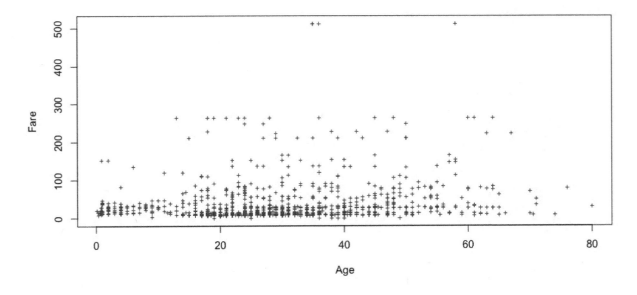

Figure 3.12: Scatter Plot

3.3 Summary

This chapter demonstrated how to create informative graphs in basic R. We have really just scratched the surface of what can be done in R. The data visualization capabilities of R are one of many reasons that it is heavily used in industry and academia. Data visualization is useful first for a researcher's understanding of the data, and then to communicate what has been learned about the data to others. There are many online resources for advanced data visualization techniques in R. Advanced graphics can be achieved with the power ggplot2 package, described in a later chapter.

3.3.1   Quick Reference

Reference 3.3.1 Change and restore graphing parameters

```
opar <- par()         # copy original settings
par(mfrow=c(1,2))     # set up 1x2 grid
hist(...     # make a plot
plot(...     # make another plot
par(opar)    # restore parameter settings
```

3.3.2   R Plot Parameters

The next few code chunks show how to change a few plot paramters.

Reference 3.3.2 Text and symbol size

```
# cex changes point size
# default is 1
# 1.5 means 50% larger
plot(mtcars$wt, mtcars$mpg, cex=1.5)
```

Reference 3.3.3 Point symbol

```
# pch is point symbol; default is open dot
# pch=19 is closed dot, filled with col

plot(mtcars$wt, mtcars$mpg,
     pch=19, col='green')
```

Reference 3.3.4 lines

```
# lty 5-long dash; 2=short dash; 3=dots
# pch=19 is closed dot, filled with col

plot(mtcars$wt, mtcars$mpg)
abline(lm(mtcars$mpg~mtcars$wt), lty=5, col='red')
```

4. The Craft 1: Planning to Learn

Learning any craft is a long-term commitment. Two keys points to keep in mind are:
- Be systematic. Develop an organized approach to learning.
- Find mentors. Mentors may be people in your company/organization with skills you wish to learn. However, you can also find mentors online by identifying people who demonstrate the kind of projects you want to create, and following them online.

Two specific recommendations are discussed below. The first is that you need to develop an organized and systematic work flow for your projects. The second is that you need to develop a plan for ongoing improvement.

4.1   Machine Learning Workflow

A systematic approach to a machine learning project is important for two reasons. First, once you set up a work flow, the process becomes almost automatic. Second, by having a systematic workflow, others (or you) can reproduce your results. The concept of *reproducible research* has gained importance in recent years to help researchers distinguish between innovation and hype. Also, when you go back to your own work months from now, you want to quickly see what you did and how you did it without having to reinvent your work.

Typical machine learning projects follow a work flow similar to Figure 4.1. In an organizational setting, the project objectives, accuracy goals and final report involve interactions with project managers (shown in green rounded, shadowed rectangles with diagonal sketch lines in the work flow diagram).

The yellow squared rectangles involve data gathering, cleaning, and exploration. Data must be organized, cleaned, and processed in order to be useful. In this phase it may be discovered that data is incomplete or inadequate for the project objectives in which case a plan for further data collection must be developed. The data collection phase may take months to complete in some cases.

After data is ready for consumption, data exploration can take place. Initial data exploration can identify trends in the data that will be useful in selecting algorithms and features.

The blue boxes (rounded corners, no diagonal sketch lines) involve the machine learning: training, testing, and evaluating. As shown in the diagram, machine learning projects are often iterative, going through model variations until acceptable results are achieved on the validation data. In reality, the iteration could involve earlier steps if project objectives and goals need to be reconsidered in light of project results.

4.1.1 The Life Cycle of a Machine Learning Project

A large machine learning project for clients involves much more than simply running data through an algorithm. The needs of various stakeholders in a project must be considered. Stakeholders in a machine learning project include, at a minimum:

1. The clients for whom the project is being prepared, who are also typically the funders of the project. These clients could be internal managers of a data science firm, or external clients from organizations and businesses who wish to obtain information that will help the entity achieve organizational objectives.

2. The technical experts and domain knowledge experts that plan and carry out the project. A wide range of expertise may be needed in larger projects. These experts could include statisticians, computer scientists, data scientists, and persons with insight into the subject area.

3. Any persons whose data was collected or who may be impacted by the machine learning project. Considerations that must be made include: Who owns the data? Who are the subjects of the data? Has the data been anonymized? Did subjects give consent for the collection of the data? How will the analysis of this data be used? How might this analysis impact the subjects in the data as well as the larger community?

4.2 Planning to Learn

Learning doesn't just happen. Going through this book in a systematic way will provide a good foundation of machine learning skills. Beyond the course or the book, you will need a plan for continued learning. Here are a few suggestions for becoming a life-long machine learning learner.

- Identify your Purpose. Where do you see your machine learning skills in 5 years? How do these skills fit into an overall career path?
- Keep a notebook. A physical or electronic notebook is important because it will chart your progress and document skills that you have learned. A notebook will avoid the frustration of knowing that you've done something before, but not remembering the file name to look up how you did it.
- Keep a schedule. Plan a regular project weekly, monthly, or whatever your time permits. Unlimited project ideas exist on sites like Kaggle.

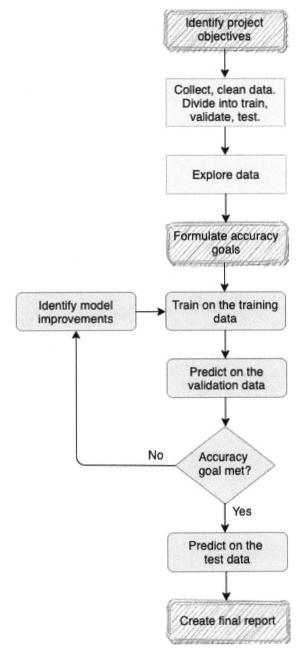

Figure 4.1: Workflow for a Machine Learning Project

Part Two: Linear Models

Preface to Part Two

Part Two explores *linear model* machine learning algorithms, including:
- linear regression
- logistic regression
- naive Bayes

These algorithms are grouped together in Part Two because they take a linear combination of inputs to estimate either a target output variable or a linear decision boundary for a given input data set $D = \{(x_1, y_1), (x_2, y_2), ..., (x_n, y_n)\}$:

$$y = \mathbf{w}\mathbf{X} + b$$

where $\mathbf{w}$ represents the weight matrix which is multiplied by the $\mathbf{X}$ input features plus the fitting parameter b. The parameters w and b are learned from the data D.

Keep in mind that *linear* does not always mean a straight line, but any line that can be created with a linear combination of inputs. For example, $y = x^2$ is a line, but not a straight line.

In linear regression, the target output y will be a real-number value. We call this kind of machine learning *regression*. In logistic regression, the target output y will be an indicator for membership in one of a finite number of classes. We call this kind of machine learning *classification*. In logistic regression and naive Bayes, the output is the *probability* of membership in one of a finite number of classes.

These models can be considered *parametric* algorithms because we have a fixed set of parameters, or weights, learned from the data. In contrast, with non-parameteric methods, the number of parameters grow with an increase in data size.

We begin with linear models because they have visual, intuitive explanations and are commonly used in machine learning tasks.

5. Linear Regression

5.1 Overview

Many machine learning algorithms have their origin in the field of statistics, and linear regression is a prime example. In fact, the fundamentals of linear regression can be traced back to mathematicians in the early 1800s. We begin with linear regression because it is relatively simple, yet powerful, and introduces foundational concepts and terminology we will use for other algorithms throughout the book. In linear regression, our data consists of predictor values, x, and target values y. We wish to find the relationship between x and y. This linear relationship can be defined by parameters w and b, with w, the slope of the line, quantifying the amount that y changes with changes in x, and b serving as an intercept.

5.2 Linear Regression in R

Let's take a look at the women data set, one of the built-in data sets in R.

```
Code 5.2.1 — women data. Height in inches and weight in pounds for 15 women.

# explore at the console:
> str(women)
'data.frame': 15 obs. of  2 variables:
 $ height: num  58 59 60 61 62 63 64 65 66 67 ...
 $ weight: num  115 117 120 123 126 129 132 135 139 142 ...
> plot(women$weight~women$height)
```

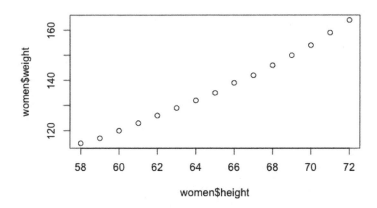

Figure 5.1: Women Data Set

This data set is from the mid-1970s, when Americans were considerably thinner than we are now. Figure 5.1 reveals a linear trend in the data: taller women weigh more than shorter women.

We will use the built-in lm() function to build a linear regression model. There are many parameters we can send to the lm() function, here we only send two: the formula, and the data. The formula *weight ~ height* says to model weight, our target, as a function of height.

Code 5.2.2 — Build a linear regression model. You can type ?lm at the console to learn more about the function.

```
> lm1 <- lm(weight~height, data=women)
> lm1

Call:
lm(formula = weight ~ height, data = women)

Coefficients:
(Intercept)          height
     -87.52            3.45
```

When we built the model, we saved it to variable lm1. If we type the model name at the console as we see in the code above, we get basic information about the model. Our parameters (coefficients) are the w and b that the algorithm learned from the data. In this model, they are $w = 3.45$, and $b = -87.52$. The intercept parameter, b, is generally not of interest to us as it is just used to fit the data. The parameter w is of more interest. In linear regression, it tells us how much we can expect the y-value to change for every one-unit change in the x-value. So for every inch taller a woman is, we expect her to weight 3.45 pounds more. We can use these values for prediction. Let's say we have a woman who is 65 inches tall. Her weight should be:

$65 * 3.45 - 87.52 = 136.7$. Check if that value makes sense given the data in Figure 5.1.

We have a model but we don't know if it is a good model. We can use the summary() function to get a glimpse of the goodness of fit achieved by this model. This is shown in the next code block. We will delve deeper into the summary() output later but now we will just point out two key elements of the output. Notice the three asterisks at the end of the line for height under Coefficients. This indicates that height was a good predictor. Notice also that the intercept received three asterisks, but again, we are not really interested in the intercept. The second thing to notice is the R-squared is about 0.99. The R-squared is a measure of goodness of fit that ranges from 0 to 1, the closer to 1 the better. This provides evidence that we have a good model for this data.

Code 5.2.3 — Model summary. Use the summary() function to learn more about the model.

```
> summary(lm1)
Call:
lm(formula = weight ~ height, data = women)

Residuals:
    Min      1Q  Median      3Q     Max
-1.7333 -1.1333 -0.3833  0.7417  3.1167

Coefficients:
             Estimate Std. Error t value Pr(>|t|)
(Intercept) -87.51667    5.93694  -14.74 1.71e-09 ***
height        3.45000    0.09114   37.85 1.09e-14 ***
---
Signif. codes:  0 '***' 0.001 '**' 0.01 '*' 0.05 '.' 0.1 ' ' 1

Residual standard error: 1.525 on 13 degrees of freedom
Multiple R-squared:  0.991,Adjusted R-squared:  0.9903
F-statistic:  1433 on 1 and 13 DF,  p-value: 1.091e-14
```

Exercise 5.1 — Building a Simple Linear Regression Model. Using the built-in data set swiss. Try the following in an R script:
- Learn more about the data by typing ?swiss at the console.
- Load the data and look at it with R data exploration functions and at least one plot.
- Build a linear regression model predicting Fertility based on Education.
- What is the mean of Education? of Fertility?
- What is the predicted Fertility, given the mean of Education? Use the coefficients from your model.
- Do you think Education is a good predictor? Why or why not?
- Do you think this is a good model? Why or why not?

5.3 Metrics

There are a lot of metrics associated with linear regression and we will start with metrics we can use in data analysis before we begin applying a machine learning algorithm.

5.3.1 Metrics for Data Analysis

In linear regression we often want to know if variables are correlated. We can use the cor() function or plot pairs() as shown in Section 2.4 earlier. For example, to see if x and y are correlated we can use this code: `cor(x, y)`.

The default method is Pearson's, which measures the linear correlation between two variables. It ranges from −1 to +1 where the former is a perfect negative correlation, the latter is a perfect positive correlation, and values close to 0 indicate little correlation. The formula for Pearson's correlation is:

$$\rho_{x,y} = Corr(x,y) = \frac{Cov(x,y)}{\sigma_x \sigma_y} \tag{5.1}$$

We see that correlation is actually covariance, scaled to $[-1,1]$. Covariance measures how changes in one variable are associated with changes in a second variable. The numbers can range wildly which is why the scaled correlation is often preferred. Here is the formula for covariance, where n is the number of data points:

$$cov(x,y) = \frac{\sum_{i=1}^{n}(x_i - \overline{x})(y_i - \overline{y})}{n-1} \tag{5.2}$$

5.3.2 Linear Regression Metrics for Model Fit

The summary() output of a linear model gives a lot of useful metrics concerning the model fit. Looking back at the output of summary() for the linear model at the Coefficients section:

```
Coefficients:
             Estimate Std. Error t value Pr(>|t|)
(Intercept) -87.51667    5.93694  -14.74 1.71e-09 ***
height        3.45000    0.09114   37.85 1.09e-14 ***
```

The estimated coefficient for height and the intercept are given, along with standard error, t value and p value. The standard error gives us an estimate of variation in the coefficient estimate and can be used to predict a confidence interval for the coefficient. So the confidence interval for w_1 would be: $w_1 \pm 2\ SE(w_1)$. Standard errors are used for the hypothesis test on the coefficient, where the null hypothesis is that there is no relationship between the predictor variable and the target variable. In other words, the true $w = 0$. This is computed using the t-statistic:

$$t = \frac{\hat{w}_1 - 0}{SE(\hat{w}_1)} \tag{5.3}$$

which measures the number of standard deviations our estimate coefficient $\hat{w}_1$ is from 0. Notice we put the hat symbol, ^, over w to remind us that it is an estimate. The distribution of the t-statistic has a bell shape which makes it easy to compute the probability of observing a t-statistic larger in absolute value than what was computed, if the null hypothesis were true. This is the p-value. If the p-value is small we can reject the null hypothesis. Typical cut-off points for the p-value are 0.05 and 0.01. One caveat about p-values is that generally you will have more confidence in them if your data size is greater than 30. That is not the case for the women data because it has only 15 observations.

The final part of the summary() output of the women linear regression model is:

```
Residual standard error: 1.525 on 13 degrees of freedom
Multiple R-squared:  0.991,Adjusted R-squared:  0.9903
F-statistic:  1433 on 1 and 13 DF,  p-value: 1.091e-14
```

Whereas the metrics for the coefficients indicate how well each coefficient modeled the true data, these statistics tell us how well the model as a whole fit the training data. The RSE, residual standard error, is computed from the RSS, residual sum of squares.

$$RSS = e_1^2 + e_2^2 + ... + e_n^2 = \sum_i (y_i - \hat{y}_i)^2 \tag{5.4}$$

The RSS is just the sum of squared errors. We square them because some will be errors in the positive direction and some will be in the negative direction. The RSE is computed from the RSS:

$$RSE = \sqrt{\frac{1}{n-2}RSS} \quad = \quad \sqrt{\frac{1}{n-2}\sum_i (y_i - \hat{y}_i)^2} \tag{5.5}$$

Why is RSS scaled by $\frac{1}{n-2}$? The value n is the number of observations and the 2 is because we have 2 estimated variables. This gives us $15 - 2 = 13$ degrees of freedom mentioned on the line with the RSE. The RSE measures how off our model was from the data, the lack of fit of the model. It is measured in units of y so in this case our RSE of 1.525 is about 1.5 pounds.

Since RSE is in terms of Y it can be hard to interpret when we have multiple predictors. For this reason the R^2 statistic is also provided:

$$R^2 = 1 - \frac{RSS}{TSS} \tag{5.6}$$

where TSS, total sum of squares, is a measure of how far off y values tend to be from the mean:

$$TSS = \sum (y_i - \bar{y})^2 \tag{5.7}$$

The R^2 statistic will always be between 0 and 1, the closer to 1 the more variance in the model is explained by the predictors. The R^2 in the summary above was 0.991, which is very high. This means that almost all the variation in weight is predicted by height. For linear regression models such as this one where there is only one predictor, R^2 will be the same as the squared correlation between the X and Y values.

The final statistic listed is the F-statistic:

$$F = \frac{(TSS - RSS)/p}{RSS/(n - p - 1)} \tag{5.8}$$

where n is the number of observations and p is the number of predictors. The F statistic takes into account all of the predictors to determine if they are significant predictors of Y. It provides evidence against the null hypothesis that the predictors are not really predictors. The advantage of the F-statistic over R^2 is that R^2 does not tell us whether it is statistically significant or not but the F-statistic does. It has an associated p-value. So we check for a F-statistic greater than 1 and a low p-value to indicate confidence in the model.

5.3.3 Metrics for Test Set Evaluation

Earlier we ran the women data set through the linear regression algorithm and looked at some metrics for judging the quality of the model. In practice, we will not run entire data sets through the algorithm, but divide the data into a training set and a test set. The model should be built on the training data and should not see the test data until evaluation time. Then the model is used to predict values for the test data, and we can use various metrics to see how far off the predictions were from the true values. We will do that in future examples. For now, we are going to just make up some test data out of the blue, making sure that the data does not fit well to the regression line so it shows up well on the graph in Figure 5.2. Again, we are only making up data for illustration purposes.

What are some metrics we can use to evaluate the prediction accuracy? For regression tasks, common metrics include mean squared error and correlation. Imagine that we randomly selected a few data observations to hold out from the training data. We call this held-out data a *test set*, or *validation set*. These observations would not have been seen by the algorithm during training and so we can use them to test the model. It is very important that the algorithm is tested on unseen data, otherwise we don't know if the algorithm learned anything or just memorized data. Using the test data to predict weight, given height, we can compute the correlation of the actual y values with the predicted y values via the R cor() function: *cor(predicted, actual)*. Correlation gives us a general idea about our model. A correlation close to +1 would mean that as height went up, weight went up as well. However, this would not tell us how much our estimates were off for the individual observations. These errors are called residuals:

```
residuals <- predicted - actual
```

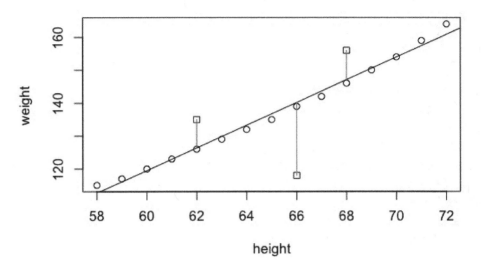

Figure 5.2: Test Set Errors

In Figure 5.2 these residuals are represented as vertical lines drawn from the data points to the regression line. Some errors may be in the positive direction and some may be in the negative direction. For this reason they are squared to find mean squared error:

$$mse = \frac{1}{n}\sum_{i=1}^{n}(y_i - \hat{y}_i)^2 \qquad (5.9)$$

This averages the squared difference between the actual values (y) and the predicted values (y-hat) over all elements in the test set. Sometimes the square root of the above is used, rmse (root mean squared error), since it will be in units of y. The metrics mse or rmse are useful in comparing two models built on the same training data.

We see in Code 5.3.1 that our correlation is 0.38 which is not good, unsurprisingly, since we purposely made up data that was far from the regression line. As you can see in Figure 5.2, the 3 test examples, shown as squares, are not that close to the regression line. Two are above the line and one is below. Red vertical lines show the residuals, the errors. We quantify the amount of error with mse and rmse. The mse value can be hard to interpret in isolation; it is most useful in comparing models. The rmse however is in units of y. In this case, we see that our test data was off by 14.67 pounds on average.

Again, it should be stressed that we normally don't hallucinate test data. We normally take our data and divide it into train and test sets.

Code 5.3.1 — Hallucinated Test Data. Women Height-Weight Model.

```
# fake test data
test <- women[c(5, 9, 11),]
test[1, 2] <- 135
test[2, 2] <- 118
test[3, 2] <- 156
# predictions on test data
pred <- predict(lm1, newdata=test)
# metrics
correlation <- cor(pred, test$weight)
print(paste("correlation: ", correlation))
mse <- mean((pred - test$weight)^2)
print(paste("mse: ", mse))
rmse <- sqrt(mse)
print(paste("rmse: ", rmse))
[1] "correlation:  0.38404402702441"
[1] "mse:  215.284722222223"
[1] "rmse:  14.6725840335717"
```

Exercise 5.2 — Exploring Metrics. Using the linear regression model you built on the swiss data, try the following. For many of the following steps you will need to refer back to the formulas in this section.

- Run the R covariance and correlation functions on Education and Fertility and discuss your observations.
- Does the order of the operands matter for these functions?
- Create R code to compute the t-value for the estimated Education coefficient, and compare to the summary output for the model.
- Create R code to compute rss, rse, and r-squared for the model, and compare to the summary output for the model.
- Make a test set of 5 randomly chosen observations from the swiss data set. Note: This is cheating! We never let the algorithm see the test data before evaluation. However, we are just using the "test" set to compute some more metrics.
- Make predictions on Fertility for this "test" data.
- Print the test and predicted values side-by-side using print() and cbind(). Are they as close in value as you would expect?
- Run cor() and compute mse on the predicted versus actual data.
- Compute the rmse and compare this to the mean of the absolute value of the residuals. Are they close? Is this surprising? Why or why not?

5.4 The Algorithm

The example above is called *simple linear regression* because it had only one predictor variable, height, for the target variable, weight. When we have more than one predictor variable as we will see below, it is called *multiple linear regression*. In general, the more predictors are added to a model, the better it will be, but that does not mean you should just add all the predictors. We will learn techniques for determining which predictors should be included as we go.

Recall that the coefficients for the simple linear regression model above were $w = 3.45$ and $b = -87.51667$. Therefore, looking at an observation where height is 64 inches, we would expect weight to be:

$$3.45 * 64 - 87.511667 = 133.28$$

and we see from Figure 5.2 that this is a reasonable estimate of weight for this height. These parameters w and b were learned from the training data, but how? We will dig deeper into the math below, but the general idea is that we want a line than minimizes the residuals, the errors, designated as e:

$$\underset{w,b}{\mathrm{argmin}} \sum_{i=1}^{n} e_1^2 = \sum_{i=1}^{n} (y_i - \hat{y}_i)^2 \tag{5.10}$$

The above equation states that we want the parameters w, b that minimize the squared errors over all n examples in the training data. The estimated values of w and b are:

$$\hat{b} = \bar{y} - \hat{w}\bar{x} \qquad\qquad \hat{w} = \frac{\sum_{i=1}^{n}(x_i - \bar{x})(y_i - \bar{y})}{\sum_{i=1}^{n}(x_i - \bar{x})^2} \tag{5.11}$$

As seen above, these equations rely on mean values of x and y to compute w and b. To prove to ourselves that these equations find the parameters w, b, let's find the mean of x and y in the women's data and plug them into the equations.

Code 5.4.1 — Verifying the equations. Manually Computing Coefficients.

```
x <- women$height
y <- women$weight
x_mean <- mean(women$height)
y_mean <- mean(women$weight)

w_hat <- sum((x-x_mean)*(y-y_mean)) / sum((x-x_mean)^2)
b_hat <- y_mean - w_hat * x_mean
print(paste("w and b estimates = ", w_hat, b_hat))

[1] "w and b estimates =  3.45 -87.5166666666667"
```

> **Exercise 5.3 — Verify the equations.** Using the formulas in this section in R, verify the coefficients for the linear model you built on the swiss data. Comment on the role of means in linear regression. ∎

The algorithm described above for linear regression is called the **ordinary least squares (OLS) method**. Next we explore how these equations are derived.

5.5 Mathematical Foundations

Our goal in the OLS method is to reduce the errors over all the training data. These errors are quantified in the residual sum of errors, RSS:

$$RSS = e_1^2 + e_2^2 + ... + e_n^2 \qquad (5.12)$$

Each error, e, in turn is the difference between the actual y value and the predicted value:

$$RSS = (y_1 - b - wx_1)^2 + (y_2 - b - wx_2)^2 + ... + (y_n - b - wx_n)^2 \qquad (5.13)$$

The **loss function** describes how much accuracy we lose in our model. The first equation below specifies the loss for one example, the second averages the loss over all the examples. By the way, you will also see this called a **cost function**. The terms loss function, cost function, and error function are used somewhat synonymously, but unfortunately inconsistently across the literature. In the equations below we see the loss function with subscript i to indicate the loss for one instance, and the loss function without the subscript indicates the loss averaged over all examples.

$$\mathcal{L}_i = (y_i - f(x_i))^2 \qquad (5.14)$$

$$\mathcal{L} = \frac{1}{N} \sum_{i=1}^{n} (y_i - f(x_i))^2 \qquad (5.15)$$

Our goal is to find the parameters (coefficients) that minimize these errors on the training data:

$$\underset{w,b}{\operatorname{argmin}} \sum_{i=1}^{n} e_1^2 = \sum_{i=1}^{n} (y_i - \hat{y}_i)^2 \qquad (5.16)$$

One method for finding the coefficients is to take the partial derivatives of the loss function, set them to zero, and solve. This produces the normal equations given in the last section. Here we show the details of how they are derived. The equations above express the loss function in algrebraic notation. We could find the derivative with this notation but it is more concise if we use matrix notation. We are now going to consider parameter b to be one of possibly many parameters (in this case only two) in a vector. Specifically, we will refer to parameter b as w_0. Additionally we will express x as a vector, making the first element 1 so that it multiplies by w_0, the intercept.

$$\mathbf{w} = \begin{bmatrix} w_0 \\ w_1 \end{bmatrix}, \quad \mathbf{x} = \begin{bmatrix} 1 \\ x_1 \end{bmatrix}$$

$$f(x) = \mathbf{w}^T \mathbf{x} = w_0 + w_1 x_1$$

In the notation above, only one predictor is used. For multiple predictors, the w and x vectors would expand accordingly. Let's visualize this matrix representation of f(x) for the women data set.

$$\mathbf{y} \begin{bmatrix} 115 \\ 117 \\ 120 \\ 123 \\ 126 \\ ... \\ 154 \\ 159 \\ 164 \end{bmatrix} = \mathbf{w} \begin{bmatrix} -87.5167 \\ 3.45 \end{bmatrix}^T \mathbf{X} \begin{bmatrix} 1 & 1 & 1 & 1 & 1 & ... & 1 & 1 & 1 \\ 58 & 59 & 60 & 61 & 62 & ... & 70 & 71 & 72 \end{bmatrix}$$

Our loss function expressed in matrix notation, with i indexing indivdual observations:

$$\mathcal{L} = \frac{1}{N} \sum_{i=1}^{n} (\mathbf{y}_i - \mathbf{w}^T \mathbf{x}_i)^2 \tag{5.17}$$

Rewriting the square term above into the form shown below uses the property that $(\mathbf{X}\mathbf{w})^T = \mathbf{w}^T \mathbf{X}^T$:

$$\mathcal{L} = \frac{1}{N} (\mathbf{y} - \mathbf{X}\mathbf{w})^T (\mathbf{y} - \mathbf{X}\mathbf{w}) \tag{5.18}$$

Next we go through a few steps to multiply out and collect terms. First, bring the transpose inside the parenthesis.

$$\mathcal{L} = \frac{1}{N} (\mathbf{y}^T - (\mathbf{X}\mathbf{w})^T)(\mathbf{y} - \mathbf{X}\mathbf{w}) \tag{5.19}$$

Multiply out:

$$\mathcal{L} = \frac{1}{N}\mathbf{y}^T\mathbf{y} - \frac{1}{N}\mathbf{X}\mathbf{w}\mathbf{y}^T - \frac{1}{N}(\mathbf{X}\mathbf{w})^T\mathbf{y} + \frac{1}{N}(\mathbf{X}\mathbf{w})^T\mathbf{X}\mathbf{w} \qquad (5.20)$$

We can combine the middle two terms because $w^T X^T y$ and $y^T X w$ are transposes of one another and scalars.

$$\mathcal{L} = \frac{1}{N}\mathbf{y}^T\mathbf{y} - \frac{2}{N}\mathbf{w}^T\mathbf{X}^T\mathbf{y} + \frac{1}{N}\mathbf{w}^T\mathbf{X}^T\mathbf{X}\mathbf{w} \qquad (5.21)$$

Before we take the partial derivative wrt w, we can get rid of the first term since it doesn't involve w.

$$\mathcal{L} = -\frac{2}{N}\mathbf{w}^T\mathbf{X}^T\mathbf{y} + \frac{1}{N}\mathbf{w}^T\mathbf{X}^T\mathbf{X}\mathbf{w} \qquad (5.22)$$

Now use the rules for matrix partial derivatives to get:

$$\frac{\partial\mathcal{L}}{\partial w} = -\frac{2}{N}\mathbf{X}^T\mathbf{y} + \frac{2}{N}\mathbf{X}^T\mathbf{X}\mathbf{w} \qquad (5.23)$$

Above, we used the fact that the partial derivative of $w^T x = x$ for the first term and $w^T w = 2w$ for the second term. We simplify the equation to:

$$\mathbf{X}^T\mathbf{y} = \mathbf{X}^T\mathbf{X}\mathbf{w} \qquad (5.24)$$

And so our estimated parameters must be:

$$\hat{\mathbf{w}} = (\mathbf{X}^T\mathbf{X})^{-1}\mathbf{X}^T\mathbf{y} \qquad (5.25)$$

In practice, finding the inverse matrix above is computationally intense, $O(n^3)$, and therefore very slow for large data sets. For this reason, R uses optimization techniques to find the parameters.

5.5.1 Gradient descent

The situation just described in which a direct mathematical approach would be computationally expensive is a common one. This has led to the development of many optimization techniques. In this section we discuss gradient descent, and as we will see through the book, it is one of the most commonly used optimization techniques. Unlike directly finding the inverse in the normal equation above, gradient descent will not get bogged down for large data sets. The algorithm starts with some value for the parameters **w** and keeps changing them in an iterative

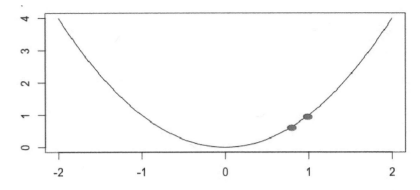

Figure 5.3: Searching for Error Minimum

loop until they find a minimum. Figure 5.3 visualizes a convex function with a random starting point symbolized by the higher red dot. One iteration may move the first dot to the second location. This is one step.

The gradient descent algorithm repeats the parameter update until convergence:

$$w_j := w_j - \alpha \frac{\partial \mathcal{L}}{\partial w} \tag{5.26}$$

Note that all parameters in w are updated at every iteration. The derivative gives us the slope and the alpha determines our step size. If alpha is too small, the algorithm will be slow. On the other hand, if it is too large we could overshoot the minimum and fail to converge.

> **Exercise 5.4 — Mathematical Foundations.** Use what you have learned in this section to answer the following questions. A good reference for R matrix operations is: `https://www.statmethods.net/advstats/matrix.html`
>
> - What is the purpose of a loss or cost function?
> - Is gradient descent guaranteed to find the optimal parameter? Why or why not?
> - Using R matrix operations, compute the w matrix of coefficients using formula 5.25 above.

5.6 Multiple Linear Regression

Next we look at another example of linear regression in R. We will use the R build-in data set ChickWeight, which has 578 rows and 4 columns of data resulting from an experiment on the effect of different types of feed on chick weight. We will use weight as our target, with the following predictors:
- Time - number of days since birth
- Diet - a factor representing 4 different diets

We will ignore the Chick column which identifies the chicken. In **simple linear regression** we use only one predictor. In **multiple linear regression** we use more than one predictor. We will do both on this data set. First, let's make a couple of plots to visualize the data.

Code 5.6.1 — **Plots.** Use par() to set up a 1x2 grid for the plots.

```
par(mfrow=c(1,2))
plot(ChickWeight$Time, ChickWeight$weight,
     xlab="Time", ylab="Weight")
plot(ChickWeight$Diet, ChickWeight$weight,
     xlab="Diet", ylab="Weight")
```

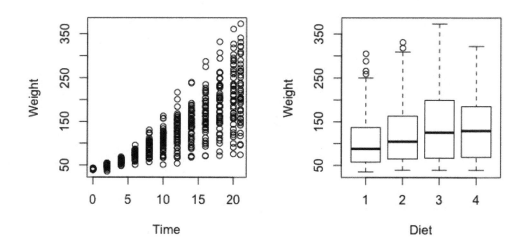

Figure 5.4: ChickWeight Weight Impacted by Time, Diet

In Figure 5.4 we see in the plot on the left that chicks gain wait over time. That is not surprising but what the plot also shows is that chicks start off at near identical weights and diverge over time. The plot on the right shows the impact of diet on weights. Box plots show the median value as the horizontal line through the box, the box itself shows the IQR (inter-quartile range from the first to the third quartile), and the horizontal lines at the end of the dashed lines show minimum and maximum values, not including suspected outliers which appear as dots beyond the horizontal lines. In this example it appears that diet 4 is slightly better than diet 3 and diet 1 appears to result in the lowest weights for chicks.

Next we divide the data into train and test sets by randomly sampling the rows. We set a seed so that each time we run this code we should get the same results. Vector i will contain the row numbers so we can subset the data frame with indices i to get a train set and *not i, or -i* to get the test set. After this 75/25 split, the train set has 433 observations and the test set has 145.

> **Code 5.6.2 — Divide data into train and test sets.** Made a 75/25 split.
>
> ```
> set.seed(1234)
> i <- sample(1:nrow(ChickWeight), nrow(ChickWeight)*0.75,
>     replace=FALSE)
> train <- ChickWeight[i,]
> test <- ChickWeight[-i,]
> ```

The sample() function as we used it above has this form: `sample(x, size, replace = FALSE)`. The first argument is a vector of elements from which to choose, in our case from 1:578, the row numbers of the data frame. The second argument specifies the size; in our case we want 75% of the row numbers. The last argument indicates that sampling should be done without replacement. To learn more about this function type `?sample()` at the console.

5.6.1 Interpreting summary() output for a linear model

Next we create a linear model on the train set, using only Time as a predictor. Let's look at the output of summary() in more detail. First it echoes back the code used to build lm1.

Next we see the distribution of the residuals, the errors. We want to see that the residuals are symmetrically distributed around the mean or median. There is a wide range here, from the minimum of -140 to the maximum of 158. That is not encouraging. The wide range of residuals confirms what we saw in Figure 5.4, that chick weight diverges widely as time goes on.

The Coefficients section lists for each predictor and the intercept, the estimated value, standard error, t value and p value, followed by significance codes. If you recall from our earlier discussion, a t-value measures variation in the data, and the associated p-value estimates confidence in that value. A low p-value indicates evidence for rejecting the null hypothesis that the predictor does not influence the target variable. We want to see low p-values and in this case we do. Time has a low p-value and correspondingly, 3 asterisks. The estimate for our one predictor, Time, is 8.952. This means we would expect chicks to gain an average of almost 9 gm a day. The standard error measures the average amount the coefficient estimate varies from the actual values. The t-value is a measure of how many standard deviations the coefficient estimate was from 0. The further it is from 0, the more confidence we have in rejecting the null hypothesis, in this case that Time has no effect on chick weight. The p-value gives the probability of observing a similar or larger t-value due to chance, given the data. A small p-value gives us confidence that there really is a relationship between our predictor(s) and the target variable. The chart for the significance codes is given at the bottom of the Coefficients section.

The last section gives some statistics on the model. The residual standard error, RSE, is in units of y. In this case our RSE was 41.4, so the average error of the model was about 41 gm. This statistic was calculated on 431 degrees of freedom: we had 433 data points minus 2 predictors. Multiple R-squared is scaled from 0 to 1 and so is easier to interpret than RSE. The adjusted R-squared is 0.6863 which is not bad. This means that 68% of the variance in the model can be explain by our predictor. The adjusted R-squared takes into account the number of predictors. This is important because R-squared tends to increase as we add predictors, and the adjusted R-squared accounts for this. Finally the F-statistic also measures whether our predictors and target are related. We want to see the F-statistic be far away from zero and its associated p-value to be low. The more data observations we have, the lower the F-statistic can be to confirm the relationship. This is why the p-value is important.

Code 5.6.3 — Linear model 1. Using only Time as a predictor.

```
lm1 <- lm(weight~Time, data=train)
summary(lm1)
```

```
Call:
lm(formula = weight ~ Time, data = train)
Residuals:
      Min      1Q   Median      3Q      Max
 -140.314  -16.648    0.778  14.682  158.686
Coefficients:
             Estimate Std. Error t value Pr(>|t|)
(Intercept)    26.318      3.743   7.031 8.06e-12 ***
Time            8.952      0.291  30.760  < 2e-16 ***
---
Signif. codes:  0 '***' 0.001 '**' 0.01 '*' 0.05 '.' 0.1 ' ' 1
Residual standard error: 41.4 on 431 degrees of freedom
Multiple R-squared:  0.687,Adjusted R-squared:  0.6863
F-statistic: 946.2 on 1 and 431 DF,  p-value: < 2.2e-16
```

5.6.2 Residuals

Plotting the residuals results in 4 plots, which we have arranged in a 2x2 grid in Figure 5.5. How do we interpret these plots? A comprehensive explanation is given here: `http://data.library.virginia.edu/diagnostic-plots/`.

Code 5.6.4 — Plot the residuals. The residuals give us information about how well the model fits the data.

```
par(mfrow=c(2,2))
plot(lm1)
```

Below we provide a brief overview of the 4 plots:
1. Plot 1 Residuals vs Fitted: This plots the residuals (errors) with a red trend line. You want to see a fairly horizontal red line. Otherwise, the plot is showing you some variation in the data that your model did not capture.
2. Plot 2 Normal Q-Q: If the residuals are normally distributed, you will see a fairly straight diagonal line following the dashed line.
3. Plot 3 Scale-Location: You want to see a fairly horizontal line with points distributed equally around it. If not, your data may not be homoscedastic (means "same variance").

4. Plot 4 Residuals vs Leverage: This plot will indicate leverage points which are influencing the regression line. They may or may not be outliers, but further investigation is warranted. An **outlier** is a data point with an unusual y value whereas a **leverage point** is a data point with an unusual x value.

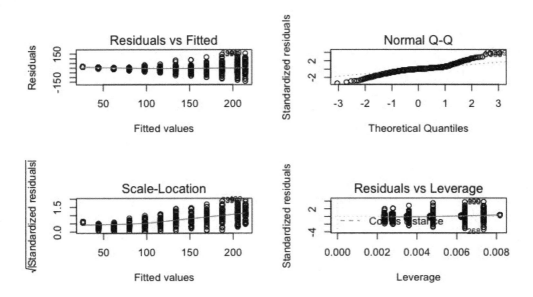

Figure 5.5: Residuals Plot

Looking at Figure 5.5 we see some problems with our model. In the first graph, the red line is horizontal but notice that the residuals vary more as we go to the right. This confirms our very first observation of the data, that chicks vary greatly in how much weight they gain. Time and even diet cannot account for this. What is not accounted for in our model is the genetic contribution. We humans start off life at an average of about 7 pounds but end up as adults in a wide range of weights. We could consider genetics a hidden or unseen variable in this experiment. Also chick gender was not included in the data, so we have no way of knowing if this influenced the weight variation. The second graph indicates that most of the residuals are normally distributed except for those in the lower range. So there is variation in the data that our model does not capture.

Let's build another model using Time and Diet as predictors. We do this with the plus sign in the formula: Time+Diet. The adjusted R-squared for lm2 is 0.7338 which is higher than the adjusted R-squared for lm1, which was 0.6863. Also, RSE has decreased to 38.13 from 41.1 in lm1. Adding Diet seems to have improved our model.

Code 5.6.5 — **Linear model 2.** Using Time and Diet as predictors.

```
lm2 <- lm(weight~Time+Diet, data=train)
summary(lm2)
```

```
Call:
lm(formula = weight ~ Time + Diet, data = train)

Residuals:
     Min       1Q   Median       3Q      Max
-137.857  -20.492   -1.685   16.955  137.365

Coefficients:
             Estimate Std. Error t value Pr(>|t|)
(Intercept)    8.4109     4.1372   2.033 0.042670 *
Time           8.9086     0.2682  33.218  < 2e-16 ***
Diet2         16.3645     4.9235   3.324 0.000965 ***
Diet3         40.1424     4.8907   8.208 2.67e-15 ***
Diet4         32.1873     5.2503   6.131 1.99e-09 ***
---
Signif. codes:  0 '***' 0.001 '**' 0.01 '*' 0.05 '.' 0.1 ' ' 1

Residual standard error: 38.13 on 428 degrees of freedom
Multiple R-squared:  0.7363, Adjusted R-squared:  0.7338
F-statistic: 298.8 on 4 and 428 DF,  p-value: < 2.2e-16
```

5.6.3 Dummy variables

Looking at the summary output for lm2, we see that Time and Diet were good predictors. Why do we have Diet2, Diet3, Diet4? Since Diet is a factor with 4 levels, R made 3 **dummy variables** for us. The base model represents Diet1, the dummy variables Diet2 - Diet 4 tell us how much each diet impacted the model compared to Diet 1. Recall from the boxplot above, that Diet1 resulted in the lowest weights and we see that confirmed in this summary, because Diet2 - Diet4 each have positive coefficients. For each data observation, only one of the dummy variables will be active with the others being zero. So for a chick on Diet 1, the dummy variables for Diets 2 through 4 would be zero.

5.6.4 The anova0 function

We can compare the summary() statistics of models to gauge their relative value. Another way to compare them is to run anova() on the two models. The anova() function lists each model and provides similar statistics as the summary() function for each model. We see that the RSS is lower for model 2, and model 2 is given a low p-value. This is confirmation that lm2 outperformed lm1.

Code 5.6.6 — **The anova() function.** Analysis of Variance.

```
anova(lm1, lm2)
```

```
Analysis of Variance Table
```

```
Model 1: weight ~ Time
Model 2: weight ~ Time + Diet
  Res.Df    RSS Df Sum of Sq       F    Pr(>F)
1    431 738546
2    428 622323  3    116222 26.644 8.107e-16 ***
```

Let's try one more thing. Recall from Figure 5.5 that there was a funnel shape in the residuals in that they became more spread out from left to right. The log function damps down x values across the axis. Perhaps this could squish the chick weights closer about the linear regression line.

Code 5.6.7 — **Linear model 3.** Linear models are not always a straight line.

```
lm3 <- lm(log(weight)~Time+Diet, data=ChickWeight)
summary(lm3)
```

```
Residual standard error: 0.2281 on 573 degrees of freedom
Multiple R-squared:  0.8484,Adjusted R-squared:  0.8474
F-statistic:   802 on 4 and 573 DF,  p-value: < 2.2e-16
```

Above we show only the statistics portion of the summary() output. Now the R-squared has increased to 0.8474, indicating that lm3 may be better than lm1 and lm2. We cannot run anova on the 3 models because lm3 has a different response: log(weight) instead of weight. But we could look at the residuals plots to look for improvement.

Exercise 5.5 — **Multiple Linear Regression.** Using the same swiss data, try the following activities:

- Run cor() and pairs() on swiss and discuss any patterns you see.
- Build a linear regression model predicting Fertility from all predictors.
- Build another model just using 2 or 3 predictors of your choice.
- Compare RSE and R-squared for the simple linear regression model and the two models you just created. Which appears best?
- Run anova() on the 3 models and discuss the results.
- Plot the residuals on your best model and discuss what you see.

5.7 Polynomial Linear Regression

To emphasize the point that linear regression is not always a straight line, we next look at polynomial linear regression. We will perform polynomial regression on the cars dataset, included in R. The data set has 50 observations and 2 variables: speed and stopping distance. The code example is from the R documentation. The plot() call at the top of the code sets up the plot. The seq() call sets up a sequence for the s values we want to plot across the horizontal axis. The for loop plots models of degree 1 through 4 in different colors. Colors 1-4 correspond to black, red, green3, blue. The poly() function is used to create orthogonal (not correlated) polynomials. Finally an anova() is run on the 4 models.

Code 5.7.1 — **Polynomial Regression.** Using the cars data set

```
plot(cars, xlab = "Speed (mph)",
    ylab = "Stopping distance (ft)", xlim = c(0, 25))
s <- seq(0, 25, length.out = 200)
for(degree in 1:4) {
  fm <- lm(dist ~ poly(speed, degree), data = cars)
  assign(paste("cars", degree, sep = "."), fm)
  lines(s, predict(fm, data.frame(speed = s)), col = degree)
}
anova(cars.1, cars.2, cars.3, cars.4)
```

```
Analysis of Variance Table

Model 1: dist ~ poly(speed, degree)
Model 2: dist ~ poly(speed, degree)
Model 3: dist ~ poly(speed, degree)
Model 4: dist ~ poly(speed, degree)
  Res.Df   RSS Df Sum of Sq      F Pr(>F)
1     48 11354
2     47 10825  1    528.81 2.3108 0.1355
3     46 10634  1    190.35 0.8318 0.3666
4     45 10298  1    336.55 1.4707 0.2316
```

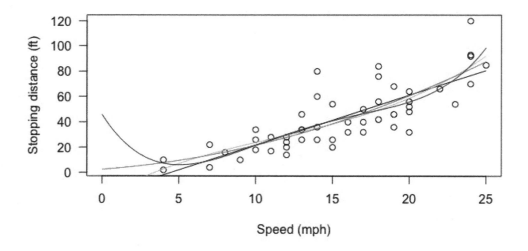

Figure 5.6: Cars with Polynomial Degree 1:4

When we look at the results above,[1] we see that the residuals of Model 2 are less than the degree-1 model. This is an indication that model 2 might be better than model 1. Residuals for models 3 and 4 are lower still, but at some point we worry about overfitting the training data, which we will discuss in the next section.

> **Exercise 5.6 — Polynomial Linear Regression.** Using the same swiss data, try the following activities:
> - Rerun the degree-1 linear regression model predicting Fertility from Education if necessary.
> - Build a degree-2 regression model predicting Fertility from Education.
> - Build a degree-3 regression model predicting Fertility from Education.
> - Run anova() on the 3 models and discuss the results.

5.8 Model Fitting and Assumptions

In this section we explore important concepts in machine learning that relate to how well a model fits the data. Overfitting is a common problem in many machine learning algorithms we will learn. And we will discuss the bias-variance tradeoff of various algorithms as we learn them.

5.8.1 Overfitting v. underfitting

The anova() results from the polynomial regression indicate the smallest RSS with the degree 4 model. However, none of the p-values are significant, and it is difficult to draw firm conclusions from such a small set of data points. However, the graph in Figure 5.6 gives us an opportunity to talk about underfitting versus overfitting. The linear degree=1 model probably underfits. In contrast the degree 3 and 4 models might be overfitting the data. When you underfit the data, your model does not have sufficient complexity to explain the data. That is what we see with the degree=1 model. The straight line is not capturing some of the complexity in the data. On the other hand, overfitting is when the model has too much complexity. The principle of **Occam's razor** tells us that when choosing between two likely explanations, choose the simpler one. In this case we might choose degree=2 since it did have a lower p-value. In a scenario where you have a train and test set, if the data performs well on the training data but poorly on the test data you may have overfit. Your model tuned itself too much to variation in the training data and this limited its ability to generalize to new data. On the other hand, if your model does poorly on the training set, you may have underfit. Figure 5.7 illustrates overfitting versus underfitting.

5.8.2 Bias and variance

A common theme throughout this handbook will be the bias-variance tradeoff which is related to underfitting and overfitting. Each algorithm that we learn will have tendencies one way or

---

[1]Reminder: Readers of the grayscale print book can find the color graphs in the github

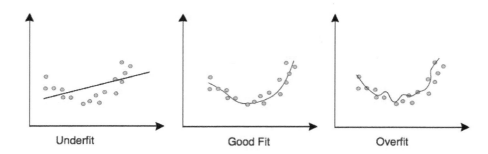

Figure 5.7: Fitting a model

the other. In the underfitting illustration in Figure 5.7, we see that the straight line underfit. It had a strong bias that the data was truly linear and is too simple a model for the data. On the other extreme, the overfitting example showed what can happen if variance is too high: the model learned random things from the data.

So bias-variance and underfitting-overfitting are related but it is important to distinguish their seperate meanings. A high bias, low variance model is likely to underfit and not capture the true shape of the data. This tends to happen more with simpler models like linear regression or logistic regression. In contrast, a low bias, high variance model captures too much complexity and noise in the data and may not generalize well to new data. This can happen with more complex models like decision trees, SVM, or neural networks.

So if you suspect your model has high bias, what can you do? We could try different algorithms. Right now, that's not helpful because we have only learned one algorithm. As we go we will learn more algorithms and learn their tendencies towards either bias or variance. We will see one tool in this chapter however that can help, and that is adding a regularization term that will help linear regression pull back its tendency towards bias. Also in this chapter we learned that a linear model doesn't necessarily mean a straight line. It can be a polynomial line or any mathematical transformation of the linear equation. One more technique we can try to reduce bias is to add more features, if available.

If you suspect your model is suffering from high variance, what can you do? More data should help. Algorithms that tend toward high variance are overly sensitive to noise in the data. Adding more data can quiet the effect of a few noisy observations. Another approach is to try fewer features if you are using a lot of features. Some features may be noiser than others so this could help.

Exercise 5.7 — **Interaction Effects.** In R, we can add interaction effects to formulas using the * operator. For example, y~x1+x2+x1*x2 has three predictors: x1, x2, and the interaction of x1 and x2. Again using the swiss data, create a linear model with all predictors plus an interaction between Education and Infant.Mortality. Is this interaction a good predictor? Is the model better?

5.8.3   Linear Model Assumptions

A linear model first and foremost assumes some linear shape in the data. Beyond that, the linear model also has an **additive assumption**, that each predictor contributes to the model independently of the other predictors. In reality, some predictors may be correlated, in which case we might consider removing one of them, since it will be hard for the model to assess the effect of them independently and thus the coefficient estimates may be erroneous. Other predictors may have an **interaction effect**, a synergy between them. Yet another concern is **confounding** variables, which are variables that correlate with both the target and a predictor. How can we detect these situations? We can use the cor() and pairs() methods in R to quantify and visualize correlations in the data set.

5.9   Advanced Topic: Regularization

An extension of the least squares approach is to add a regularization term to the RSS, with its importance controlled by another parameter, lambda. This extra term penalizes large coefficients. When lambda=0 it is the same as the least squares estimate. As lambda gets larger, the coefficients will shrink. The intercept does not shrink because the goal is to reduce the coefficients associated with predictors. The notation $\|w\|^2$ denotes the $l2$ norm, which is $\sqrt{(\sum_{j=1}^{p})}w_j^2$.   Regularization can help prevent overfitting when you have relatively complex models on a small data set.

$$\mathbf{RSS} = \sum_{i=1}^{n}(\mathbf{y}_i - \mathbf{w}^T\mathbf{x}_i)^2 + \lambda\|\mathbf{w}\|^2 \qquad (5.27)$$

We can implement ridge regression with the R package glmnet. We will use the airquality data set. Since airquality has a lot of NAs we will omit observations with NAs in the columns we care about with the complete.cases() function. Before performing ridge regression, we build a multiple linear regression model as usual.

Code 5.9.1 — **Linear Regression.** Multiple Linear Regression on Airquality

```
df <- airquality[complete.cases(airquality[, 1:5]),]
df <- df[,-6]
set.seed(1234)
i <- sample(1:nrow(df), .75*nrow(df), replace=FALSE)
train <- df[i,]
test <- df[-i,]
lm1 <- lm(Ozone~., data=train)
pred <- predict(lm1, newdata=test)
mse1 <- mean((pred-test$Ozone)^2)
```

The output above for the mse is 409.3799. Let's see if we can beat that with ridge regression. First we use the model.matrix() function to create a matrix of the predictors. Then we split into the same train and test observations as for lm1.

Code 5.9.2 — **Regularization.** Ridge Regression On Airquality

```
library(glmnet)
x <- model.matrix(Ozone~., df)[,-1]
y <- df$Ozone
train_x <- x[i,]
train_y <- y[i]
test_x <- x[-i,]
test_y <- y[-i]

# build a ridge regression model
rm <- glmnet(train_x, train_y, alpha=0)

# use cv to see which lambda is best
set.seed(1)
cv_results <- cv.glmnet(train_x, train_y, alpha=0)
l <- cv_results$lambda.min

# get data for best lambda, which is the 99th
pred2 <- predict(rm, s=l, newx=test_x)
mse2 <- mean((pred2-test_y)^2)
coef2 <- coef(rm)[,99]
```

The mse for the ridge regression was 371.0138, which is about 10% lower than for the regular multiple regression. Let's confirm that the ridge regression shrunk our coefficients. It appears that all the coefficients shrunk a bit.

```
> lm1$coefficients
  (Intercept)       Solar.R          Wind          Temp         Month
-66.85709002    0.08314323   -3.75229006    1.98524049   -3.27749222


> coef2
  (Intercept)       Solar.R          Wind          Temp         Month
-60.80449134    0.08165752   -3.61256523    1.83183505   -2.60738344
```

5.10 Summary

In this chapter we learned the supervised regression technique of linear regression, where our target was a real number variable and our predictors could be any combination of quantitative or qualitative variables. Linear regression has a strong bias in that it assumes that the relationship between the target and the predictors is linear. Keep in mind that *linear* does not always mean a straight line as we saw in the examples.

When we run the linear regression algorithm on training data, we create a *model* of the data that can then be used for predictions on new data. Our model gives us the coefficients which quantify the effect of each predictor on the target variable. As we explore many more algorithms for regression in the book, we will typically use linear regression as a baseline algorithm to see if other algorithms can beat it. If the data is linear, linear regression is quite hard to beat.

Linear regression strengths and weaknesses:

Strengths:
- Relatively simple algorithm with an intuitive explanation because the coefficients quantify the effect of predictors on the target variable.
- Works well when the data follows a linear pattern.
- Has low variance.

Weaknesses:
- High bias because it assumes a linear shape to the data.

5.10.1 Terminology

This chapter introduces a lot of terminology as we explored simple linear regression, multiple linear regression, and polynomial linear regression. There is a glossary at the end of the book but you might want to read back through the chapter again if you are unsure of the meaning of any of the following terms.

Terms related to the data:
- outlier
- leverage point
- dummy variables
- confounding variables

Terms related to the algorithm:
- coefficients
- residuals
- loss function, or cost function
- gradient descent
- additive assumption of linear regression
- interaction effect in linear predictors

Terms related to metrics:
- correlation
- covariance
- mse mean squared error
- rmse root mean squared error
- rss residual sum of squared errors
- rse residual standard error
- R^2 and adjusted R squared
- F-statistic
- p-value

Terms relevant to all machine learning algorithms:

- overfitting
- underfitting
- bias
- variance
- regularization

5.10.2   Quick Reference

Reference 5.10.1 Create Train and Test Sets
```
set.seed(...)
i <- sample(1:nrow(df), nrow(df)*0.8, replace=FALSE)
train <- df[i,]
test <- df[-i,]
```

Reference 5.10.2 Build and Examine a Linear Regression Model
```
lmName <- lm(formula, data=train)
summary(lmName)
```

Reference 5.10.3 Predict on Test Data
```
# predict using the test data
pred <- predict(lmName, newdata=test)

# predict for a single value
#   where the formula was target~predictor
pred <- predict(lm1, data.frame(predictor=5))
```

Reference 5.10.4 Evaluate Regression Predictions
```
# pred is a vector of real-number predictions
mse1 <- mean((pred - test$y)^2)
cor1 <- cor(pred, test$y)
```

Reference 5.10.5 Comparing Models with anova()
```
anova(model1, model2, ..., modeln)
```

Reference 5.10.6 Building formulas
```
lm1 <- lm(y~., data=train)  # y~. means use all predictors
lm1 <- lm(y~.-x1, data=train) # y~.-x1 all  except x1
lm1 <- lm(y~x1+x2, data=train)  # y~x1+x2 use x1 and x2
lm1 <- lm(y~x1+x2+x1*x2, data=train)  # x1*x2 interaction effect
lm1 <- lm(y~I(x^2), data=train)  # I() needed for x^2
```

5.10.3 Lab

Problem 5.1 — Practice on the Abalone Data. Try the following:

1. Download the Abalone data from the UCI Machine Learning Repository, `http://archive.ics.uci.edu/ml/datasets/Abalone`.
2. The data does not have column names so you will have to create them. Use meaningful names based on your reading about the data on the UCI site.
3. Check if there are missing values.
4. Run cor() and pairs() to see if there are any columns you might consider getting rid of.
5. Divide the data into 80-20 train-test, setting a seed for reproducibility.
6. Create a linear regression model with all predictors. What is the correlation of the predicted and actual values? What is the mse?
7. Create at least 2 more models, trying different features and combinations of features to see if you can improve these results.

5.10.4 Exploring Concepts

Problem 5.2 Based on your experience with the linear regression algorithm in R, does removing predictors with low p-values necessarily improve performance? Discuss possible reasons for your answer.

Problem 5.3 If you found that some predictors had high p-values, what reasons might you give for leaving them in? What reasons might you give for taking them out?

5.10.5 Going Further

There are entire statistics courses devoted to linear regression and scores of books if you have time for a deep exploration. Here are some recommendations:

- Free online linear regression tutorial here: `https://onlinecourses.science.psu.edu/stat501/node/250`
- *Linear Models in Statistics* by Rencher and Schaalje.
- *Linear Models with R* by Faraway.

6. Logistic Regression

6.1 Overview

Despite its name, when we use logistic regression, we are performing **classification**, not regression. Whereas in linear regression, our target variable was a *quantitative* variable, in logistic regression, our target variable is *qualitative*: we want to know what class an observation is in. In the most common classification scenario, the target variable is a binary output so that we classify into one class or the other. As we will see later in the chapter, there are techniques that allow classification into more than two classes.

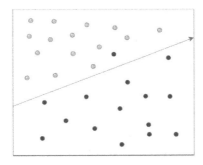

Figure 6.1: Decision Boundary for Binary Classification

Linear models for classification create decision boundaries to separate the observations into regions in which most observations are of the same class. The decision boundary is a linear combination of the X parameters. As we see in Figure 6.1 the two classes are almost perfectly separated by the decision boundary. There is one misclassified observation.

6.2 Logistic Regression in R

Let's take a look at the plasma data set in package HSAUR. This is a blood screening data set for 32 patients that gives measures of two plasma proteins, fibrinogen and globulin, and a binary indicator associated with the two protein levels. The fibrinogen and globulin variables are quantitative. The qualitative variable ESR>20 indicates whether the erythrocyte sedimentation rate, the rate at which red blood cells settle in blood plasma, is over 20 or not. In logistic regression our target needs to be a qualitative variable. In this data set, ESR>20 is our target. It has been coded as a factor in R so that ESR>20 = 2 means that ESR is over 20 and 1 means otherwise. We want to learn to predict whether ESR>20 or not, based on the levels of the plasma proteins fibrinogen and globulin. Values >20 indicate some possible associations with various health conditions.

6.2.1 Plotting factor data

Code 6.2.1 shows how the plots in Figure 6.2 were generated. First, we specify a 1x2 layout for the plots, then use the plot(x, y) command. The parameter `varwidth=TRUE` makes the boxplot widths proportional to the square root of the samples sizes. This easily lets us see that ESR<20 is more common than ESR>20. More importantly, the box plots show that ESR>20 observations are associated with slightly higher levels of globulin and significantly higher levels of fibronogen.

> **Code 6.2.1 — Plotting Factors.** Boxplots.
>
> ```
> par(mfrow=c(1,2))
> plot(ESR, fibrinogen, data=plasma, main="Fibrinogen",
>     varwidth=TRUE)
> plot(ESR, globulin, data=plasma, main="Globulin", varwidth=TRUE)
> ```

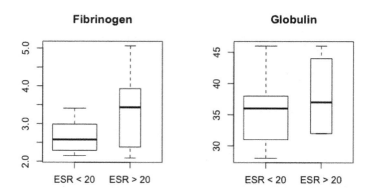

Figure 6.2: Box Plots

(R) **Plotting Qualitative Data**

If you use the R plot() function with command:

```
plot(globulin, ESR, data=plasma)
```

you will see a row of points at y=1 and another row of points at y=0 on the y axis. This should be your first clue that you need to rethink your plot. A boxplot is created if X is the qualitative variable and Y is the quantitative variable.

In Code 6.2.2 we make two conditional density (CD) plots, shown in Figure 6.3. We can make the same observations as we did when looking at the box plots. Here they are just visualized differently. The total probability space is the rectangle, with the lighter grey indicating ESR>20.

> **Code 6.2.2 — Plotting Factors.** CD Plots.
>
> ```
> par(mfrow=c(1,2))
> cdplot(ESR~fibrinogen)
> cdplot(ESR~globulin)
> ```

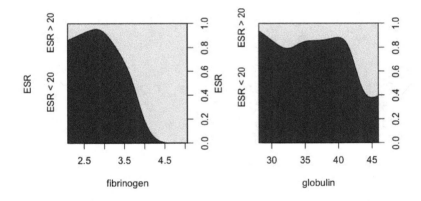

Figure 6.3: Conditional Density Plots

6.2.2 Train and Test on the Plasma Data

Even though this data set is very small, only 32 observations, we divided it into train and test sets, then created a logistic regression model using fibrinogen to predict ESR>20. The full notebook is available online.

For logistic regression we use the glm() *generalized* linear function instead of lm() that we used for linear regression. Also we need the parameter `family=binomial` for logistic regression. Otherwise the glm() function call looks similar to what we have done previously for lm(). The first argument is the formula, which seeks to learn the target ESR with one predictor, fibrinogen.

```
Code 6.2.3 — Logistic Regression. Using glm().

set.seed(1234)
i <- sample(1:nrow(plasma), 0.75*nrow(plasma), replace=FALSE)
train <- plasma[i,]
test <- plasma[-i,]
glm1 <- glm(ESR~fibrinogen, data=train, family=binomial)
summary(glm1)
```

You will notice that the output of the summary() function is very similar to the output we saw for linear regression, with 4 sections:
- the glm() call
- the residual distribution
- the coefficients with statistical significance metrics
- metrics for the model

Here is the summary output:

```
Call:
glm(formula = ESR ~ fibrinogen, family = binomial, data = train)

Deviance Residuals:
    Min       1Q    Median        3Q       Max
-0.9852  -0.7375   -0.5074   -0.1920    2.2554

Coefficients:
            Estimate Std. Error z value Pr(>|z|)
(Intercept)  -5.6141     2.6591  -2.111   0.0347 *
fibrinogen    1.5084     0.8543   1.766   0.0775 .
---
Signif. codes:  0 '***' 0.001 '**' 0.01 '*' 0.05 '.' 0.1 ' ' 1

(Dispersion parameter for binomial family taken to be 1)

    Null deviance: 26.992  on 23  degrees of freedom
Residual deviance: 22.716  on 22  degrees of freedom
AIC: 26.716

Number of Fisher Scoring iterations: 4
```

6.2.3 Interpreting summary() in Logistical Regression

For the logistic regression output, it is important to note that the residuals are *deviance residuals*. What does that mean? The deviance residual is a mathematical transformation of the loss function (discussed in a later section) and quantifies a given point's contribution to the overall likelihood. These deviance residuals can then be used to form RSS-like statistics.

At the bottom of the output, the statistics section is quite different. We have null deviance and residual deviance for metrics. The null deviance measures the lack of fit of the model, considering only the intercept. The residual deviance measures the lack of fit of the entire model. We want to see that the Residual deviance is much lower than the Null deviance. The AIC is most useful in comparing models, the lower the AIC the better. AIC stands for Akaike Information Criterion and is based on deviance. AIC shows a preference for less complex models with fewer predictors. The Fisher scoring algorithm is a modified form of Newton's method of solving a maximum likelihood problem.

Interpreting coefficients of a logistic regression model is quite different from interpreting them in a linear regression model. Whereas the coefficient of a linear regression predictor quantifies the difference in the target variable as the predictor changes, in logistic regression, the coefficient quantifies the difference in the log odds of the target variable. We will discuss odds, log odds, and probability in the Metrics section.

6.2.4 Evaluation on the Test Data

Next, we look at the output of predict() for logistic regression created in Code 6.2.4. Notice the parameter `type="response"`. This is important to get probabilities out of the model. The model outputs log-odds but by requesting "response" we get these numbers converted to probabilities. The probabilities for the first few test observations are:

```
> head(probs)
         1          3         10         11         22         24
0.14028110 0.09023866 0.15547539 0.10341103 0.16563738 0.10202084
```

The ifelse() function is needed to convert these probabilities to 1 or 2, the internal coding for the target variable. Once the predictions are in variable pred, we can compare them to the actual values in the test observations to get accuracy, the percentage of observations that were classified correctly. The code also outputs a table of predictions and actual values. All the predictions were of class 1. All 8 actual values in this tiny test set were of class 1, giving 100% accuracy. On such a small and unbalanced data set, we should be skeptical about this seemingly good accuracy.

Code 6.2.4 — **Logistic Regression.** Evaluating the output.

```
probs <- predict(glm1, newdata=test, type="response")
pred <- ifelse(probs>0.5, 2, 1)
acc1 <- mean(pred==as.integer(test$ESR))
print(paste("glm1 accuracy = ", acc1))
table(pred, as.integer(test$ESR))
```

```
[1] "glm1 accuracy =  1"


pred 1
   1 8
```

6.2.5 Learning (or Not) From Data

Note one odd thing about the table above: the model always predicted class 1 (ESR<20). Even though 100% accuracy sounds great, we cannot be impressed. There are two problems here: (1) a small amount of data, (2) an unbalanced data set.

The first problem is that we have a very small data set. In order to create a stronger model, much more data would have to be collected. Data collection can be expensive and require domain expert assistance. In the case of this data set, more blood samples would have to be drawn from a random population, analyzed by technicians, and supervised by a hematologist or other clinician.

When additional data cannot be obtained, another but less preferable option is to use sampling techniques. Consider our example above, with 8 test cases randomly sampled from the data. What if we randomly sampled the data multiple times? By randomly sampling iteratively, each time we would have a different test set. We could average our test accuracy over all these samples and get a better idea of the accuracy of our model. One such sampling technique is cross-validation which we will explore later in the book.

The second problem with the data set is that it is unbalanced. Of the 32 observations, only 6 have ESR>20. This is a 81% ESR<20 to 19% ESR>20 ratio. Unbalanced data sets can pose problems for some classification algorithms while others can rise above it. Again, more data would be helpful. If that additional data is still unbalanced, sampling techniques may be of help. The idea is to oversample from the minority class and undersample from the majority class to come up with a data set that is more balanced. We will explore techniques for doing this in future chapters, and discuss when it might be helpful. For now, we will take our model as created, but take it with a grain of salt.

> **Exercise 6.1 — Logistic Regression.** Practice on the PimaIndiansDiabetes2 data set from package mlbench. First, create an 80-20 split into train and test sets. What is your accuracy predicting diabetes from glucose?
>
> By the way, this data set has a lot of missing NA values. If you get NA for your accuracy, it means that one or more of the predictions was NA. Check this with code: `sum(is.na(pred))`. If you have NAs, compute your mean accuracy using parameter `na.rm=TRUE` in the mean() function.   ∎

6.3 Metrics

Classification can be evaluated by many measures. In this section we will look at accuracy, sensitivity and specificity, Kappa, AUC, and ROC curves.

6.3.1 Accuracy, sensitivity and specificity

The most common metric to evaluate results in classification is accuracy:

$$acc = \frac{C}{N} \qquad\qquad (6.1)$$

where C is the number of correct predictions, and N is the total number of test observations. The output of the table() command above was limited because the model predicted all test cases to be in one class. Normally it should look something like this:

```
pred 1 2
   1 7 1
   2 1 5
```

Such a table is also called a confusion matrix. The diagonal values from the upper left to the lower right are the correctly classified instances, 7 and 5 in this case. The other values are errors, 1 and 1. The flip side of accuracy is the error rate, calculated by subtracting accuracy from 1.

We can break down each component of the confusion matrix as follows:

```
pred T  F
   T TP FP
   F FN TN
```

- TP - true positive: these items are true and were classified as true
- FP - false positive: these items are false but were classified as true
- TN - true negative: these items are false and were classified as false
- FN - false negative: these items are true but were classified as false

$$accuracy = \frac{TP+TN}{TP+TN+FP+FN} \tag{6.2}$$

$$error\ rate = \frac{FP+FN}{TP+TN+FP+FN} = 1 - accuracy \tag{6.3}$$

The **sensitivity** measures the true positive rate:

$$sensitivity = \frac{TP}{TP+FN} \tag{6.4}$$

The **specificity** measures the true negative rate:

$$specificity = \frac{TN}{TN+FP} \tag{6.5}$$

Sensitivity and specificity range from 0 to 1, just as accuracy does, with values closer to 1 being better. They help to quantify the extent to which a given class was misclassified.

6.3.2   Kappa

Cohen's Kappa is a statistic that attempts to adjust accuracy by accounting for the possibility of a correct prediction by chance alone. Kappa is often used to quantify agreement between two annotators of data. Here we are quantifying agreement between our predictions and the actual values. Kappa is computed as follows:

$$\kappa = \frac{Pr(a) - Pr(e)}{1 - Pr(e)} \qquad (6.6)$$

where Pr(a) is the actual agreement and Pr(e) is the expected agreement based on the distribution of the classes. The following interpretation of Kappa is often used but there is not universal agreement on this. Kappa scores:

- <2.0 poor agreement
- 0.2 to 0.4 fair agreement
- 0.4 to 0.6 moderate agreement
- 0.6 to 0.8 good agreement
- 0.8 to 1.0 very good agreement

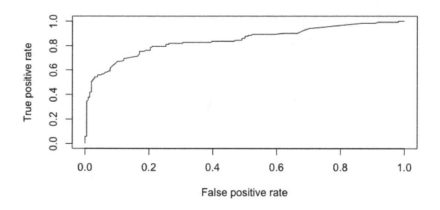

Figure 6.4: ROC Curve

6.3.3   ROC Curves and AUC

The ROC curve is a visualization of the performance of machine learning algorithms. The name ROC stands for Receiver Operating Characteristics which reflects its origin in communication technology in WWII in detecting between true signals and false alarms. The ROC curve shows the tradeoff between predicting true positives while avoiding false positives.

Figure 6.4 shows an ROC curve. This figure is taken from the Titanic logistic regression notebook on the github. The y axis is the true positive rate while the x axis is the false positive rate. The predictions are first sorted according to the estimation probability of the positive class. A perfect classifier would shoot straight up from the origin since it classified all correctly. We want to see the classifier shoot up and leave little space at the top left. Starting at the orgin, each prediction's impact on the curve is vertical for correct predictions and horizontal for incorrect ones. If we see a diagonal line from the lower left to the upper right, then our classifier had no predictive value.

A related metric is AUC, the area under the curve. AUC values range from 0.5 for a classifier with no predictive value to 1.0 for a perfect classifier.

6.3.4 Probability, odds, and log odds

What is the difference between odds and probability? Let's look at this using a sports outcome example. Imagine we played 10 games with a friend and won 7. That means we lost 3 of course. Assuming we will do as well next time, our odds are 7 to 3:

$$odds = \frac{number\ of\ wins}{number\ of\ losses} = \frac{7}{3} \tag{6.7}$$

If we want to express the same data as a probability:

$$probability = \frac{number\ of\ wins}{number\ of\ games} = \frac{7}{10} \tag{6.8}$$

Notice that probability will always range from 0 to 1, whereas odds will not. Recall that the glm() algorithm coefficients represent a change in log odds. Just as it sounds, log odds are the log of the odds: log(odds). So to find the odds, we use the inverse of log, the exp() function. And to convert odds to probability, we use the following:

$$probability = \frac{odds}{1 + odds} \tag{6.9}$$

Let's see what this means in terms of the plasma data logistic regression model above. The predictor is fibrinogen, which ranges from around 2.09 to 5.06 in this data set. Let's compare the effect of fibrinogen across values from 2.25 to 5.0. Figure 6.5 plots the log odds across this range of values on the left, and on the right, the associated probabilities across the same range of values. Observe that the results of the logistic regression model (the log odd) are linear in the parameters (w, b) but that the associated probabilities are not linear.

The coefficient for fibrinogen in the linear regression model was 2.34. For every one-unit increase in x, the probability of ESR>20 changes by exp(2.34)/[1+exp(2.34)]. Let's look at some sample values in Table 6.1. The X column is fibrinogen for a range of values. The log odds is found by plugging in the value of x for the logistic regression formula given by: 2.34 * x - 8.383.

As you see in Table 6.1 and more clearly in Figure 6.5, the log odds are linear in the parameters but the probability is not linear, we can discern a subtle S-shape in the probabilities.

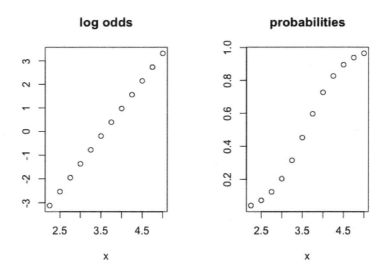

Figure 6.5: Log Odds versus Probability

X	Log Odds	Probability
2.5	-2.53	0.07
3.0	-1.36	0.20
3.5	-0.19	0.45
4.0	0.977	0.73
4.5	2.147	0.89

Table 6.1: Log Odds and Probability for Plasma Data

Ⓡ **Logistic Regression Coefficients**

In linear regression we interpret a predictor coefficient as the amount of change in y for a 1-unit change in x. We cannot make this intepretation in logistic regression. The predictor coefficient in a logistic regression model specifies the change in log-odds for a 1-unit change in x.

Exercise 6.2 — Metrics for Classification. Using your model created for the Pima Indians data, compute the following in R using the formulas above:
- TP, TN, FP and FN
- accuracy using TP, TN, FP, FN
- error rate using accuracy
- sensitivity
- specificity

Next, use the confusionMatrix() function in package `caret` to confirm your results. ∎

6.4 The Algorithm

The linear regression output was a quantitative value that could range over all the real numbers. What we need for logistic regression classification is a function that will output probabilities in the range [0, 1]. The sigmoid, or logistic, function is used for this purpose and of course is where the algorithm gets its name. When real numbers are input to the logistic function, the output is squashed into the range [0,1] as seen in Figure 6.6. The logistic function is:

$$f(x) = \frac{1}{1 + e^{-x}} \tag{6.10}$$

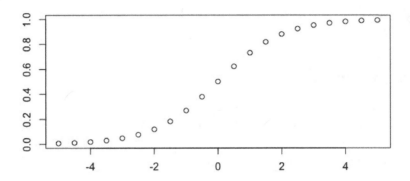

Figure 6.6: The Logistic Function

The logistic regression algorithm computes the log odds from the estimated parameters. The log odds is just log(odds). The odds are the probability of the positive class, p(x), over the probability of the negative class (1 - p(x)). If we have a single predictor w_1 and an intercept w_0, the log odds are:

$$log\frac{p(x)}{1 - p(x)} = w_o + w_1 x \tag{6.11}$$

Solving for p gives us the logistic function:

$$p(x) = \frac{e^{-(w_0 + w_1 x)}}{1 + e^{-(w_0 + w_1 x)}} = \frac{1}{1 + e^{-(w_0 + w_1 x)}} \tag{6.12}$$

We can see in Equation 6.11 why logistic regression is considered a linear classifier. It creates a linear boundary between classes in which the distance from the boundary determines the probability. When we use the logistic function for classification, the cut-off point is usually

0.5. Notice in Figure 6.6 that this is the inflection point of the S-curve. Probabilities greater than 0.5 are classified as the positive class and probabilities less than 0.5 are classified in the other class.

> **Exercise 6.3 — Logistic Regression Algorithm.** Using the coefficients and data from the logistic regression Check-Your-Understanding above, try the following:
>   - Compute the probabilities in R using only the glucose column from the test data and the coefficients of the model.
>   - Compare these to the output of predict() you did earlier. Are they the same?
>   - Create a plot with test glucose on the x axis and the probabilities you calculated for the test set on the y axis. What do you observe?
>   - Create a vector of x values: 60, 100, 140, 180, 220
>   - Compute probabilities for these values using the same formula as above.
>   - Are these probabilities consistent with the graph you just created?

6.5   Mathematical Foundations

How are the parameters, **w**, found for logistic regression? First an appropriate loss function is established, then an optimization technique such as gradient descent is used to find optimal parameters.

Recall the loss function for linear regression:

$$\mathcal{L} = \frac{1}{N} \sum_{i=1}^{n} (y_i - f(x_i))^2 \tag{6.13}$$

If we plug in the logistic function for f(x), it will not be a convex function. That is a problem because gradient descent works only for convex functions. A suitable loss function for logistic regression can be found by starting with the likelihood function, L:

$$L(w_0, w_1) = \prod_{i=1}^{n} f(x_i)^{y_i} (1 - f(x_i))^{1 - y_i} \tag{6.14}$$

Notice in the likelihood equation that one of the terms in the product will always reduce to 1 because the y values are either 0 or 1. To simplify the likelihood equation we will take the log of it to find the log-likelihood, ℓ:

$$\ell = \sum_{i=1}^{n} y_i \, log f(x_i) + (1 - y_i) \, log(1 - f(x_i)) \tag{6.15}$$

The log-likelihood equation for each instance:

$$\ell = y \, log f(x) + (1 - y) \, log(1 - f(x)) \tag{6.16}$$

In training the classifier, we want to penalize it for wrong classifications. This is our loss function. The penalties follow directly from Equation 6.16. Our Loss is:

$$\mathcal{L} = -log(f(x)) \; if \; y = 1 \qquad \mathcal{L} = -log(1 - f(x)) \; if \; y = 0 \tag{6.17}$$

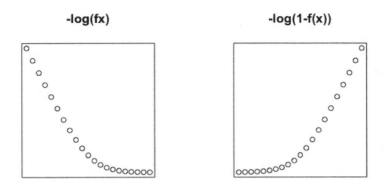

-log(fx)   **-log(1-f(x))**

Figure 6.7: Loss Function for Logistic Regression

These two loss functions are visualized in Figure 6.7. In the leftmost graph which represents -log(fx), the closer the function gets to 1, the smaller the penalty but the closer it gets to 0, the higher. We want to penalize -log(f(x)) severely if it classifies as 0 when the true target is 1. The reverse is true when the true target is 0. This is shown in the rightmost graph. Here we penalize -log(1-f(x)) severely as it moves toward 1 because the true target is 0.

We can put the two loss functions into one equation as shown below, where they are summed over all observations. Notice that one of the terms will always be zero because y will be either 0 or 1.

$$\mathcal{L} = -\left[\sum_{i=i}^{N} y_i log(f(x_i)) \quad + \quad (1 - y_i)log(1 - f(x_i)) \right] \tag{6.18}$$

where f(x) =

$$f(x) = \frac{1}{1 + e^{-(w^T x)}} \tag{6.19}$$

The parameters w are then determined using gradient descent. You can see from Figure 6.7 that when you put together the two loss functions you will have a convex function suitable for gradient descent. Once the parameters are known, classifying new instances is done by plugging in the instance into the logistic function shown in Equation 6.19. This returns a probability in the range [0, 1]. Typically we establish a threshold such as 0.5. Values over that threshold are classified as 1, values below are classified as 0.

(R) **Likelihood versus Probability**

In common speech we use the terms likelihood and probability interchangeably, but in statistics they have different meanings. Likelihood is looking backward in time. Likelihood is the probability that an event which already happened would yield a specific outcome. Probability looks forward in time. Probability is estimating a future outcome given known values. Probabilities for all possible values sum to 1. Likelihoods do not have this limit. We'll discuss this more in the next chapter.

6.6 Logistic Regression with Multiple Predictors

The github repo for the book has a logistic regression example on a Titanic data set. We will just cover a few points here. The first is that the data had a lot of NA values. NA values can cause a lot of problems for many classifiers and it is a good idea to remove them. There are a couple of approaches to take. One is to simple remove rows with NAs which is a good choice if you have lots of remaining data. We saw an example of that using R's complete.cases() function in the linear regression chapter. Another approach is to replace NA values with either the mean or median of the variable for quantitative variables, or the most common factor for qualitative variables. The code below shows the detection of NAs with the sapply() function.

```
Code 6.6.1 — Detecing NAs. Using sapply().

sapply(df, function(x) sum(is.na(x)==TRUE))
   pclass  survived      sex      age
        0         0        0      263
```

The output shows that almost a third of the examples in the data set have missing values for age. Getting rid of these rows would leave a much smaller data set. Instead, we replace NAs with the median value. That is shown in the code below. The median() function needs the argument 'na.rm=T' in order to compute the median of the values that are not NA.

```
Code 6.6.2 — Removing NAs. By deleting rows or replacing with the median.

df$age[is.na(df$age)] <- median(df$age,na.rm=T)
```

One concern about replacing age NAs with median values is that there were so many NAs, almost one-third of the data. By replacing so many NAs with the mean or median, we are diminishing the predictive power of age. An alternative is to replace age NAs for observations that survived with the mean or median for age of those who survived, and then do something similar for NAs for observations that did not survive. This approach is somewhat problematic as well. We are manipulating our data. Whatever decisions you make should be thoroughly documented in your RStudio notebook and any other reporting you do on your results.

In the online notebook you will see that we divided the data into train and test sets and build a logistic regression model which achieved 76.5% accuracy. The code also gives an example of using the `caret` package to output the confusion matrix and other statistics including the Kappa. The ROC curve for our predictions is the ROC curve shown in the Metrics section above. The AUC for that curve was 0.81. The following is the key output of summary() for the model predicting survival with all predictors.

```
Call:
glm(formula = survived ~ ., family = "binomial", data = train)

Deviance Residuals:
    Min       1Q    Median       3Q       Max
-1.9509  -0.6567   -0.4336   0.6703    2.4834

Coefficients:
             Estimate Std. Error z value Pr(>|z|)
(Intercept)  3.858516   0.360478  10.704  < 2e-16 ***
pclass2     -1.417739   0.249787  -5.676 1.38e-08 ***
pclass3     -2.437512   0.233637 -10.433  < 2e-16 ***
sexmale     -2.552619   0.175795 -14.520  < 2e-16 ***
age         -0.042339   0.007198  -5.882 4.06e-09 ***
---
Signif. codes:  0 '***' 0.001 '**' 0.01 '*' 0.05 '.' 0.1 ' ' 1

(Dispersion parameter for binomial family taken to be 1)

    Null deviance: 1305.05  on 980  degrees of freedom
Residual deviance:  897.03  on 976  degrees of freedom
AIC: 907.03

Number of Fisher Scoring iterations: 4
```

Consider the summary shown above. All of the predictors seem to be good predictors. Notice that pclass has dummy variables for class 2 and class 3. How do we interpret this? If a person is pclass 2 instead of 1, the log odds of their survival decreases by 1.4 and if they are pclass 3 instead of 1, the log odds of their survival decreases by 2.4. A similar interpretation can be made for male over female. In this example, age is our only quantitative predictor. The coefficient is telling us that log odds of survival decrease a little for every year. Notice also the large drop in deviance from the null deviance which considers the intercept alone, and the residual deviance, which considers all predictors. This drop indicates that our predictors are good predictors.

Below we have the code for generating the ROC plot and computing AUC. The AUC is .81.

Code 6.6.3 — **ROC and AUC.** On the Titanic Data.

```
library(ROCR)
p <- predict(glm1, newdata=test, type="response")
pr <- prediction(p, test$survived)
# TPR = sensitivity, FPR=specificity
prf <- performance(pr, measure = "tpr", x.measure = "fpr")
plot(prf)
# compute AUC
auc <- performance(pr, measure = "auc")
auc <- auc@y.values[[1]]
```

Exercise 6.4 — **Logistic Regression with Multiple Predictors.** In this example, you will build a logistic regression model using multiple predictors on the Pima Indian data. Try the following:

- Build a model with all predictors, using the same train and test set as you used with only glucose as a predictor. Is your accuracy higher or lower?
- Use R functions to count how many NAs are in each column.
- Replace NAs in the triceps and insulin columns with the mean of each column in both train and test. Now replace train and test with rows that have complete data using complete.cases().
- Build a second model with all predictors on the train and test that have been cleaned up.
- Compare the accuracies of the two models.
- Compare the residual deviance and degrees of freedom for each model. Which model do you think is best, and why?

6.7 Advanced Topic: Optimization Methods

Earlier we specified our log-loss function for logistic regression as follows:

$$\ell = \sum_{i=1}^{n} y_i \, log f(x_i) + (1 - y_i) \, log(1 - f(x_i)) \tag{6.20}$$

where f(x) =

$$f(x) = \frac{1}{1 + e^{-(w^T x)}} \tag{6.21}$$

Next we find the gradient of the log likelihood. The gradient, g, is the partial derivative with respect to the parameters **w**. The gradient is the slope which is going to tell the algorithm which direction to move to find the minimum. The gradient equation is given below. Notice that it is really the X matrix multiplied by how wrong f(x) is at this point in predicting the true y.

$$g = \frac{\partial \ell}{\partial \mathbf{w}} = \sum_i (f(x_i) - y_i)\mathbf{x}_i = \mathbf{X}^T (f(x) - \mathbf{y}) \tag{6.22}$$

All we need for gradient descent is the first derivative, the gradient. For other optimization methods we will also need the second derivative, the Hessian, H. The Hessian is a square matrix of second partial derivatives that gives the local curvature of a function. Note that in the following equation for the Hessian, the S represents $S \triangleq diag(p_i(1 - p_i))$

$$H = \frac{\partial}{\partial \mathbf{w}} g(\mathbf{w})^T = \sum_i (\nabla_w f(x_i))\mathbf{x}_i^T = \sum_i f(x_i) (1 - f(x_i) \mathbf{x}_i \mathbf{x}_i^T = \mathbf{X}^T \mathbf{S} \mathbf{X} \tag{6.23}$$

There are many algorithms to find the optimal parameters, **w**. The first one we examine is gradient descent.

6.7.1 Gradient Descent

Gradient descent is an iterative approach where at each step the estminated parameters, θ get closer to the optimal values. We can express this as follows:

$$\theta_{k+1} = \theta_k - \eta_k \, g_k \tag{6.24}$$

where η is the learning rate, which specifies how big of a step to take at each iteration. If the eta (step size) is too slow the algorithm will take a long time to converge. If eta is too large, the true minimum can be stepped over and then the algorithm will not be able to converge.

6.7.2 Stochastic Gradient Descent

For large data sets, gradient descent can bog down. An alternative is *stochastic gradient descent* which processes the data either one at a time or in small batches instead of all at once. It is stochastic because the observations are chosen randomly. If the data is processed one at a time it means that the gradient has to be computed at each step. It turns out that the gradient will reflect the underlying function better if it is computed from a small batch. This also improves computation time.

6.7.3 Newton's Method

Gradient descent finds the optimal parameters using the first derivative. Newton's method is another approach; it uses the second derivative, the Hessian defined above. Newton's method (also called Newton-Raphson) is also an iterative method. At each step either the full Hessian is recalculated, or it is updated in which we call the method quasi-Newton. In a well-behaved convex function, Newton's method will converge faster.

A key insight in Newton's method is that if it is computationally difficult to compute a minimum for a given function, then come up with a function that shares important properties with the original function but is easier to minimize. At each iteration, Newton's method constructs a quadratic approximation to the objective function in which the first and second derivatives are the same. The approximate function is minimized instead of the original.

How is this approximate function found? A Taylor series about the point is used, but ignores derivatives past the second. A Taylor series converts a function into a power function and the first few terms can be used to get an approximate value for a function.

6.7.4 Optimization from Scratch

We are going to take a closer look at gradient descent by finding our optimal coefficients in the plasma data set from scratch. The R Notebook for this is available online. First we recreate the logistic regression model from earlier in the chapter. Our coefficients were $w_0 = -5.6141$ and $w_1 = 1.5084$.

The first thing we need to do is define our sigmoid/logistic function that will take an input matrix and return a vector of sigmoid values for each observation. We initialize w_0 and w_1 to 1. We make a data matrix where column 1 is all 1s that will be multiplied by the intercept, and column 2 is fibrinogen which will be multiplied by w_1. We will also need the labels but since they were coded as 1-2 instead of 0-1 we subtract 1.

Code 6.7.1 — **Logistic Regression from Scratch.** Set up code.

```
sigmoid <- function(z){
  1.0 / (1+exp(-z))
}
# set up weight vector, label vector, and data matrix
weights <- c(1, 1)
data_matrix <- cbind(rep(1, nrow(train)), train$fibrinogen)
labels <- as.integer(train$ESR) - 1
```

Now we are ready to iterate. The code below iterates 500,000 times. In each iteration it does the following:

1. multiplies the data by the weights to get the log likelihood, then runs these values through the sigmoid() function to get a vector of probabilities
2. computes the error: the true values (0 or 1) minus the probabilities
3. updates the weights by weights plus the learning rate times the gradient; Recall that the gradient is the X values times the errors as shown in Equation 6.22; Notice also the operator for matrix multiplication is an asterisk surrounded by percent signs.

Code 6.7.2 — **Gradient Descent from Scratch.** Three steps per iteration.

```
learning_rate <- 0.001
for (i in 1:500000){
  prob_vector <- sigmoid(data_matrix %*% weights)
  error <- labels - prob_vector
  weights <- weights + learning_rate * t(data_matrix) %*% error
}
weights
```

Try running this code several times, changing the number of iterations. The following table shows the weights af various numbers of iterations.

No. Iterations	(w_0)	(w_1)
50	0.483	-0.328
500	-0.097	-0.267
5000	-3.26	0.763
50000	-5.61	1.50
500000	-5.6141	1.5084

Table 6.2: Optimized Weights by Number of Iterations

The 500,000 iterations gives use the same coefficients as R's glm(). However, it was slow compared to R's optimized code. R functions are heavily optimized and will reliably give good performance.

Finally, we create a plot that confirms Equation 6.11. The linear combination of the weights we calculated in the code above and X values give us the log odds.

Code 6.7.3 — **Log Odds.** Linear combination of $w_0 + w_1 x$

```
plasma_log_odds <- cbind(rep(1, 32), plasma$fibrinogen) %*% weights
plot(plasma$fibrinogen, plasma_log_odds, col=plasma$ESR)
abline(weights[1], weights[2])
```

6.8 Multiclass Classification

The classification examples we have seen so far have been binary, classifying into one of two possible classes. What if we want to classify in a scenario where there are more than two classes? One technique that can be used is **one-versus-all** classification in which we perform multiple binary classifications. Let's look at the iris data set as an example. The notebook for this is in github as usual. The iris data set contains 150 observations of flower measurements. There are 50 observations each of 3 species: virginica, setosa, and versicolor. First we look at a couple of graphs for data exploration. Figure 6.9 shows the pairs() output for the predictor

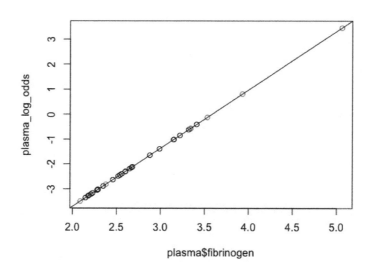

Figure 6.8: LogOdds is a Linear Combination of the Parameters

columns with the color of each observation representing one of the 3 classes. Figure 6.10 plots petal width and length, color coded as well. The code for these plots is given below. The as.integer() function was used to make Species an integer 1, 2, or 3, which in turn is used to match colors red, yellow and blue.

Code 6.8.1 — Code to Generate Plots. Using as.integer()

```
pairs(iris[1:4], pch = 21,
    bg = c("red", "yellow", "blue")[as.integer(Species)])
plot(Petal.Length, Petal.Width, pch=21,
    bg=c("red","yellow","blue")as.integer(Species)])
```

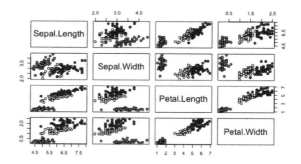

Figure 6.9: Iris Pairs

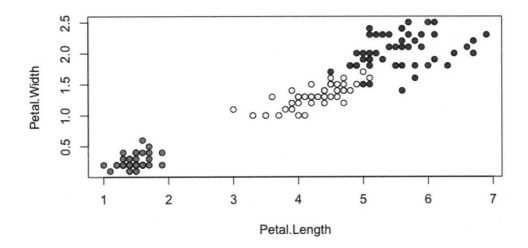

Figure 6.10: Iris Petal Length and Width

To perform one-versus-all classification for 3 classes, we have to create 3 data sets, one for each class as shown next. Each time we copy the original data set, then set the Species column to be a binary factor for that species or not.

Code 6.8.2 — **Make a data set for each class.** With a binary target.

```
# recode as virginica or not
iris_virginica <- iris
iris_virginica$Species <-
    as.factor(ifelse (iris_virginica$Species=="virginica",1,0))

# recode as setosa or not
iris_setosa <- iris
iris_setosa$Species <-
    as.factor(ifelse (iris_setosa$Species=="setosa",1,0))

# recode as versicolor or not
iris_versicolor <- iris
iris_versicolor$Species <-
    as.factor(ifelse (iris_versicolor$Species=="versicolor",1,0))
```

We next write a function to enable us to run the same code 3 times.

Machine Learning Handbook with R and Python © Karen Mazidi 2020

Code 6.8.3 — **Function Definition.** For repeated code.

```r
fun <- function(df, i){
    train <- df[i,]
    test <- df[-i,]
    glm1 <- glm(Species~., data=train, family="binomial")
    probs <- predict(glm1, newdata=test)
    pred <- ifelse(probs>0.5, 1, 0)
    acc <- mean(pred==test$Species)
    print(paste("accuracy = ", acc))
    table(pred, test$Species)
}
```

Next we make one set of indices to divide the train and test sets, and run the function on each data set.

Code 6.8.4 — **Run the function.** On each data set.

```r
set.seed(1234)
i <- sample(1:150, 100, replace=FALSE)
fun(iris_virginica, i)
fun(iris_setosa, i)
fun(iris_versicolor, i)
```

The accuracies for the 3 runs were: 0.98, 1.0, and 0.62. The average gives 87% overall accuracy. From the figures above it is clear that separating setosa (yellow) and versicolor (blue) is challenging and it looks like the versicolor classifier is the weakest one.

How well does this one-versus-all approach scale up? You can imagine that it would be troublesome for classifying 10 classes, as in digit recognition. You would have to build 10 classifiers. As we will see in the deep learning chapter, neural networks can be built to output probabilities for 10 classes, as in this problem scenario. The kNN algorithm is another example of an algorithm that can handle multi-class problems.

(R) **Warnings in glm()**

For logistic regression, if your training data is perfectly or nearly perfectly linearly separable, R will throw out several warning messages. This is due to the inability to maximize the likelihood which already has separated the data perfectly. For example, for the iris data which is too easy to classify, the sample notebook on github shows the error messages:

```
## Warning: glm.fit: algorithm did not converge
## Warning: glm.fit: fitted probabilities numerically 0 or 1 occurred
```

Since there are just warnings, they do not stop the algorithm from producing a model.

6.9 Generalized Linear Models

Logistic regression is part of the GLM (generalized linear model) family because its response is determined by a predictor in which the parameters are linear. In R's glm() function we used the family parameter to specify the family and link function.

```
glm1 <- glm(ESR~fibrinogen, data=train, family=binomial)
```

For binomial, the link function is "logit". Other available families include gaussian, gamma, poisson and more, as indicated in the R documentation.

Why do we need a link function? In linear regression the algorithm assumes that the target variable is normally distributed over the real numbers. This is not the case for logistic regression and other generalized linear models. The link function links the mean of the target $\mu_i = E(Y_i)$ to the linear term $x_i^T w$. The link function "links" the linear predictors to the response. The canonical link for mapping real numbers to [0,1] is the logit.

6.10 Summary

Logistic regression is something of a misnomer because we use it for classification, not regression. It is considered a linear model because it is linear in the parameters. The sigmoid function shapes the output to be in range [0, 1] for probabilities. Here are the stengths and weaknesses of logistic regression:

Strengths:
- Separates classes well if they are linearly separable
- Computationally inexpensive
- Nice probabilistic output

Weaknesses:
- Prone to underfitting; Not flexible enough to capture complex non-linear decision boundaries

In this chapter we showed how to perform logistic regression with one predictor or multiple predictors. In addition, we discussed how to use the one-versus-all technique for multi-class classification.

6.10.1 New Terminology in this Chapter

Refer back to the chapter or look at the glossary if you are unsure of the meaning of these terms.

New metrics:
- accuracy
- error rate
- sensitivity
- specificity
- Kappa
- ROC Curves
- AUC

Mathematical terms:
- probability
- odds
- log odds

6.10.2 Quick Reference

Reference 6.10.1 Build and Examine a Logistic Regression Model
```
glmName <- glm(formula, data=train, family=binomial)
summary(glmName)
```

Reference 6.10.2 Predict on Test Data
```
probs <- predict(glmName, newdata=test, type="response")
pred <- ifelse(probs>0.5, 1, 0)
table(pred, test$target)
acc <- mean(pred==test$target)
```

Reference 6.10.3 Confusion Matrix
```
library(caret)
confusionMatrix(predictions, test$target)
```

Reference 6.10.4 ROC and AUC
```
library(ROCR)
p <- predict(glm1, newdata=test, type="response")
pr <- prediction(p, test$survived)
# TPR = sensitivity, FPR=specificity
prf <- performance(pr, measure = "tpr", x.measure = "fpr")
plot(prf)
# compute AUC
auc <- performance(pr, measure = "auc")
auc <- auc@y.values[[1]]
```

6.10.3 Lab

Problem 6.1 — **Practice on the Abalone Data.** Try the following:

1. Download the Abalone data from the UCI Machine Learning Repository, `http://archive.ics.uci.edu/ml/datasets/Abalone`.
2. The data does not have column names so you will have to create them. Use meaningful names based on your reading about the data on the UCI site.
3. Check if there are missing values.
4. Examine the rings column with range(), median(), and hist() to determine where you would like to split the data into two classes: large and small.
5. Create a new factor column for binary large/small based on the rings column and your cut-off decision.
6. Divide the data into 80-20 train-test, setting a seed for reproducibility.
7. Create a logistic regression model with all predictors except rings. What is the accuracy of the model? Do you think this is a good model? Why or why not?
8. Create at least 2 more models, trying different features, and combinations of features to see if you can improve these results.

Problem 6.2 — **Practice on the Heart Data.** Try the following:

1. Download the Heart data from the UCI Machine Learning Repository, `http://archive.ics.uci.edu/ml/datasets/Heart+Disease`.
2. The data does not have column names so you will have to create them. Use meaningful names based on your reading about the data on the UCI site.
3. Make sure that columns are of the correct type: factors, integer, etc.
4. Check if there are missing values, and how many per column.
5. Divide the data into 80-20 train-test, setting a seed for reproducibility.
6. Create a logistic regression model with all predictors. What is the accuracy of the model? Do you think this is a good model? Why or why not?
7. Create at least one more model, trying different features, and combinations of features to see if you can improve these results.

6.10.4 Exploring Concepts

Problem 6.3 Based on your experience with the logistic regression algorithm in R, does removing predictors with low p-values necessarily improve performance? Discuss possible reasons for your answer.

Problem 6.4 If you found that some predictors were not adding to the performance of the model, what reasons might you give for leaving them in? What reasons might you give for taking them out?

6.10.5 Going Further

A free online lesson on Logistic Regression is available here: `https://onlinecourses.science.psu.edu/stat504/node/149`

A good discussion of the AIC metric is available here: `https://www.r-bloggers.com/how-do-i-interpret-the-aic/`

7. Naive Bayes

7.1 Overview

Naive Bayes is a popular classification algorithm. The mathematical foundations of Naive Bayes go back to the 18th Century and the mathematician and minister, Thomas Bayes, who formalized this probabilistic equation that bears his name. Bayes theorem:

$$P(Y|X) = \frac{P(X|Y)P(Y)}{P(X)} \quad aka: \quad \textbf{posterior} = \frac{\textbf{likelihood} \times \textbf{prior}}{\textbf{marginal}} \tag{7.1}$$

Let's consider the above equation in terms of the Titanic data.

$$P(survived|data) = \frac{P(data|survived)P(survived)}{P(data)} \tag{7.2}$$

The quantity $P(data|survived)$ is called the **likelihood**. It is calculated from the training data by determining the joint probabilities of Survived and the Data. It quantifies how likely it is that we would see the data given the Survived instances. The quantity $P(survived)$ is called the **prior** and the distribution of this data is also learned from the training set. The denominator $P(data)$ is used to normalize the fraction to a probability in the range 0 to 1. It is also called the marginal. The quantity to the left of the equal sign is called the **posterior** and it will be the probability of the positive class for a given observation.

7.2 Naive Bayes in R

We will apply the naive Bayes algorithm to the same Titanic data set as we applied logistic regression in the previous chapter. The same steps were used for data cleaning and creating the train/test split, so we will skip those here. In the code below we see that we first load package e1071 which contains the naiveBayes() function. Then we call Naive Bayes on the training data using a formula the same as other algorithms we have used. When we type the name of the model we have built, the information below the code is output.

Code 7.2.1 — **Naive Bayes.** Requires package e1071.

```
library(e1071)
nb1 <- naiveBayes(survived~., data=train)
nb1
```

```
Naive Bayes Classifier for Discrete Predictors

Call:
naiveBayes.default(x = X, y = Y, laplace = laplace)

A-priori probabilities:
Y
        0        1
0.617737 0.382263

Conditional probabilities:
   pclass
Y           1          2          3
  0 0.1468647 0.1930693 0.6600660
  1 0.3946667 0.2426667 0.3626667

   sex
Y      female       male
  0 0.1584158 0.8415842
  1 0.6773333 0.3226667

   age
Y        [,1]       [,2]
  0 30.32109 12.32909
  1 28.14467 13.83251
```

Earlier we stated that the prior and likelihood data was calculated from the training set. The output above shows this. The prior for Survived, called A-priori above, is .617 not-Survived and .382 Survived. The likelihood data is shown in the output as conditional probabilities. For discrete variables, this is a breakdown by survived/not for each possible value of the attribute.

For continuous data like age we are given the mean and standard deviation for the two classes. Notice also the reference at the top of the output about laplace. More about that in a later section.

In the output above there are 2 discrete variables, pclass and sex. Notice that each row sums to 1, indicating that they are probabilities. The probabilities of survival=1 for the 3 classes are 39%, 24%, and 36% respectively. The probability of surviving for females was 67.7% compared to 32% for males. The age variable is continuous. The mean for not surviving is 30 and for surviving is 28. These values are very close, so just looking at age alone does not tell us much. However, when we preprocessed this data (see the online notebook) we had a lot of NAs for age that were replaced with the median of age. This could have muddied the waters.

We calculated accuracy on the test set after predicting with parameter type="class". The accuracy for naive Bayes was slightly higher than for logistic regression. Note that we can extract the raw probabilities from the predictions using type="raw".

Code 7.2.2 — Raw Probabilities. With type="raw"

```
p2_raw <- predict(nb1, newdata=test, type="raw")
head(p2_raw, n=2)
```

```
              0          1
[1,] 0.06305836 0.9369416
[2,] 0.12856023 0.8714398
```

Exercise 7.1 — Pima Diabetes Data. Try the following:
- Load the PimaIndiansDiabetes2 data set from package mlbench into variable df.
- Use str() to familiarize yourself with the data and attach the data.
- Use sapply() to get counts of NAs per column.
- Fix the NAs as follows. Replace NAs in triceps and insulin with the mean value of the column. Then remove final NAs with complete.cases().
- Divide the data into a 80/20 train/test split using seed 1234.
- Compare the results of a logistic regression and naive Bayes model.
- Evaluate on the test data. What is your accuracy?

This data set had extremely large numbers of NAs for insulin and triceps, almost a third to one half of the data. By replacing these NAs with the mean of each column we could have diminished their predictive power. What if instead of replacing with the mean, we replace with the class-conditional mean? First we check to see if there is much difference in the means when diabetes is positive versus negative:

```
n <- which(df$diabetes=="pos")
mean(df$insulin[n], na.rm=TRUE)   # 206.8
mean(df$insulin[-n], na.rm=TRUE)  # 130
```

Yes, there is. Let's run the algorithms again on updated data:
- Reload the data into df and redivide into train and test using the same i as before.
- Replace NAs for insulin and triceps with the class conditional means. An example is shown below of one of the four lines you will need.
- Run logistic regression and naive Bayes on this updated data.
- Were your results significantly different? Which models do you prefer and why?

```
# Replace NAs on triceps with class-conditional means:
df$triceps[which(df$diabetes=="pos" & is.na(df$triceps))] <-
        mean(df$triceps[n], na.rm=TRUE)
```

7.3   Probability Foundations

This book assumes that readers have had a prior course on probability but we will review some key concepts here. Random variables, often denoted by capital letters such as X, can be discrete or continuous. The probability of two variables X and Y is called the *joint* distribution, determined jointly by X and Y, $P(X,Y)$. The *conditional* distribution of P(X|Y) is given by:

$$P(X|Y) = \frac{P(X,Y)}{P(Y)} \tag{7.3}$$

Two important probability rules are the product rule and the sum rule. The product rule says that the joint probability of A and B can be calculated by multiplying the conditional probability of A given B by the probability of B.

$$p(A,B) = p(A|B)p(B) \tag{7.4}$$

The sum rule says that we can calculate the probability of A by finding the joint probability with B and summing over all possible values of b.

$$p(A) = \sum_b p(A,B) = \sum_b p(A|B=b)P(B=b) \tag{7.5}$$

The chain rule lets us take the joint probability of many variables as follows:

$$p(X_{1:D}) = p(X_1)p(X_2|X_1)p(X_3|X_2,X_1)...p(X_D|X_{1:D-1}) \tag{7.6}$$

The expectation of a random variable is also known as the mean, or first moment. The expectation of a discrete random variable is:

$$E(X) = \sum_i X_i P(X_i) \tag{7.7}$$

Machine Learning Handbook with R and Python © Karen Mazidi 2020

So the expected value of a fair die is 3.5:

$$E(X) = 1 \times \frac{1}{6} + 2 \times \frac{1}{6} + 3 \times \frac{1}{6} + 4 \times \frac{1}{6} + 5 \times \frac{1}{6} + 6 \times \frac{1}{6} = 3.5 \qquad (7.8)$$

The variance of a distribution is also called its second moment, and is represented by σ^2. When we take it's square root, we have the standard deviation.

$$\sigma^2 = E[(X - \mu)^2] \qquad (7.9)$$

The log trick is often used when multiplying probabilities to prevent underflow and possibly multiplying by 0. Instead of multiplying the probabilities, the log trick says to add the log of the probabilities.

7.4 Probability Distributions

There are a few probability distributions that occur frequently in Bayesian approaches so it would be a good idea to review them here. Many of these are discussed also in context of their conjugate prior. Conjugate distributions are in the same family.

7.4.1 Bernoulli, Binomial, and Beta Distributions

These distributions concern binary variables representing such things as the flip of a coin, wins and losses, and so forth. Our example will be shooting baskets for practice, where x=1 means that we made a basket and x=0 means that we missed. Let's say that I am shooting hoops for the first time and I made 2 baskets out of 10 tries. Given this data, my probability of making a basket is 0.2. The Bernoulli distribution describes binary outcomes like this example. The Bernoulli distribution has a parameter, μ, which specifies the average probability of the positive class.

$$Bernoulli(x|\mu) = \mu^x(1 - \mu)^{1-x} \qquad (7.10)$$

This gives us the probability that x is 1: $p(x = 1) = 0.2^1 * .8^0 = 0.2$. And the probability that x is 0: $p(x = 0) = 0.2^0 * .8^1 = 0.8$.

The Bernoulli distribution is a special case of the binomial distribution in which the number of trials, N = 1. Now suppose we run our Bernoulli trial N=100 times, that is, I shoot 100 baskets. Let X be the random variable which represents the number of baskets made. The binomial distribution of X where I made k baskets in N trials has the following probability mass function (pmf):

$$Binomial(k|N,\mu) = \binom{N}{k} \mu^k(1 - \mu)^{N-k} \qquad (7.11)$$

Let's let k=20 for our 100 trials. Will the outcome of the binomial be 0.2?

$$Binomial(20|100, 0.2) = \binom{100}{20} 0.2^{20}(1 - 0.2)^{80} = 0.09930021 \quad (7.12)$$

No, it is not because there are many ways we can get 20 baskets out of 100 trials, 100 choose 20, to be exact. You can get out your calculator to confirm that or use R command `dbinom(20, 100, 0.2)`.

What is the expected mean of our 100 trials? Our expected value will be $N\mu$ which in our case is $100*0.2 = 20$. Let's derive these values using R. First we make a vector of possible values for k, the number of baskets made. We could make anywhere from 0 to 100 baskets. Then we multiply each k by its probability and add them together following Equation 6.7 above for the mean of a discrete distribution. E is 20, as we expected. The plot in Figure 7.1 shows the expected value at the center with the variance, calculated as $N\mu(1 - \mu)$, which is 16 in our example. If you `sum(dbinom(k, 100, 0.2))` you get 1.0 of course because this represents the total probability space.

Code 7.4.1 — **Basketball.** A Binomial Distribution.

```
k <- 0:100   # possible number of baskets for 100 tries
E <- sum(k * dbinom(k, 100, 0.2))
v <- 100 * .2 * .8
plot(k, dbinom(k, 100, 0.2))
```

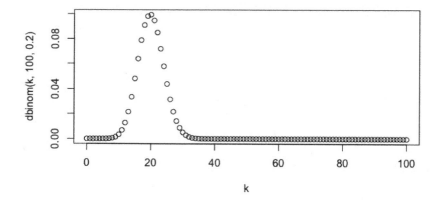

Figure 7.1: Binomial Distribution for 0.2

Now suppose that I got really lucky when I shot my first 3 hoops and made all 3 baskets. This gives me $\mu = 1.0$. It's unlikely I can keep this probability over the long haul. In fact, small sample sizes serve poorly as prior estimates of probabilities. Instead of a prior μ we really need a prior distribution over μ. We want this prior distribution to be a *conjugate* of our binomial distribution, meaning that we want it to be proportional to $\mu^x(1-\mu)^{1-x}$. The beta distribution is a good choice:

$$Beta(\mu|a,b) = \frac{\Gamma(a+b)}{\Gamma(a)\Gamma(b)}\mu^{a-1}(1-\mu)^{b-1} \tag{7.13}$$

In the above equation, the first term with the gammas serves as a normalizing constant to make sure that the total probability integrates to 1. The gamma function is commonly used in probability, and is an extension of the factorial function to the real numbers: $\Gamma(n) = (n-1)!$ and is also extended to complex numbers. The parameters a and b in our example will be the number of baskets made and missed, respectively. Beta distributions are commonly used in Bayesian approaches to represent prior knowledge of a parameter. The gamma function is defined as follows for positive real numbers or complex numbers with a positive real portion:

$$\Gamma(x) \equiv \int_0^\infty u^{x-1}e^{-u}du \tag{7.14}$$

Let's look at the beta distribution for our example in R. We use the rbeta() function to create 100 random beta samples with shape parameters 20 and 80. Then we plot this curve as the black line in Figure 7.2. Now suppose I take 15 more shots and make 5 of them. This will make a=30 and b=85. This updated curve is shown in red in Figure 7.2. The code below shows how to create the random beta samples with `rbeta(n, shape1, shape2)`. What will x look like? it is a vector of 100 random numbers drawn from a beta distribution with parameters a=20 and b=80. The mean will be 0.2 with the min around 0.1 and the max around 0.3. The code then draws the original curve in black and the updated curve in red. The `par(new=TRUE))` is used when you want to plot over an existing plot.

Code 7.4.2 — **Basketball.** A Beta Distribution.

```
x <- rbeta(100, 20, 80)
curve(dbeta(x, 20, 80), xlab=" ", ylab=" ", xlim=c(0.1,0.6),
    ylim=c(0,10))
par(new=TRUE)
curve(dbeta(x, 30, 85), xlab=" ", ylab=" ", xlim=c(0.1,0.6),
    ylim=c(0,10), col="red")
```

In the code and plot above, we updated the original black curve by adding baskets to a and misses to b. Our new probability given our data will be:

$$p(x=1|D) = \frac{a+m}{a+b+m+l} \tag{7.15}$$

where m represents the number of new baskets and l represents the number of new losses.

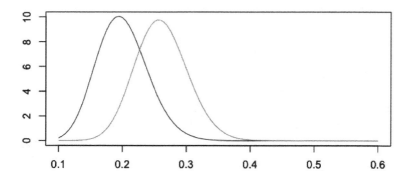

Figure 7.2: Beta Distribution for a=20, b=80

The equation above is a Bayesian estimate. In contrast, note that the MLE estimate is simply m/N. As m and l approach infinity, the Bayesian estimate converges to the MLE. For a finite data set, the posterior probability with be between the prior and the MLE.

7.4.2   Multinomial and Dirichlet Distributions

We can extend the binomial distribution to the case where we have variables that are not binary but can take on more than 2 values. This is a multinomial distribution. The probability mass function of a multinomial distribution is:

$$Multinomial(m_1, m_2, ..., m_k | N, \mu) = \left(\frac{N}{m_1! m_2! ... m_k!} \right) \prod_{k=1}^{K} \mu_k^{m_k} \tag{7.16}$$

Where k indexes over the number of classes, K, and each of the m_i represent the probability of that class, with the sum of all $m_i = 1$.

The iris data is an example of a multinomial distribution. There are 3 classes, and the data set has 50 examples of each class, an even distribution. If we want to put the 150 flowers in 3 boxes (classes) with even probability of being in each class, we could use the following R command.

```
Code 7.4.3 — Multinomial. Iris Example

rmultinom(n=10, size=150, prob=c(1/3, 1/3, 1/3))
     [,1] [,2] [,3] [,4] [,5] [,6] [,7] [,8] [,9] [,10]
[1,]  56   44   51   55   54   47   49   60   61    42
[2,]  36   48   54   44   42   46   58   50   40    61
[3,]  58   58   45   51   54   57   43   40   49    47
```

The output above shows us 10 vectors, left to right, because we said "n=10". Our size is 150 for each of our iris flowers, and they have an even distribution. What we see in each column are distributions of the 150 flowers. Each column sums to 150. What we see in each row are the number of flowers in each box (class). The mean values for the 3 classes are 54, 50.1, and 45.9.

If we selected 6 flowers at random, what is the probability that there will be 1 flower from class 1, 2 flowers from class 2, and 3 flowers from class 3?

Code 7.4.4 — Multinomial. Use dmultinom() for probabilities.

```
dmultinom(x=c(1,2,3), prob=c(1/3, 1/3, 1/3))
[1] 0.08230453
# check:
factorial(6)/(factorial(3)*factorial(2)*factorial(1))*
    0.333333^1*0.333333^2*0.333333^3
[1] 0.08230403
```

The Dirichlet distribution is the conjugate prior of the multinomial distribution. The Dirichlet distribution has k parameters, α, one for each class. So instead of X being 0 or 1, it can take on k values. In the following, α_0 is the sum of all alphas. The Dirichlet distribution:

$$Dir(\mu|\alpha) = \frac{\Gamma(\alpha_0)}{\Gamma(\alpha_1)...\Gamma(\alpha_k)} \prod_{k=1}^{K} \mu_k^{\alpha_k-1} \tag{7.17}$$

Consider a magic bag containing balls of K=3 colors: red, blue, yellow. For each of N draws, you place the ball back in the bag with an *additional* ball of the same color. As N approaches infinity, the colored balls in the magically expanded bag will be $Dir(\alpha_1, \alpha_2, \alpha_3)$.

You can think of the Dirichlet distribution as a multinomial factory.

Code 7.4.5 — Dirichlet. Output Distribution.

```
library(MCMCpack) # for function rdirichlet()
m <- rdirichlet(10, c(1, 1, 1))
m
             [,1]         [,2]        [,3]
 [1,] 0.015740801 0.3900641 0.59419507
 [2,] 0.295649733 0.3622780 0.34207224
 [3,] 0.464984547 0.4516325 0.08338300
 [4,] 0.365099590 0.3074731 0.32742729
 [5,] 0.065993901 0.2832624 0.65074371
 [6,] 0.252786635 0.6786473 0.06856608
 [7,] 0.049175200 0.4904748 0.46034997
 [8,] 0.297815089 0.2121868 0.48999815
 [9,] 0.005201826 0.3076536 0.68714457
[10,] 0.326711959 0.4160060 0.25728208
```

```
mean(m[,1])
[1] 0.2139159
> mean(m[,2])
[1] 0.3899679
> mean(m[,3])
[1] 0.3961162
```

We asked for 10 distributions with our alphas all equal to 1. The sum of every row, which is every distribution, is 1.0. The mean of the columns for these 10 examples are 0.2, 0.38, and 0.39. When run with 1000 examples the means were 0.34, 0.33 and 0.32.

7.4.3 Gaussian

The Gaussian or normal distribution is used for quantitative variables. Two parameters define its shape: the mean μ and the variance σ^2. The probability density function is:

$$f(x) = \frac{1}{\sqrt{2\pi}\sigma} exp\left(-\frac{(x-\mu)^2}{2\sigma^2}\right) \tag{7.18}$$

Let's plot a few Gaussians to see how the mean and variance influence the shape. All 3 distributions are generated with the dnorm() function, and all have a mean of 0. Different means would shift the curves right or left. The three curves have different standard deviations.

Code 7.4.6 — **Gaussians.** Normal distributions.

```
curve( dnorm(x,0,1), xlim=c(-4,4), ylim=c(0,1) )
curve( dnorm(x,0,2), add=T, col='blue' )
curve( dnorm(x,0,.5), add=T, col='orange' )
```

The rnorm() function in R generates random numbers, following a normal distribution. The d in the dnorm() function is for density, as in pdf, probability density function. The dnorm() function returns the pdf for the normal distribution specified by the parameters.

The pdf of the Gaussian above in Equation 5.18 is for a single variable x. The Gaussian can be extended to a D-dimensional vector **x** in which case it is called a multivariate Gaussian and has the pdf shown below where μ is now a vector of means, Σ is a DxD covariance matrix, $|\Sigma|$ is the determinant.

$$f(x) = \frac{1}{\sqrt[D/2]{2\pi}\,\sqrt{|\Sigma|}} exp\left(-\frac{(x-\mu)^T(x-\mu)}{2\Sigma}\right) \tag{7.19}$$

7.5 Likelihood versus Probability

The sum of probabilities for all outcomes of an experiment is 1. This is a binomial distribution. This block of code computes this manually.

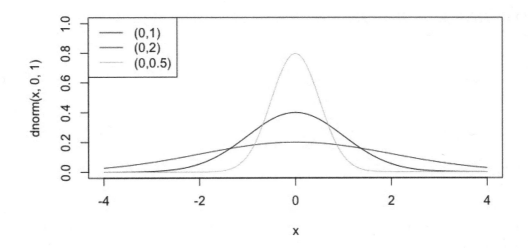

Figure 7.3: Gaussian Distributions

```
# 4 coin tosses, 5 possible outcomes

heads <- c(0, 1, 2, 3, 4)  # number of heads
tails <- c(4, 3, 2, 1, 0) # number of tails
binomial_coeff <- c(1, 4, 6, 4, 1)  # binomial coefficient
p_head <- 0.5
p_tail <- 0.5

# sum probability
p_vector <- rep(0, 5)  # 5 possible outcomes
for (i in 1:5){
  p_vector[i] <- binomial_coeff[i] * p_head^heads[i]  * p_tail^tails[i]
}
print(p_vector)  # prob for each possible event
[1] 0.0625 0.2500 0.3750 0.2500 0.0625
print(sum_prob) # sum of all probabilities
[1] 1
```

Now, let's try to find p_head given some coin tosses. Let's say for 4 coin tosses, there were 3 heads.

```
# out of 4 coin tosses, 3 were heads
# p = .75, the most likely value of p given the outcome
# compare this to p = .5 to see which is more likely
```

```
# look at the case where heads=3 tails=1
p <- 0.75
lh1 <- 6 * p^3 * (1 - p)^1
lh1
> lh1
[1] 0.6328125

p <- 0.5
lh2 <- 6 * p^3 * (1 - p)^1
lh2
[1] 0.375
```

The likelihood that p=0.75 is greater, given the data that we have seen.

Probability looks forward in time. We have p and can estimate outcomes based on p. Likelihood looks backward in time. We observe some data, and try to find the parameter p which most likely resulted in this outcome.

7.6　The Algorithm

Calculating joint probabilities with the chain rule above would be mathematically intractable. The simplifying assumption of the naive Bayes algorithm is that each of the predictors is independent. Therefore:

$$p(X_1, X_2, ...X_D|Y) = \prod_{i=1}^{D} p(X_i|Y) \tag{7.20}$$

The naive assumption of the independence of the predictors is typically not true, but perhaps surprisingly, naive Bayes works well. Naive Bayes forms a good baseline for comparing other classifiers.

The algorithm requires a single read through the data to estimate parameters. There are two sets of parameters to estimate from the data and two ways we can estimate the from the test data. The two methods are maximum likelihood estimates (MLE) and maximum apriori (MAP). MLE simply involves counting instances in the training data while MAP additionally makes some estimates based on prior distributions of the data. The two sets of parameters are counts for the probability of each class, and parameters for each predictor.

The first set of parameters to estimate is the probability of each class. If we estimate this with MLE, we just calculate the number of observations in each class. The estimate for class c will be the count of observations with class c divided by the number of observations:

$$MLE_c = \frac{|Y = y_c|}{|N|} \tag{7.21}$$

Estimating parameters for predictors depends upon their type. Binary features can use the mean of the Bernoulli distribution to get probabilities for each class. For discrete variables with more than 2 categories, the mean of the multinoulli distribution for each category can be used. Parameters for quantitative predictors are estimated from the mean and variance of the Gaussian distribution.

The MLE for the likelihood of a predictor given the class is also achieved by counting the data for discrete predictors. For predictor X_i and class c:

$$\hat{\theta}_{ic} = \frac{|X_{ic}|}{|N_c|} \tag{7.22}$$

It is possible that a given predictor for a given class may have 0 observations. In this case the estimate is 0 which is a problem given the multiplication of predictor likelihoods. An approach that eliminates this problem is smoothing, which involves adding a little to the numerator and denominator:

$$\hat{\theta}_{ic} = \frac{|X_{ic}| + l}{|N_c| + lm} \tag{7.23}$$

The value added to the denominator, m, represents the number of categories of X_i. If l=1 it is called Laplace or add-one smoothing. If we let l be a larger value this corresponds to a MAP estimate for the likelihood. We can add smoothing in a similar way to the MLE for the prior, in effect making it a MAP estimate.

For continuous variables, the mean and standard deviation of the predictor can be estimated but we would really like these values as they are associated with each class. Therefore separate mean, μ, and standard deviation, σ^2, values are computed by class. This is called a Gaussian naive Bayes classifier.

$$\hat{\theta}_{ic} = \frac{1}{\sqrt{2\pi\sigma^2}} e^{-\frac{(x-\mu)^2}{2\sigma^2}} \tag{7.24}$$

7.7 Applying the Bayes Theorem

There are a lot of misconceptions about probabilities. Let's walk through an example to illustrate some of the subtleties. Suppose that a given test for cancer has a sensitivity of 80% which means that if you have cancer, it will be positive with p=0.8. If your test is positive this does not mean you have an 80% chance of having cancer. Other data points we need: the probability of a false positive rate for the test is 10%, and the overall probability of having cancer is 0.4%. By plugging in the numbers into the theorem we say that the probability of actually having cancer given this positive test is 3.1%.

$$p(cancer|positive\_test) = \frac{0.8*0.004}{0.8*0004 + 0.1*0.996} = 0.031 \tag{7.25}$$

7.8   Handling Text Data

Previously all of our data has been numeric. However, machine learning with text is a hot topic in the field of Natural Language Processing. That's a separate course but we will talk a little about how text can be handled numerically now and revisit this in the data wrangling chapter. Any kind of natural language processing involves a lot of preprocessing. In a bag of words model, the text is tokenized, meaning that it is divided into individual words. The sentence structure is lost but just looking at counts of words can be informative. Additional preprocessing may involve removing punctuation, numbers, and making all text lowercase. Further, stop words are often removed. Stop words are common words that glue a sentence together but don't add much content. In this sentence, the stop words might be: *in, this, the, might, be.* Finally, the vocabulary size may be reduced since rare words don't have predictive value.

Often a document-term matrix is created in which each row represents a document and each column represents a term in the vocabulary. The intersection gives the count of a specific term in a given document. This is a sparse matrix in that each document has relatively few words out of the total vocabulary. Sometimes it is converted to a binary matrix with counts being replaced by 1 indicating the presense of that word in the document. The github site has a couple of examples of handling text data in the Data Wrangling section.

7.9   Naive Bayes v. Logistic Regression

Next we look at a classification data set in package mlbench. This package collects several real-world and artificial data sets for benchmarking. You can see the list of data sets by typing `data(package="mlbench")` at the console. We will use the BreastCancer data set, sometimes called the Wisconsin breast cancer data since the data originated from clinical practice at the Univeristy of Madison Wisconsin hospital. This data set has 669 observations with 11 columns. Column 1 is an ID that will be ignored, columns 2-10 are factors specifying information gleaned from biopsies. The final column is the label: benign or malignant.

7.9.1   Compare to Logistic Regression

Of the 669 observations in the breast cancer data set, approximately 64% are benign to 36% malignant. This is a reasonably balanced data set. We can easily use the summary() function to get the numbers: `summary(BreastCancer$Class)` gives us 458 benign and 241 malignant. Although breast cancer is rare in the general population, the data is fairly balanced, probably because patients going for a biopsy are likely to have suspicious lumps or other symptoms, and therefore be more likely to have cancer than the general population. In the notebook available online we first divide into 80% train and 20% test data, after removing the Id column. Then we perform logistic regression and get 91% accuracy on predicting benign or malignant on the test data. The accuracy of a classifier on test data can be further examined by breaking it down into sensitivity and specificity.

7.9.2 Naive Bayes Model

Next we build a Naive Bayes model on the same train and test data. The accuracy was 96%, higher than for the logistic regression model.

Code 7.9.1 — **Naive Bayes.** On the Breast Cancer Data.

```
nb1 <- naiveBayes(train[,-10], train[,10])
pred2 <- predict(nb1, newdata=test[,-10], type="class")
confusionMatrix(pred2, test$Class, positive="malignant")
```

7.9.3 Sparse data issues

Although both algorithms learned well from this data, digging into the training results shows some signs of difficulty. For example, there are 10 levels to the Cell.shape predictor, the Cell.size predictor and multiple levels for all other predictors. Let's say an average of 7 levels for each of 10 predictors, that's essentially 70 predictors. The training data has a little over 500 examples, that averages to about 7 examples per predictor level if they were distributed evenly, which they are not. This is a data sparseness problem. Ideally the number of examples should be much higher than the number of predictors. Fortunately, logistic regression and Naive Bayes are two algorithm that deal well with sparse data.

Looking in the online notebook at the summary for logistic regression, none of the 70+ predictors got a low p-value. Actually they all got p-values of 1.0! The summary shows that coefficients were assigned but that the standard error for each one is very large.

Looking at the results for the naive Bayes trained model, we see that the probabilities have to be spread out among the many levels. Look at the probabilities for Cell.size:

```
Cell.size
Y                       1           2           3           4
   benign      0.835616438 0.082191781 0.057534247 0.010958904
   malignant 0.010309278 0.036082474 0.113402062 0.139175258
            Cell.size
Y                       5           6           7           8
   benign      0.000000000 0.005479452 0.002739726 0.002739726
   malignant 0.118556701 0.103092784 0.082474227 0.113402062
            Cell.size
Y                       9          10
   benign      0.002739726 0.000000000
   malignant 0.015463918 0.268041237
```

Notice that nearly 84% of the probability for benign is taken by Cell.size 1, with diminishing values all the way to a zero probability for Cell.size 10. The malignant probabilities are more evenly distributed with the highest probability of 27% being for Cell.size 10.

7.9.4 Data preprocessing

Let's see how the two algorithms perform on a simplified version of the data set. THe data set was first subset to 3 columns: Class and two predictors: Cell.size and Cell.shape. Then the two predictors were converted to binary factors 0/1 where 1 indicates levels > 5. The code is shown below. These two predictors were chosen out of the 9 predictors randomly. Important predictors could have been omitted, and the arbitrary cut-off point at level 5 may not be optimal. All these types of decisions should be made with domain experts.

Code 7.9.2 — **Data Preprocessing.** Simplified train/test

```
df2 <- df[, c(2:3, 10)]    # just Cell.size Cell.shape and Class
df2$Cell.size <- as.factor(ifelse(df$Cell.size > 5, 1, 0))
df2$Cell.shape <- as.factor(ifelse(df$Cell.shape > 5, 1, 0))
str(df2)

train2 <- df2[i,]
test2 <- df2[-i,]
```

Running the logistic regression model on this data increased the accuracy from .91 to .92 but more significantly, the two predictors had p-values near 0. Running naive Bayes on the reduced data *decreased* the accuracy from .96 to .92. The naive Bayes algorithm was able to get the best model on all the data levels while logistic regression struggled to assign appropriate coefficients to each level of each predictor. The advantage to both models of the second simpler data set is that they are more interpretable.

One concern in looking at the conditional probabilities of the second naive Bayes model is that the two predictors separated well for the benign class but not so much for the malignant class. Notice that for the malignant class, it was almost as bad as tossing a coin. That's not what most of us would want for a diagnostic.

```
A-priori probabilities:
Y
   benign malignant
0.6529517 0.3470483

Conditional probabilities:
          Cell.size
Y                  0          1
  benign    0.98630137 0.01369863
  malignant 0.41752577 0.58247423

          Cell.shape
Y                  0          1
  benign    0.98630137 0.01369863
  malignant 0.40721649 0.59278351
```

7.9.5 Generative v. Discriminative Classifiers

In this example Naive Bayes outperformed logistic regression. It is important to keep in mind that these are two quite different classifiers. Logistic regression directly estimates the parameters of P(Y|X). This is called a *discriminative classifier*. Naive Bayes directly estimates parameters for P(Y) and P(X|Y). This is called a *generative classifier*. If the naive Bayes independence assumptions hold, and the number of training examples grows towards infinity, the naive Bayes and logistic regression converge toward similar classifiers. In general, Naive Bayes will do better with small data sets and logistic regression will do better as the size of the data grows. Naive Bayes has higher bias but lower variance than logistic regression. In this example, if you look at the output of the summary() function for the logistic regression model online you will see dozens of predictors because each of the 9 predictor columns are broken down into their factors. None of these almost 100 predictors achieved a low p-value and many factor levels were not included in the model. Further, five of the 9 predictor columns are ordinal factors which not only classify different values but there is an order to the values. The logistic regression function may have been overwhelmed by the sheer number of factors and levels whereas the simpicity of the Naive Bayes approach may have worked in its favor.

7.10 Naive Bayes from Scratch

In order to understand Naive Bayes on a deeper level, we will explore creating the algorithm from scratch. This will be applied to the Titanic data. The notebook online first loads and cleans the data, then runs the naiveBayes() function on the data.

7.10.1 Probability Tables

Here are the probability tables from the naiveBayes() function:

```
A-priori probabilities:
df[, 2]
        0        1
0.618029 0.381971
Conditional probabilities:
       pclass
df[, 2]         1         2         3
      0 0.1520396 0.1953028 0.6526576
      1 0.4000000 0.2380000 0.3620000
       sex
df[, 2]   female      male
      0 0.1569839 0.8430161
      1 0.6780000 0.3220000
       age
df[, 2]      [,1]      [,2]
      0 29.94757 12.22384
      1 28.78417 13.92003
```

Calculating the prior (apriori) probabilities of survived or perished is easy. It is simply dividing the counts of survived or perished by the total number of observations, as shown here:

```
apriori <- c(
  nrow(df[df$survived=="0",])/nrow(df),
  nrow(df[df$survived=="1",])/nrow(df)
  )
print("Prior probability, survived=no, survived=yes:")
[1] 0.618029 0.381971
```

7.10.2 Conditional Probability for Discrete Data

The conditional probability tables are also quite simple to create for qualitative data. Following Equation 7.21, we have a count for each level of each predictor.

```
# get survived counts for no and yes
count_survived <- c(
  length(df$survived[df$survived=="0"]),
  length(df$survived[df$survived=="1"])
)

# likelihood for pclass
lh_pclass <- matrix(rep(0,6), ncol=3)
for (sv in c("0", "1")){
  for (pc in c("1","2","3")) {
    lh_pclass[as.integer(sv)+1, as.integer(pc)] <-
      nrow(df[df$pclass==pc & df$survived==sv,]) /
        count_survived[as.integer(sv)+1]
  }
}              [,1]      [,2]      [,3]
[1,] 0.1520396 0.1953028 0.6526576
[2,] 0.4000000 0.2380000 0.3620000

# likelihood for sex
lh_sex <- matrix(rep(0,4), ncol=2)
for (sv in c("0", "1")){
  for (sx in c(2, 3)) {
    lh_sex[as.integer(sv)+1, sx-1] <-
      nrow(df[as.integer(df$sex)==sx & df$survived==sv,]) /
        count_survived[as.integer(sv)+1]
  }
}              [,1]      [,2]
[1,] 0.1569839 0.8430161
[2,] 0.6780000 0.3220000
```

7.10.3 Likelihood for Continuous Data

To calculate the likelihood for age we first need the mean and variance.

```
age_mean <- c(0, 0)
age_var <- c(0, 0)
for (sv in c("0", "1")){
    age_mean[as.integer(sv)+1] <-
      mean(df$age[df$survived==sv])
    age_var[as.integer(sv)+1] <-
      var(df$age[df$survived==sv])
}
age_mean
[1] 29.94757 28.78417
> age_var
[1] 149.4223 193.7673
```

Now we plug these values into Equation 7.23. We will write a function to calculate this, using the R built-in functions exp( ).

```
calc_age_lh <- function(v, mean_v, var_v){
  # run like this: calc_age_lh(6, 25.9, 138)
  1 / sqrt(2 * pi * var_v) * exp(-((v-mean_v)^2)/(2 * var_v))
}
```

7.10.4 Putting it All Together

Now we need a function to caculate Bayes' theorem for us.

```
calc_raw_prob <- function(pclass, sex, age) {
  # pclass=1,2,3  sex=1,2   age=numeric
  num_s <- lh_pclass[2, pclass] * lh_sex[2, sex] * apriori[2] *
      calc_age_lh(age, age_mean[2], age_var[2])
  num_p <- lh_pclass[1, pclass] * lh_sex[1, sex] * apriori[1] *
      calc_age_lh(age, age_mean[1], age_var[1])
  denominator <- lh_pclass[2, pclass]  * lh_sex[2, sex] *
   calc_age_lh(age, age_mean[2], age_var[2]) * apriori[2] +
      lh_pclass[1, pclass]  * lh_sex[1, sex] *
      calc_age_lh(age, age_mean[1], age_var[1]) * apriori[1]
  return (list(prob_survived <- num_s / denominator,
          prob_perished <- num_p / denominator))
}
}
```

Separately, we create a numerator for survived, and one for perished. The denominator multiplies the likelihood for pclass times sex times age for perishing times the prior probability of perishing, then does the same for surviving, adding these two values together.

Let's call this function for the first 5 test observations.

```
for (i in 1:5){
  raw <- calc_raw_prob(test[i,1], as.integer(test[i,3]), test[i,4])
  print(paste(raw[2], raw[1]))
}
```

7.10.5 Results

The following shows the predictions:

```
[1] "0.134219499226771 0.865780500773229"
[1] "0.119544295476936 0.880455704523064"
[1] "0.135715780701606 0.864284219298394"
[1] "0.267316737470339 0.732683262529661"
[1] "0.649768435768306 0.350231564231694"
```

Below are the raw probabilities from the Naive Bayes model. Notice they are the same.

```
> pred[1:5,]
              0         1
[1,] 0.1342195 0.8657805
[2,] 0.1195443 0.8804557
[3,] 0.1357158 0.8642842
[4,] 0.2673167 0.7326833
[5,] 0.6497684 0.3502316
```

The above code detailed how the algorithm works: counting and simple math. The code was not written in the most efficient way for R but in the way that makes how the algorithm works most clear to human readers.

7.11 Summary

Naive Bayes is a dependable classifier that is often used as a baseline for more sophisticated algorithms that are expected to outperform it. However, Naive Bayes is a reliable classifier in its own right. Its simple, probabilistic results make interpretation of the learning easy. Naive Bayes may outperform more sophisticated algorithms on small data sets. Next we look at the strengths and weaknesses of Naive Bayes.

Strengths:
- Works well with small data sets
- Easy to implement
- Easy to interpret
- Handles high dimensions well

Weaknesses:
- May be outperformed by other classifiers for larger data sets
- Guesses are made for values in the test set that did not occur in the training data
- If the predictors are not independent, the naive assumption that they are may limit the performance of the algorithm

7.11.1 New Terminology in this Chapter

This chapter used a lot of terminology from probability theory:
- likelihood v. probability
- prior probability v. posterior probability
- Bayes Theorem
- conditional probability
- joint probability
- marginal probability
- expected values, mean and variance

In addition we reviewed several probability distributions by family:
- Bernoulli, binomial and beta distributions
- Multinomial and Dirichlet distributions
- Gaussian distributions

Finally, there are a few terms related to techniques:
- MLE maximum likelihood estimate
- MAP maximum apriori estimate
- Laplace smoothing
- Discriminative v. generative classifiers

7.11.2 Quick Reference

Reference 7.11.1 Build a Naive Bayes Model
```
library(e1071)
# method one: use a formula
nb_model <- naiveBayes(formula, data=train)
```

Reference 7.11.2 Build a Naive Bayes Model
```
# method two: X, Y
nb_model <- naiveBayes(predictor_cols, target_col, data=train
```

Reference 7.11.3 Predict
```
raw <- predict(model, newdata=test, type="raw")
pred <- predict(model, newdata=test, type="class"
```

Reference 7.11.4 Confusion Matrix
```
library(caret)
confusionMatrix(predictions, test$target, positive="2")
```

7.11.3 Labs

Problem 7.1 — **Classification on the Abalone Data.** Try the following:
- Re-run your code from the Chapter 5 Lab on classifying the Abalone data using Logistic regression, or follow those instructions to create the model.
- Create a naive Bayes model on the same train/test split.
- Compare the performance of the two algorithms.
- Compare the confusion matrix tables of the two algorithms. What do you observe? Was one better at predicting true positives versus true negatives? Why might this be important?

Problem 7.2 — **Classification on the Heart Data.** Try the following:
- Re-run your code from the Chapter 5 Lab on classifying the Heart data using Logistic regression, or follow those instructions to create the model.
- Create a naive Bayes model on the same train/test split.
- Compare the performance of the two algorithms.
- Compare the confusion matrix tables of the two algorithms. What do you observe? Was one better at predicting true positives versus true negatives? Why might this be important? How many NAs were predicted for each algorithm?

Problem 7.3 — **Classification on the Sonar Data.** Try the following:
- Load the Sonar data set from package mlbench. Research this data set and write a brief description of the columns.
- Divide the data into 80-20 train-test.
- Create a logistic regression model of the data. What is the accuracy?
- Create a naive Bayes model of the data. Compare the accuracy to the logistic regression model.
- Compare the confusion matrix tables for each. Discuss what you find.

7.11.4 Exploring Concepts

Problem 7.4 Compare how logistic regression makes classification predictions compared to naive Bayes.

Problem 7.5 Briefly summarize why logistic regression is called a discriminative classifier and naive Bayes is called a generative classifier.

Problem 7.6 What is the naive assumption in Naive Bayes?

7.11.5 Going Further

Tom Mitchell's classic book, *Machine Learning* Chapter 3 discusses Naive Bayes and Logistic Regression. Tom Mitchell has provided free access to this chapter here:

`http://www.cs.cmu.edu/~tom/mlbook/NBayesLogReg.pdf`

A well-regarded paper comparing discriminative and generative classifiers by Andrew Ng and Michael Jordan can be found here:

`https://ai.stanford.edu/~ang/papers/nips01-discriminativegenerative.pdf`

8. The Craft 2: Inductive Learning

Machine-learning expert Pedro Domingos summarizes machine learning as follows:

```
Learning = Representation + Evaluation + Optimization
```

Representation, evaluation, and optimization are the major tasks of machine learning. We have done all of them in the previous chapters, although we never explicitly said so. The algorithms we have used in R rely on internal metrics to *evaluate* how well the training is proceeding. Internal *optimization* code ensures that the best model is produced, given the training data.

In machine learning, we need to figure out two kinds of representation. First, we need to be able to state the problem in a formal language, so that computation can take place. Second, we need to decide how the input data will be represented.

For the algorithms learned so far, the input data was represented as (x, y) pairs of data, where **x** is a matrix of features, and y is the target value. The learning problem for linear classifiers is represented as:

$$y = \mathbf{w}\mathbf{X} + b \tag{8.1}$$

where **w** represents the weight matrix which is multiplied by the **X** input features plus the fitting parameter b. The parameters w and b are learned from the data.

8.1 How learning happens

Figure 8.1 gives a big-picture view of learning for optimization algorithms such as logistic regression and neural networks. Given a problem specification, an initial hypothesis can be created, h_0. The first hypothesis is not likely to be the best, it may just be a random guess in some algorithms. The results of this first hypothesis are evaluated, using an error function, E, which measures the distance between the predicted value and the actual value for y. This error is used to optimize the next hypothesis, h_1, which should be an improvement over the initial hypothesis. This process continues until a hypothesis is found that fits the training data to some acceptable threshold level.

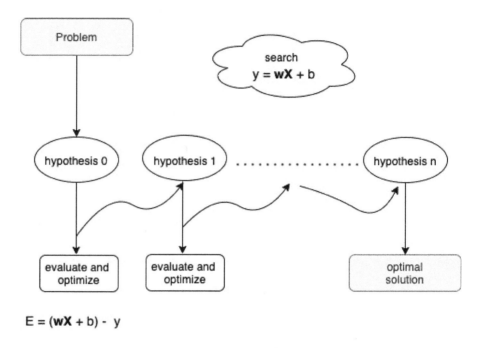

Figure 8.1: Learning as Search

Each hypothesis for a linear model, is a matrix of values **w** that is learned from the data. We can think of machine learning as a search through the hypothesis space for the optimal hypothesis.

This form of machine learning is *inductive learning*. The algorithm is given examples of training data, and has to learn a hypothesis (or function) that models the data. Once this model or function is learned, it can be used to make predictions on previously unseen data that is from a similar distribution as the training data. The extent to which a model can generalize to new data, the better it will perform. Unfortunately, machine learning algorithms can have some degree of *inductive bias*, the assumptions that the model makes about the incoming data.

A recent article from MIT Technology Review[1] observed that real-world performance on machine learning models is often disappointing compared to results in the lab because the real-world data may be different. This is the *data shift* problem. Another reason for disappointing real-world results is *underspecification*, a term borrowed from statistics where it indicates that some missing or hidden variables are unaccounted for in the model. In machine

---

[1]`https://www.technologyreview.com/2020/11/18/1012234/`

learning, underspecification can also result from the way that some algorithms learning by starting from random parameter settings. One proposed solution is to move away from the train-test-deploy paradigm. Instead, multiple models would be created that perform well on in-lab testing data. Then, these models would be deployed to operate on real-world data. A period of real-world evaluation could identify the best model.

8.2 Feature Selection

Another problem in machine learning is determining whether to use all available features, or to select a subset of them. Many of the algorithms we have used have embedded methods to determine the usefulness of predictors. For example, linear and logistic regression give us p-values so that we can gauge confidence in the predictive value of variables. Others do not so we need to use external methods.

8.2.1 Feature Selection with caret

The caret package has several useful functions for feature selection, we will explore a couple of them here. First, the findCorrelation() function which returns a list of columns that can be removed due to their correlation with other variables. We will use the PimaIndiansDiabetes2 data from package mlbench. First we remove rows that have NAs, then compute a correlation matrix with cor() and input this into the findCorrelation() function. The function lets you specify the cutoff point. In this case we had a cutoff of .5 correlation. We also set verbose to TRUE to get fuller information from the function.

Code 8.2.1 — **Find Correlated Variables.** PimaIndiansDiabetes2.

```
library(caret)
library(mlbench)
data("PimaIndiansDiabetes2")
df <- PimaIndiansDiabetes2[complete.cases(PimaIndiansDiabetes2[]),]
corMatrix <- cor(df[,1:7])
findCorrelation(corMatrix, cutoff=0.5, verbose=TRUE)
```

```
Compare row 6  and column  4 with corr  0.664
  Means:  0.265 vs 0.187 so flagging column 6
Compare row 2  and column  5 with corr  0.581
  Means:  0.266 vs 0.161 so flagging column 2
All correlations <= 0.5
[1] 6 2
```

The output of findCorrelation() recommended that we remove column 6, mass, because it correlates with triceps. It also recommended that we remove column 2, glucose, because it correlates with insulin. This is easily done with: df <- df[,-c(2,6)] Recall that in this data set we had a lot of NAs for triceps. Therfore, knowing that mass correlates with triceps but mass has very few NAs might cause us to remove triceps instead of mass.

8.2.2 Ranking Feature Importance

Of the variables we have left, which ones are most important? The caret package was used in the code below to train a model and extract variable importance. We show the output below the code and the plot in Figure 8.2.

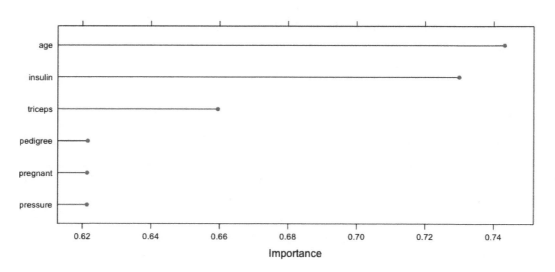

Figure 8.2: Plot of Variable Importance

Code 8.2.2 — Ranking Feature Importance. PimaIndiansDiabetes2.

```
ctrl <- trainControl(method="repeatedcv", repeats=5)
model <- train(diabetes~., data=df, method="knn",
    preProcess="scale", trControl=ctrl)
importance <- varImp(model, scale=FALSE)
importance
plot(importance)
```

```
ROC curve variable importance

          Importance
age          0.7432
insulin      0.7299
triceps      0.6594
pedigree     0.6215
pregnant     0.6214
pressure     0.6213
```

8.2.3 Recursive Feature Selection

Another option in caret is recursive feature selection. This recursively eleminates features to find a subset of predictors that perform well. We start will all the original features. This gave us different advice than the findCorrelation() function above. Here we are told we can eliminate mass and pedigree but it left in both glucose and insulin which we know are highly correlated.

Code 8.2.3 — Recursive Feature Selection. PimaIndiansDiabetes2.

```
df <- PimaIndiansDiabetes2[complete.cases(PimaIndiansDiabetes2[]),]
ctrl <- rfeControl(functions=rfFuncs, method="cv", number=10)
rfe_out <- rfe(df[,1:7], df[,8], sizes=c(1:7), rfeControl=ctrl)
rfe_out
```

```
Recursive feature selection
Outer resampling method: Cross-Validated (10 fold)
Resampling performance over subset size:
```

Variables	RMSE	Rsquared	MAE	RMSESD	RsquaredSD	MAESD	Selected
1	7.177	0.5144	5.176	1.768	0.1737	1.0658	
2	7.602	0.4676	5.433	1.738	0.1501	0.9455	
3	7.358	0.4916	5.350	1.754	0.1532	0.9457	
4	7.363	0.4949	5.372	1.760	0.1562	1.0373	
5	7.416	0.4909	5.432	1.650	0.1367	0.9637	
6	7.221	0.5120	5.276	1.658	0.1413	1.0005	
7	6.999	0.5459	5.126	1.725	0.1463	0.9692	*

```
The top 5 variables (out of 7):
   pregnant, glucose, insulin, triceps, pressure
```

8.3 FSelector

Another package that can help with feature selection is FSelector. Here is a sample run :

Code 8.3.1 — FSelector. PimaIndiansDiabetes2.

```
library(FSelector)
var_scores <- random.forest.importance(diabetes~., df)
```

```
pregnant 12.41986326
glucose 50.53806586
pressure 0.03753078
triceps 8.39019322
insulin 18.00908543
mass 14.08434636
pedigree 7.30103768
age 24.80577317
```

The best predictor was glucose, followed by age. Recall that caret recommended removing glucose because it correlated highly with insulin. As with any diagnosis, a second opinion never hurts.

8.4 Predictive Modeling

The previous chapters described regression and classification algorithms that can be used to model data, and then predict results on future unseen data. The approach described so far in the book has a good deal of overlap with the field of predictive modeling. A definition from the Gartner Glossary:[2]

> **Predictive modeling** is a commonly used statistical technique to predict future behavior. Predictive modeling solutions are a form of data-mining technology that works by analyzing historical and current data and generating a model to help predict future outcomes. In predictive modeling, data is collected, a statistical model is formulated, predictions are made, and the model is validated (or revised) as additional data becomes available.

The examples in this book are one-and-done small projects to illustrate a concept or technique. In a real-world predictive modeling project, the analysis continues in a cyclic manner, ever-evaluating and improving the model. Predictive modeling involves many techniques covered in this book: data preparation, model building, model evaluation, model improvement. Predictive modeling often starts with an objective. For example, a mobile phone service company may want to understand their customers who churn in order to predict customers that are likely to switch to another carrier. Notice that this model would not necessarily be useful for another carrier because the dynamics that make customers leave can be quite different between companies. The objective is typically defined by organization managers who may have little technical knowledge or experience with machine learning. It is important to set realistic expectations with management about the level of accuracy that can be built from the data at hand. Improving accuracy increases in difficulty the higher you go. Going from 98 to 99% accuracy may require much more data and more complex models. The more input features that are used, the more data is needed in order to let the algorithm see all possible values of all features.

Predictive modeling focuses on accuracy in prediction over other considerations such as interpretability. The three algorithms covered in the last three chapters are all highly interpretable. In linear regression, for example, the coefficients quantify the change in y for a one-unit change in x. Other algorithms covered later in the book are not very interpretable, but are more like black boxes.

A definitive guide to predictive modeling is *Applied Predictive Modeling* by Max Kuhn and Kjell Johnson. Max Kuhn is also the author of several R packages, including the caret package.

---

[2]https://www.gartner.com/en/information-technology/glossary/predictive-modeling)

III

Part Three: Modern R

Preface to Part Three

Parts One and Two of the book introduced you to R, often called Base R. This is the R language that has been in use since the 1980s. The importance of learning base R is to be able to read and use legacy code. Base R is all you really *have* to know to use R for machine learning. However, your skill set is greatly enhanced by learning new additions to R syntax, Modern R. This is the purpose of Part Three.

Part Three introduces you to the Tidyverse, a collection of integrated R packages for data wrangling, visualization, and more.

9. Modern R

This handbook has used basic R throughout in order to focus on the algorithms and to make the code as accessible as possible to a wide audience. However, as you continue in R after working through this book, you should learn to use recent extensions to the language that fall under the general title of the **tidyverse**. The tidyverse is a set of R packages designed for improved data manipulation, exploration, and visualization. The packages work together well because they have common data representations and a common API design. All of them can be installed at once with command: `install.packages("tidyverse")`.

The packages include:
- dplyr - provides a grammar of data manipulation
- tibble - creates and manipulates a modern data frame
- tidyr - helps you create tidy data
- readr - is a fast reader of rectangular data
- purr - enhances R's functional programmming (FP) toolkit
- ggplot2 - implements a grammar of graphics for data visualization
- stringr - makes working with strings easier
- forcats - work with factors
- haven - helps read data from other statistical programs such as SAS, SPS, Stata

These extensions to the language are exciting because they have updated R to be more competitive with newer languages. The Base R language was developed in the 1980s when data was smaller and computing power was limited compared to today. In comparison, the tidyverse is fast, and better able to handle larger data.

This chapter explores tidyverse syntax for data manipulation and the next chapter looks at ggplot2 for creating graphs. A terrific online resource for learning to code in the tidyverse is Garrett Grolemund and Hadley Wickham's book *R for Data Science*, most of which is available on the web site: `http://r4ds.had.co.nz/index.html`

The tidyverse packages can be installed as follows: `install.packages("tidyverse")`. Once installed, the tidyverse is loaded like any other library: `library(tidyverse)`.

9.1 Tibble

A tibble is the tidyverse update to the Base R data frame. A tibble is backwardly compatible with the data frame, so you can use a tibble anywhere you previously used a data frame. A tibble is the central data structure for the tidyverse. The documentation states that the general ethos of tibbles is that tibbles are lazy, because they do less, and surly, because they complain more to alert you to problems in the data.

A tibble behaves a little differently under the hood which will not be noticeable to the average user. Two differences you will notice are:

- A tibble will print only a screen at a time of the data.
- A subset of a tibble always returns a tibble. Subsetting a data frame could return a data frame or just a vector.

The code below loads a data frame into memory and converts it to a tibble with the tbl_df() function.

Code 9.1.1 — **tibble.** Create a tibble.

```
library(tidyverse)
library(mlbench)
data("PimaIndiansDiabetes2")   # load the data into memory
tb <- tbl_df(PimaIndiansDiabetes2)   # convert df to tbl
rm(PimaIndiansDiabetes2)   # remove df from memory
tb # display the tibble
```

```
# A tibble: 768 x 9
    pregnant glucose pressure triceps insulin  mass pedigree  age diabetes
       <dbl>   <dbl>    <dbl>   <dbl>   <dbl> <dbl>    <dbl> <dbl> <fct>
  1        6     148       72      35      NA  33.6    0.627    50 pos
  2        1      85       66      29      NA  26.6    0.351    31 neg
  3        8     183       64      NA      NA  23.3    0.672    32 pos
  4        1      89       66      23      94  28.1    0.167    21 neg
  5        0     137       40      35     168  43.1    2.29     33 pos
  6        5     116       74      NA      NA  25.6    0.201    30 neg
# ...
```

A slightly different view is available with the `glimpse(tb)` function. The output is similar to that of str() in Base R.

```
>glimpse(tb)

Observations: 768
Variables: 9
$ pregnant <dbl> 6, 1, 8, 1, 0, 5, 3, 10, 2, 8, 4, . . .
$ glucose  <dbl> 148, 85, 183, 89, 137, 116, . . .
$ pressure <dbl> 72, 66, 64, 66, 40, 74, 50, . . .
$ triceps  <dbl> 35, 29, NA, 23, 35, NA, 32, . . .
$ insulin  <dbl> NA, NA, NA, 94, 168, NA, 88, . . .
$ mass     <dbl> 33.6, 26.6, 23.3, 28.1, 43.1, . . .
$ pedigree <dbl> 0.627, 0.351, 0.672, 0.167,. . .
$ age      <dbl> 50, 31, 32, 21, 33, 30, 26, 29, . . .
$ diabetes <fct> pos, neg, pos, neg, pos, neg, . . .
```

9.2   Pipes

The pipe symbol, %>%, works like the unix pipe. It makes code easier to read as you can combine several commands in a neat group of lines instead of nesting functions in the typical R fashion. The pipe symbol can be typed as you see it, or you can use the shortcut shift+command+M. Pipes are most useful when performing a series of data manipulations on a tibble, but can be used in other places as well.

Recall the code we used to compute rmse: $rmse < -sqrt(mean((pred - test)^2))$. To understand this code you have to start from the inner ( ) and work outward. In pipes, you just read down:

```
# compute rmse with pipes
rmse <- (pred - test)^2  %>%
    mean   %>%
    sqrt
```

9.3   Package dplyr

According to the package author, Hadley Wickham, the d in dplyr is for data and the rest is to evoke pliers. So dplyr is used to manipulate data efficiently. The dplyr packages has several functions for data manipulation. Some of the functions work on columns, such as select, rename, and mutate. Others work on rows, such as filter and arrange. There are also variations of a join function to combine multiple data frames into one tibble.

9.3.1 **Select**

The select function selects columns, returning a tibble
with just those columns. The following code uses select() to extract two columns from the
data frame and send them to the print function. Although select() returns a new tibble, in this
case we didn't save it to another variable so it does not exist in memory.

Code 9.3.1 — **dplyr.** Select.

```
select(tb, diabetes, pregnant) %>%
    glimpse

    Observations: 768
Variables: 2
$ diabetes <fct> pos, neg, pos, neg, pos, neg, pos, neg, ...
$ pregnant <dbl> 6, 1, 8, 1, 0, 5, 3, 10, 2, 8, 4, 10, 10, ...
```

9.3.2 **Mutate**

You can use mutate to create new columns from the existing data. In the code example below
we created a new binary factor columns that is 1 if glucose is above average for the population
and 0 otherwise. The mutate() function returns a tibble, the code below replaces the tibble.
Notice that you can use square brackets to subset a tibble just as you can for data frames.

Code 9.3.2 — **dplyr.** Mutate.

```
tb <- tb %>%
    mutate(glucose_high = factor(
        ifelse(glucose>mean(glucose, na.rm=TRUE), 1, 0)))

tb[1:5, c(2, 10)]  # display glucose and glucose_high for 5 rows

glucose    glucose_high
<dbl>      <fctr>
    148        1
     85        0
    183        1
     89        0
    137        1
```

Mutate can also be used to delete a column by setting it to null. The following code would
remove the column created in the previous code:

```
tb <- tb %>%
    mutate(glucose_high = NULL)
```

```
names(tb)  # verify that the column is gone
[1] "pregnant" "glucose"  "pressure" "triceps"  "insulin"  "mass"
    "pedigree" "age"       "diabetes"
```

9.3.3 Rename

Rename a column using syntax: new = old.

```
tb <- rename(tb, blood_pressure = pressure)
```

9.3.4 Filter

The filter function is used to remove rows. Below we filter rows out that have NAs in either glucose or mass, then glimpse the data. The data now has 752 rows instead of 768.

> **Code 9.3.3 — dplyr.** Filter.
>
> ```
> tb <- filter(tb, !is.na(glucose), !is.na(mass))
> dim(tb)
>
>
> [1] 752 9
> ```

9.3.5 Arrange

Arrange is used to control the order of rows. Here we arrange by mass in descending order.

> **Code 9.3.4 — dplyr.** Arrange.
>
> ```
> arrange(tb, desc(mass)) # descending order
> ```

```
## # A tibble: 752 x 9
##    pregnant glucose pressure triceps insulin  mass pedigree   age diabetes
##       <dbl>   <dbl>    <dbl>   <dbl>   <dbl> <dbl>    <dbl> <dbl> <fct>
## 1        0     129      110    46.0     130  67.1    0.319  26.0 pos
## 2        0     180     78.0    63.0    14.0  59.4    2.42   25.0 pos
## 3     3.00     123      100    35.0     240  57.3    0.880  22.0 neg
## 4     1.00    88.0     30.0    42.0    99.0  55.0    0.496  26.0 pos
## 5        0     162     76.0    56.0     100  53.2    0.759  25.0 pos
## 6     5.00     115     98.0      NA      NA  52.9    0.209  28.0 pos
## 7     11.0     135       NA      NA      NA  52.3    0.578  40.0 pos
## 8        0     165     90.0    33.0     680  52.3    0.427  23.0 neg
## 9     7.00     152     88.0    44.0      NA  50.0    0.337  36.0 pos
## 10    1.00     122     90.0    51.0     220  49.7    0.325  31.0 pos
```

9.3.6 Summarize

The summarize function is a powerful way to get summary statistics. Below we have two examples. Note that you can spell it the American or British way: summarize or summarise. The syntax is: label=function

```
tb %>%
  summarize(min=min(mass), max=max(mass), sd=sd(mass))
```

```
min      max       sd
18.2     67.1      6.928926
```

```
tb %>%
  summarize(num_diabetic = sum(diabetes=="pos"),
       num_healthy = sum(diabetes=="neg"))
```

```
num_diabetic      num_healthy
<int>             <int>
264               488
```

9.3.7 Grouping

The group_by provides a way to summarize selected subsets of the data.

```
tb %>%
  group_by(diabetes) %>%
  summarize(median_BMI = median(mass, na.rm=TRUE))
```

The output (see the online notebook), shows that the median BMI for people with diabetes was 34.3 in contrast to the median BMI of 30.1 for those without a diagnosis of diabetes.

9.4 Shiny

An overview of modern R would not be complete without a mention of Shiny, an R package that helps you make interactive web apps. Shiny apps have two components: the user interface and the server function. The shiny package has eleven built-in demos to show how it works. If you are interested in creating Shiny web apps, there is ample information to get started here: https://shiny.rstudio.com/

9.4.1 Going Further with dplyr

- The book *R for Data Science* by Garrett Grolemund and Hadley Wickham is available here: http://r4ds.had.co.nz/. It provides a thorough introduction to R and the tidyverse.

10. ggplot2

Hadley Wickham developed ggplot2 in 2005, inspired by a grammar of graphics developed by Leland Wildinson in 1999. The ggplot2 functions are much more powerful than standard R graphs but also slower.

Some R users prefer to use base R plots for data exploration, the plots that only they will see that give insight into the data. Then later they can spend the time producing a pretty showpiece graph for publication.

The gglot2 package can be loaded with the library() function but is also loaded automatically when the tidyverse is loaded:
`library(tidyverse)`

There are 7 grammatical elements in ggplot2, the first 3 of these are essential to getting something plotted.
- data = the data being plotted should be the first argument, or specify data=...
- aesthetics - the scales onto which we plot; use aes() to specify at least x= and y= if needed as well as other parameters for customization
- geometries - visual elements such as points, lines, etc.
- facets - for plotting multiples
- statistics - representations to aid understanding
- coordinates - space on which data will be plotted
- themes - you can customize your own theme to use over and over

To get started, the code below shows the important components of building a ggplot:

- the data
- the aesthetics which are how the data is represented
- the geometry
- labels

The full code is available in the GitHub. The graph is visible to the right. As you can see, the graph is a little blah. A little color would be nice. Also, the points seem to be a blob and it's hard to find a trend. We can add a smoothing line to show that as BMI increases, glucose increases. The code is shown in the second code block below, with the graph underneath.

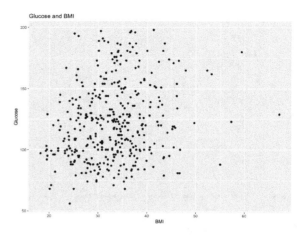

Figure 10.1: Scatterplot of BMI and Glucose

Code 10.0.1 — **ggplot.** Basic Scatterplot Using PimaIndiansDiabetes2 data.

```
ggplot(df, aes(x=mass, y=glucose)) +
  geom_point() +
  labs(title="Glucose and BMI", x="BMI", y="Glucose")
```

Code 10.0.2 — **ggplot.** Scatterplot and Smoothing Line.

```
ggplot(df, aes(x=mass, y=glucose)) +
  geom_point(pch=20, color='blue', size=1.5) +
  geom_smooth(method='lm', color='red', linetype=2) +
  labs(title="Glucose and BMI", x="BMI", y="Glucose")
```

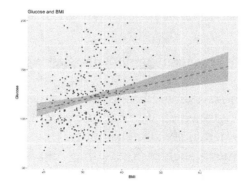

Figure 10.2: Scatterplot with Smoothing Line

10.0.1 Facet Grid

In the notebook on the github, we made two new factor columns, glucose_high and insulin_high which are 1 if the value is above the mean and 0 otherwise. Then we plot with mass on the x axis and age on the y axis. We have 4 plots within the space based on the two new factor columns. Also the points are shaped according to whether the observation has diabetes or not and the color indicates the number of pregnancies.

Code 10.0.3 — **ggplot.** Facet Grid.

```
ggplot(df,
  aes(x=df$mass, y=df$age, shape=diabetes, col=pregnant)) +
  geom_point(size=2) +
  facet_grid(df$glucose_high~df$insulin_high)
```

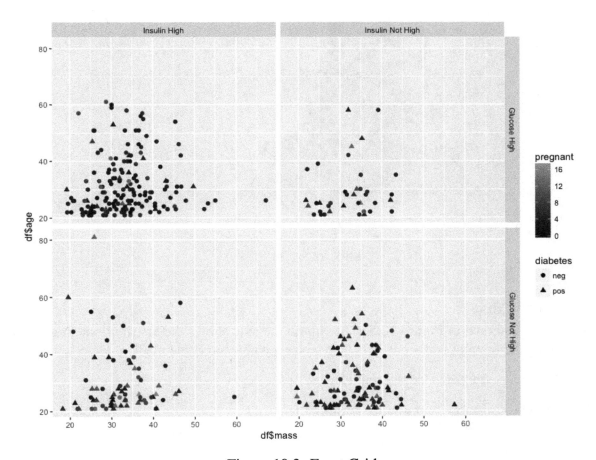

Figure 10.3: Facet Grid

Machine Learning Handbook with R and Python © Karen Mazidi 2020

10.0.2 Histogram

We have seen many histograms throughout the book with base R but ggplot has its own take on the histogram, boxplot, and other graph types.

Code 10.0.4 — **ggplot.** Histogram.

```
ggplot(df, aes(x=mass)) +
  geom_histogram(fill="cornsilk4")
```

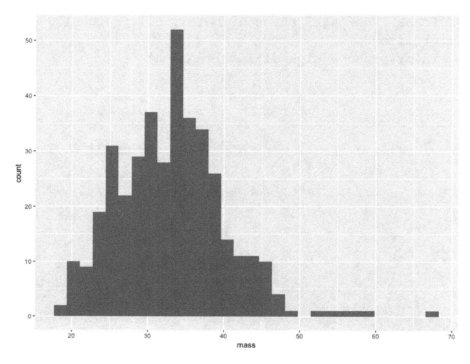

Figure 10.4: Histogram

10.0.3 Boxplot and Rug

A Boxplot is shown in Figure 10.5. The rug on the side shows the distribution. The points overlaying the boxplot add more info. The boxes are notched at the median. Here is the code:

Code 10.0.5 — **ggplot.** Boxplot and Rug.

```
ggplot(df, aes(x=diabetes, y=mass)) +
  geom_boxplot(notch=TRUE) +
  geom_point(position="jitter", color="cornflowerblue", alpha=.5) +
  geom_rug(color="cornflowerblue")
```

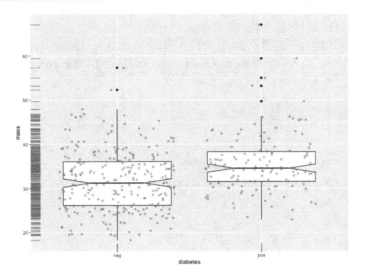

Figure 10.5: Boxplot and Rug

10.0.4 Density Plot

This plot lets you see the density of diabetes positive and negative overlapping each other because the alpha parameter makes them semi translucent. See Figure 10.6.

Code 10.0.6 — **ggplot.** Density Plot.

```
ggplot(df, aes(x=mass, fill=diabetes)) +
  geom_density(alpha=0.4)
```

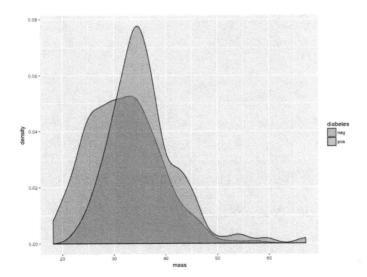

Figure 10.6: Density Plot

10.0.5 Bubble Chart

The bubble size is indicative of the number of pregnancies. The `size=pregnant` argument makes the size of shape 21 vary for each point according to the magnitude of the pregnant collumn. See Figure 10.7.

> **Code 10.0.7 — ggplot.** Bubble Chart.
>
> ```
> ggplot(df,
>        aes(x=mass, y=glucose, size=pregnant)) +
>   geom_point(shape=21, fill="cornflowerblue")
> ```

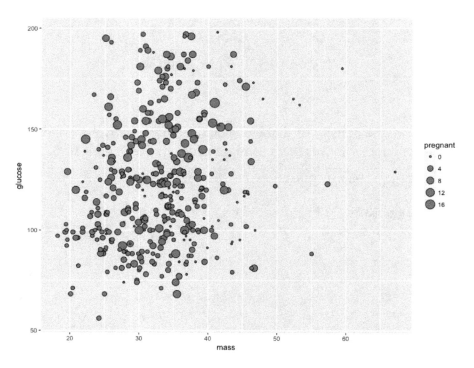

Figure 10.7: Bubble Chart

10.0.6 Grid

In standard R we arrange plots in a grid layour with par(). In ggplot we use grid.arrange().

> **Code 10.0.8 — ggplot.** Grid Arrange.
>
> ```
> library(gridExtra)
> p1 <- ggplot(df, aes(x=insulin_high)) + geom_bar(fill="blue")
> p2 <- ggplot(df, aes(x=glucose_high)) + geom_bar(fill="blue")
> grid.arrange(p1, p2, ncol=2)
> ```

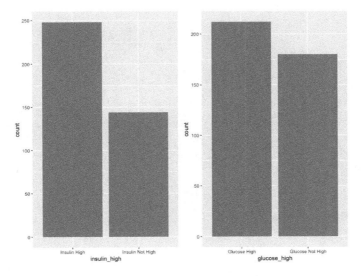

Figure 10.8: Grid Arrange

10.0.7 Going Further with Graphs

- A cheat sheet for ggplot2 from RStudio: `https://www.rstudio.com/wp-content/uploads/2015/03/ggplot2-cheatsheet.pdf`
- Colors in R can be referenced numerically or by name. Here is a list of names: R colors
- Quick-R reference for things like plotting symbols in base R and ggplot: `https://www.statmethods.net/advgraphs/parameters.html`

11. The Craft 3: Data Wrangling with R

The examples presented in this book use data sets that have previously been curated by others. These include data sets built into R, data sets in R packages, and data sets available on the web from sites such as www.kaggle.com. These ready-to-go data sets are used because our focus is on the algorithms, not the data wrangling. It is important to emphasize that data is not so easily obtained in the real world. The data gathering and cleaning phases in real-world machine learning projects can last months or even years. We can divide the data cleaning itself into two phases:

- data organization - compiling data into a form that can be read into an R data frame or other structure with functions such as read.csv() and read.table()
- data standardization - making sure that the values in the data frame make sense and are internally consistent

11.1 Data Organization

Raw data can be gathered from many sources: data bases, unstructured data bases, xml files, or even scraped from the web. Programs to gather the data and put it in an R-compatible form can be written within R but R is probably not the best language for text processing and we will not discuss it here. Rather, other common computer programming languages and libraries can be used for data gathering and organization.

11.1.1 Reproducible Research

It is critically important to document each step of your data gathering and organization. This is important for your own sake in case you need to redo some steps. It is also important if and when you want to publish your results or report results to others. You will need to summarize how the data was collected and make detailed notes available for reviewers and fellow researchers. The most important reason to document is to create **reproducible research**. Anyone should be able to take your original data and follow your instructions to get the same results you reported.

11.2 Data Standardization with Base R

Once the data is gathered into a file in some regular format it can be read with read.csv or read.table. These functions read a file in table form and create a data frame. The assumption is that observations are organized into rows and columns represent attributes. You can use the help features of R to learn more about the read functions. You can use read.csv() like this:

```
df <- read.csv("data/myfile.csv")
```

There are numerous other arguments you can add. Here are a few of the most common ones:

- header=FALSE - use this if your file does not have a header row
- na.strings="NA" - use this to encode empty cells with NA
- stringsAsFactors = FALSE - this is the default since R 4.0; previously the default was TRUE

R automatically creates dummy variables for factors with more than 2 levels. You can check the coding with contrasts() or levels(). If R didn't interpret a column the way you intended, you can change this with the as.factor(), as.integer(), etc. functions as needed. Don't assume anything! Check your data with R functions such as str() and head().

11.2.1 Dealing with NAs

Another problem is missing data, the NAs. We have discussed this before but repeat the code here for easy reference. First, you can check if NAs are going to be a problem by summing the number of NAs by column:

```
sapply(df, function(x) sum(is.na(x)==TRUE)
```

One option to get rid of NAs is to use the complete.cases() function. This will remove any row in which there is any NA in any column:

```
df <- df[complete.cases(df),]fix_NA
```

This may remove too much data. You should get rid of columns you don't care about before moving complete.cases() to limit how much data is lost. A less drastic option is to replace NAs with either the mean or median of the column. Here is a function to do this:

```
fix_NA <- function(x, mean_mode){
# sample call: df$x <- fix_NA(df$x, 1)
    if (mean_mode == 1) {  # use mean
        ifelse(!is.na(x), x, mean(x, na.rm=TRUE))
    } else {
        ifelse(!is.na(x), x, median(x, na.rm=TRUE))
    }
}
df$col <- fix_NA(df$col, 1)  # sample call
```

11.2.2 Outliers

An *outlier* is a data point that exists far outside the range of the majority of the data. Outliers can be errors that were introduced at some point into the data gathering process. Determining whether data is truly an outlier or not takes some expertise beyond the scope of this book. The most important thing to keep in mind for the sake of reproducible research is to document every decision you make. If it is determined that a few values are truly outliers, they may be removed by replacing them with the mean or median values. Or, it may be best to remove that observation entirely by deleting the entire row. Again: document every decision made along with justifications that reflect your thinking at the time.

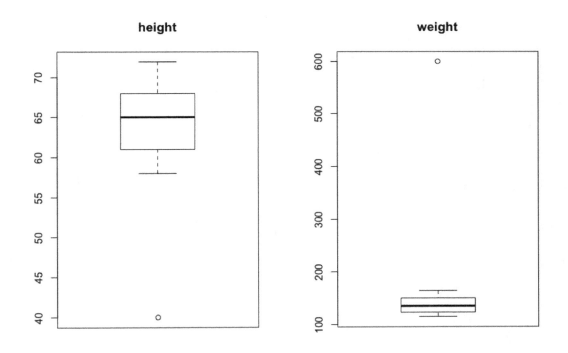

Figure 11.1: Outliers in Height and Weight Data

The boxplot() function can be used to plot the variable and detect outliers. In a boxplot, the circles at either the top or bottom of the plot may be outliers. Care must be taken to not remove data just because it is inconvenient. In the plot above, there is one observation with a height well above the norm, and one observation with a weight well below the norm. To find which row is the suspected outlier, the which() function can be used, which.max(), and which.min() functions can be used, as shown in the sample code and output below.

Is it possible that a person could be 40 inches tall and weigh 120 pounds, or be 65 inches tall and weigh 600 pounds? Yes, these could be legitimate numbers. However, if the number of such outliers are very small, it will distort any attempt to learn something about average heights and weights of a population. For this reason, a researcher may decide to toss out these two examples, after thoroughly documenting their justification for doing so.

```
i <- which.min(df$height)
print(df[i,])
i <- which.max(df$weight)
print(df[i, ])


        height weight
16      40     120


        height weight
17      65     600
```

Sorting data can also help identify max and min values. The R order() function has the following parameters and default values as shown in this example which creates a new sorted data frame with the NAs last.

```
df_sorted <- order(df$colname, na.last=TRUE, decreasing=FALSE)

> head(df[order(df$height),], n=2)
   height weight
16    40     120
1     58     115
> head(df[order(df$weight, decreasing=TRUE),], n=2)
   height weight
17    65     600
15    72     164
```

11.3 Time Data in Base R

In base R, dates are stored internally as the number of days since January 1, 1970. Dates prior to this will be negative numbers. We can use the as.Date() function to convert a character date into an internally stored date. Interestingly, base R doesn't have a native time class. If you need one, look at package hms.

Here are a few examples of processing dates and times in base R. Note the built-in as.Date() and Sys.Date() functions. We can do basic arithmetic on days as shown below, and use the difftime() function with units of secs, mins, hours, days, or weeks.

```
Code 11.3.1 — Base R. Times and Dates.

# processing dates
hire_date <- as.Date("2016-09-01")
days_employed <- Sys.Date() - hire_date
print(days_employed)  # Time difference of 623 days

# processing time
birth_date <- as.Date("1989-04-18")
difftime(Sys.Date(), birth_date, units="secs")
# Time difference of 917654400 secs
```

11.3.1 Lubridate

The lubridate package contains functions to simplify time and date processing. Lubridate is part of the tidyverse.

```
Code 11.3.2 — Lubridate. Basics.

library(lubridate)
today()    # example: "2018-05-17"
now()      # example: "2018-05-17 15:51:37 CDT"
```

Next we show a couple of things you can do with lubridate and a data set. The airquality data set has a month and a day column. The year is 1973 as stated in the description of the data set. We pasted these together and used the ymd() function to create a date column which we added to the data frame.

```
Code 11.3.3 — Lubridate. Airquality data.

df <- airquality[]
df$date <- ymd(paste("1973",airquality$Month,airquality$Day))
print(range(df$date))
# "1973-05-01" "1973-09-30"
df$date[nrow(df)] - df$date[1]
# Time difference of 152 days
```

11.4 Text Data

Before we talk about text data, a caveat: good prediction results on text data are hard to get. Your first attempts are likely to be disappointing. For example, the online notebook for this section used Naive Bayes to classify Amazon reviews as positive and negative and achieved only 56% accuracy. Why is this so hard? Primarily because language is complex and ambiguous. Words have multiple meanings and it is difficult to train a machine to know the intended meaning, much less things like sarcasm. A fuller understanding of the field of Natural Language Processing (NLP) is required to do quality work in machine language with text data. That is beyond the scope of this book. However, for the curious we will discuss how text data can be prepared for machine learning algorithms. There are various ways to handle text data, and different packages. In this section, we will look at two packages: tm and RTextTools that can be used for text processing.

11.4.1 Text Mining Packages tm

The text mining package, tm, uses vocabulary from the field of natural language processing, so we need to discuss that as we go. In NLP, a *corpus* is a body of text. It can be a set of documents, a set of text messages, any set of text examples. The online notebook gives an example of creating a corpus from an Amazon revew data set using the Corpus() function. After the corpus is created, some data cleaning is done: putting all text in lowercase, removing numbers and punctuation, stripping white space, and removing stopwords which are common function words that don't carry content like *the, an, this, it, in*, etc. Then a document-term matrix is created. This is a matrix in which each row represents a document in the corpus and each column represents a unique token (word) in the corpus. The cells hold word counts. Cell x, y holds the count of word y in document x. In the online notebook we see that the corpus contains about 4K documents and over 21K unique words. The document term matrix will be sparse: most cells are 0, indicating that the majority of words do not occur in the document. Inspecting a portion of the document term matrix reveals this sparseness:

Docs	bought	send	someone	spent	term	thing	unless	want	worst	written
50	0	0	0	0	0	0	0	0	0	0
51	0	1	0	0	0	0	0	0	0	0
52	0	2	0	0	0	0	0	0	0	0
53	0	1	0	0	0	0	0	0	0	0
54	0	0	0	0	0	0	0	0	0	0
55	0	0	0	0	0	0	0	0	0	0

An alternative representation is to create a one-hot matrix. This involves replacing counts with 1 so that we have a binary present/not-present encoding of words in matrices.

As you can see in the online notebook, the reviews were divided into train and test sets and converted to one-hot matrix representations. The train matrix was used to train a naive Bayes algorithm and the test set was used to generate predictions. The naive Bayes algorithm had to learn probabilities for each word in the corpus. Below we show a couple of words. Most of the words had this kind of distribution, in that they provide as much evidence for a low rating as they do for a high rating. This approach was not sophisticated enough to learn anything from the words in the reviews, and is best suited to problems in which classes are more easily separable.

```
> nb1$tables$worst
                     worst
factor(train_labels)           0                1
                   1 0.9976470588 0.0023529412
                   2 0.9992877493 0.0007122507

> nb1$tables$best
                     best
factor(train_labels)          0               1
                   1 0.998235294 0.001764706
                   2 0.997863248 0.002136752
```

The tm package has some unique features that are interesting to experiment with. For example you can create a word cloud with selected words where the size of the word is based on the frequency of the word in the corpus.

11.4.2 RTextTools

Another online notebook provides examples of working with package RTextTools. This package was designed for non-technical people to do text analysis. Therefore it is simple to use but gives you less freedom to fine-tune the process. In the online notebook, the same Amazon reviews data is read in and a document-term matrix is created as in the previous section. The RTextTools package uses the tm package for this. Then a container is created. This container holds the train and test split as well as the labels and will be fed into the machine learning algorithms. The algorithms included in the package are svm, glmnet, maxent, slda, boosting, bagging, rf, nnet, and tree. In the online notebook we used svm, maxent and glmnet. After classifying on the test data, the summary analytics can be printed as shown below:

```
ENSEMBLE SUMMARY
         n-ENSEMBLE COVERAGE n-ENSEMBLE RECALL
n >= 1                  1.00              0.83
n >= 2                  1.00              0.83
n >= 3                  0.78              0.89


ALGORITHM PERFORMANCE
        SVM_PRECISION          SVM_RECALL           SVM_FSCORE
                0.820               0.815                0.815
     GLMNET_PRECISION       GLMNET_RECALL        GLMNET_FSCORE
                0.815               0.810                0.810
 MAXENTROPY_PRECISION   MAXENTROPY_RECALL    MAXENTROPY_FSCORE
                0.805               0.805                0.800
```

For more about machine learning on text data, see my book *Exploring NLP with Python:* https://www.amazon.com/dp/B08P8QKDZK

IV Part Four: Searching for Similarity

Preface to Part Four

Part Four explores machine learning algorithms that group observations by similarity. These algorithms are quite diverse, some using supervised and other unsupervised approaches. Some of the supervised techniques can be used for regression or classification. Some are often used for data analysis. These algorithms will form an important part of your skill set in learning from data.

- Chapter 12 looks at the kNN, k Nearest Neighbor algorithm, which can be used for regression or classification
- Chapter 13 looks at two different clustering algorithms: k-means and hierarchical clustering, both are unsupervised methods
- Chapter 14 explores decision trees, which can be used for regression or classification

12. Instance-Based Learning with kNN

12.1 Overview

The kNN algorithm is a supervised learning algorithm but it does not form a model of the input data. Instead, all the training observations are simply stored in memory. When a new observation needs to be evaluated, the algorithm compares it with the observations stored in memory, finding the closest k neighbors.

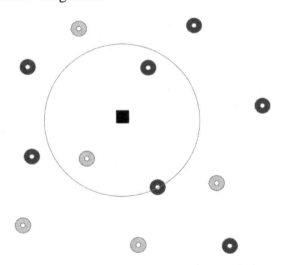

Figure 12.1: Finding k=3 Nearest Neighbors

As illustrated in Figure 12.1, the new observation is the black square. The three nearest neighbors were found and the observation will be classified as green because the majority of near neighbors were green. If this had been a regression task, the black square would be predicted to have a value that is the average target value of the nearest neighbors.

12.2 kNN in R

Using the familiar iris data set we will run the kNN algorithm. Notice in Figure 12.2 that we have 3 classes. One of the nice things about the kNN algorithm is that it can predict class membership in a multi-class data set.

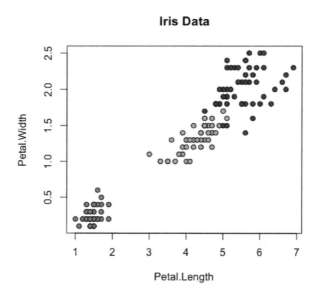

Figure 12.2: The Three Iris Classes

The code for running the knn algorithm on the iris data is shown below. In the notebook online, we have first randomly divided the 150 observations into 67% training and 33% test. We have also separated out the labels in both train and test into new vectors and removed the labels from train and test. There are 4 arguments to the knn() function below: the training data, the test data, the training labels and the chosen value of k. Notice that we do not build a model, we are loading into memory and predicting on the test data all in one command.

Code 12.2.1 — **kNN Classification.** The Iris Data.

```
library(class)
iris_pred <- knn(train=iris.train, test=iris.test,
    cl=iris.trainLabels, k=3)
```

After running the above code, the iris_pred variable will be a vector of class labels: setosa, virginica or versicolor. An optional parameter for knn() is to set prob=TRUE which will return probabilities rather than class predictions. The algorithm achieved 98% prediction accuracy on the test data, but as we have seen before, and as you can observe in Figure 12.2, this is an easy data set to classify. The notebook code to compute accuracy was:

```
acc <- length(which(iris_pred == iris.testLabels)) /
       length(iris_pred)
```

R code can sometimes seem like those Russian nesting dolls so let's unpack from the inner function out. The which(*iris_pred* == *iris.testLabels*) returns a vector of indices for test items that were correct. The length() function surrounding this returned 49. This 49 was divided by the length of the predictions, 50, to get the 98% accuracy. The online notebook compares this result to performing one-versus-all classification with logistic regression.

> **Exercise 12.1 — kNN Classification on Wine Data.** You can find the data set wine_all.csv in the github site. It is a 6497x13 data set of the chemical composition of red and white wines. This data set was edited from the wine data sets on the UCI ML Repository. Your task is to use kNN to classify red/white wine.
> - Divide the data into train and test sets, setting a seed first for reproducibility.
> - Use R commands to make sure that the train and test sets have distributions of white and red types similar to the overall data.
> - For comparison, first build a logistic regression model predicting wine type (red or white) based on all other columns. What is your acccuracy?
> - Run knn() with k=3 on the data and compare the accuracies of the two algorithms.

12.3 The Algorithm

In kNN learning, an observation is known by the company it keeps. For a given test observation x_i, the kNN classifier will identify the k closest points, the neighbors, and estimate the conditional probability for class j as the fraction of neighbors that have that class.

$$P(Y = j|X) = \frac{1}{k} \sum_i I(y_i = j) \tag{12.1}$$

where I() is an indicator function returning TRUE or FALSE.

For regression, an average of the neighbors' target value is taken to be the predicted value for an instance.

$$\hat{y} = \frac{1}{k} \sum_{i \in NB} y_i \tag{12.2}$$

where NB is the set of neighbors.

12.3.1 Choosing K

The choice of a value for k needs to be done before the algorithm is run. The choice of k is critical to the bias-variance tradeoff of the algorithm. If k is very small, the classifier will have low bias but high variance. As k grows, the algorithm becomes less flexible and bias increases while variance decreases. The optimal value for k is often found by cross validation.

A rule-of-thumb that is sometimes stated says to choose a k that is the square root of the number of observations. We have not noticed this to be an effective heuristic. Cross validation is much more reliable. If you are doing classification, it makes sense to let k be an odd number. If k is too small the algorithm will be susceptible to noise but if k is too large the computation time increases.

12.3.2 Curse of Dimensionality

The kNN algorithm works best when we have few predictors. If we have 3 predictors, it will be easier to find neighbors in this 3-dimensional space. If we have 20 predictors, it will be harder to find neighbors in this 20-dimensional space. This is referred to as the curse of dimensionality. Some algorithms, like Naive Bayes, do not suffer in high dimensions but kNN will bog down.

12.4 Mathematical Foundations

What does it mean for an instance to be near another? Often Euclidean distance is used:

$$dist = \sqrt{\sum_i (q_i - p_i)^2} \tag{12.3}$$

However, simple variance is more computationally efficient. In computing the distance or variance, the predictors need to be numeric. If a column is a factor, it should be either be ignored or converted to an integer for kNN.

12.4.1 Scaling Data

The terms scaling and normalization are used inconsistently in the literature. Generally, *normalization* means applying transformations to the data so that it follows a normal distribution while *scaling* implies some linear transformation of the data that may or may not result in a normal distribution. The R scale() function, using the default settings, will transform data to have a mean of 0 and a standard deviation of 1. If the data is normally distributed this should be sufficient. You can easily look at the distribution with a hist() graph. If data is highly skewed then you might get better results with something like this:

```
normalize <- function(x) {
  return((x - min(x)) / (max(x) - min(x)))
}
# apply to all columns
data_norm <- as.data.frame(lapply(df, normalize))
```

Another nice thing about the R scale() function is that there is an unscale() function to convert scaled data back to the original by doing the inverse operations that scaled it. The unscale() function uses information stored with the scaled data.

```
library(DMwR)
scaled <- scale(df)
predictions <- predict(...)
original <- unscale(predictions, scaled)
```

In the sample code above we scaled all the data, including the targets, before dividing into train and test. Another approach is to divide the data, then scale train and test separately. When doing this, many experts advise to do scaling on both train and test using the mean and standard deviation of the train set. Why? Some experts feel that allowing the test data to be scaled by information from the entire data set is leaking information about the data to the test set, which is prohibited. Here is an approach that follows this advice:

```
# normalize data
means <- sapply(train, mean)
stdvs <- sapply(train, sd)
train <- scale(train, center=means, scale=stdvs)
test <- scale(test, center=means, scale=stdvs)
```

Using the approach above, train and test contain just the predictor columns. There is no need to scale the targets, which are held in other vectors. It is only the predictors that need to be scaled.

In the knn classification problem above on the iris data, we did not need to scale the predictors because all measurements are in the same units. As we will see in the next example, when predictors are not in the same units, scaling usually improves performance.

> Exercise 12.2 — **Scaling Data.** Using the same wine data set as above:
> - Scale the data and see if the knn performance improves.
> - See if reducing the number of predictors (reducing the curse of dimensionality) improves the results of the knn algorithm.

12.5 kNN Regression

Next we perform regression on the Auto data set in package ISLR. In the online notebook, first we do linear regression to predict mpg, miles per gallon, based on weight, year, and origin. The linear regression model gets a correlation of 0.89 and an mse of 14.6. The rmse will be around 3.8 mpg. Let's see if kNN can do better.

The first kNN attempt in the online notebook did not scale the data and got worse results than linear regression: correlation of 0.88 and mse of 17. Then we scaled the data. Running kNN on the scaled data resulted in a correlation of 0.91, which is better than the linear model, and an mse of 14. This is the best of the 3 models, the rmse tells us we are off an average of 3.8 mpg. Note that we use the knnreg() function in package caret.

Code 12.5.1 — **kNN Regression.** Auto Data.

```
library(caret)
fit <- knnreg(train[,2:4],train[,1],k=3)
predictions <- predict(fit, test[,2:4])
cor(predictions, test$mpg)
mse <- mean((predictions - test$mpg)^2)
```

Exercise 12.3 — **kNN Regression.** Using the same wine data set as above, we now try to predict the quality.
- Remove the red/wine column from the scaled train and test sets.
- Run knnreg() on the data.
- What is the cor() and mse?
- Create a linear regression model.
- Compare linear regression and knn model performance on the test set.

12.6   Find the Best K

The results with k=3 were good on the Auto data, but how do we know if a different k would produce even better results? We can try various values for k to find out. First we fill two vectors with 20 zeroes. These will hold our results for each level of k. Then we let k be 1, 3, 5, ..., 39. At each iteration in the for loop we store the correlation and mse and also print them out. Trying 1 to 39, skipping by 2, is purely arbitrary. You might try a larger range or skipping more or fewer possible k values.

Code 12.6.1 — **Find the Best K.** Auto Data

```
cor_k <- rep(0, 20)
mse_k <- rep(0, 20)
i <- 1
for (k in seq(1, 39, 2)){
  fit_k <- knnreg(train[,2:4],train[,1], k=k)
  pred_k <- predict(fit_k, test[,2:4])
  cor_k[i] <- cor(pred_k, test$mpg)
  mse_k[i] <- mean((pred_k - test$mpg)^2)
  print(paste("k=", k, cor_k[i], mse_k[i]))
  i <- i + 1
}
```

We can either visually go down the printed values to find the minimum mse and the maximum correlation or we can use the following commands at the console:

```
> which.min(mse_k)
```

```
[1] 8
> which.max(cor_k)
[1] 8
```

It looks like the 8th element is best. That corresponds to k=15. Let's plot this to get a visual understanding. The plot in Figure 12.3 confirms that k=15 (the 8th run) gives the best results. The MSE is in blue, we want that to be as low as possible. The correlation is in red, we want that to be as high as possible. The code below generated this plot. Notice the command par(new=TRUE). This causes the next plot() to be added to the existing plot.

Code 12.6.2 — **Plot mse and cor.** For various k.

```
plot(1:20, cor_k, lwd=2, col='red')
par(new=TRUE)
plot(1:20, mse_k,lwd=2,col='blue',labels=FALSE,ylab="",yaxt='n')
```

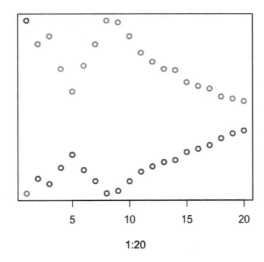

Figure 12.3: MSE (blue) and Correlation (red) for Various K

Exercise 12.4 — **Finding the Best k.** Using the same regression task as above, predicting quality from other variables, try the following:
- Find the best k for your model.
- What is the cor() and mse for this model? How does it compare to the linear regression model?

Machine Learning Handbook with R and Python © Karen Mazidi 2020

12.7   k-fold Cross Validation

The code sample in the last section ran through several values of k to find the optimal k. Running the model many times gave us more information about the data that running only once with k=3 would have. Techniques where algorithms are run different times to find the best or the most accurate parameters fall in the category of resampling methods. In effect the kNN algorithm is "sampling" neighbors. As seen in Figure 12.3 above, the results vary with the value of k. This shows how kNN is sensitive to the data. If we sampled the data many times to get different test sets, the results would vary quite a bit from sample to sample. There are many statistical approaches to sampling. In this section we will talk about k-fold cross validation.

12.7.1   Creating k Folds

Figure 12.4 illustrates 10-fold cross validation. In k-fold cross validation, the entire data set is divided into k (10 in this case) equal portions. For k iterations, the algorithm is trained on all but one portion of the data, leaving the held-out data for test. The test metrics for the k runs are then averaged together to get an overall estimate of test error. Common values of k are 5 and 10. Don't confuse k-NN with k-fold cross validation. The k values don't mean the same thing, it is simply an unfortunate coincidence that both use k.

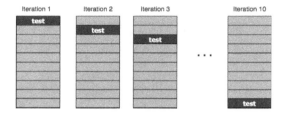

Figure 12.4: 10-fold Cross Validation

Since k-fold cross validation is computationally expensive, why do it? There are a few situations where it will be useful. One is if you have a very small data set and your algorithm is prone to high variance. By running the algorithm many times on different subsets of test data you will get a better idea of how the algorithm will generalize to new data. With just one sampling of the test data you may have gotten lucky or unlucky with the selection of observations in the test set.

Another reason to use cross validation is to select algorithm parameters. In the case of kNN we have to select a value for k. In the last section we selected this value based on how well it performed on this test set. Will that value of k also be good for other random draws of test data? Cross validation can answer that question. This is sometimes called *parameter tuning*.

Cross validation is a technique that can be used with any algorithm. For example, we could use it in linear regression by trying different polynomial regression lines to find the model that best fits the data. This is sometimes called *model selection*.

Next we use 10-fold cross validation on the knn regression problem we discussed earlier. This is in a kNN notebook in the github. After loading the Auto data and subsetting it to just mpg, weight, year, and origin, we need to divide the data into folds. We could easily write the code ourselves but the `caret` package already has a nice function for that, `createFolds`. The first argument to createFolds() is the target column and the second tells it we want 10 folds. Since there are 392 observations in Auto, we expect a little less than 40 indices in each fold. We confirm that with sapply().

Code 12.7.1 — Cross Validation. Divide Data into Folds.

```
library(caret)
set.seed(1234)
folds <- createFolds(df$mpg, k=10)
sapply(folds, length)
Fold01 Fold02 Fold03 Fold04 Fold05 Fold06 Fold07 . . . Fold10
    39     41     37     40     39     39     39 . . .     39
```

You can look at the indices in the first fold with `folds[[i]]`. Recall that double square brackets are used with lists.

```
> folds[[3]]
 [1]  13  15  24  42  54  55  57  60  73  76  84  91 113 126 131 138
     143 144 157 159
[21] 164 173 191 197 204 206 207 218 225 230 270 278 298 310 339 351
     362 366
```

12.7.2 Run knnreg() on each Fold

Now that we have the folds, we can run knnreg() on each fold and average the results. For now we just let k=3.

Code 12.7.2 — Cross Validation. Run 10 times.

```
test_mse <- rep(0, 10)
test_cor <- rep(0, 10)
for (i in 1:10){
  fit <- knnreg(df[-folds[[i]], 2:4], df$mpg[-folds[[i]]], k=3)
  pred <- predict(fit, df[folds[[i]], 2:4])
  test_cor[i] <- cor(pred, df$mpg[folds[[i]]])
  test_mse[i] <- mean((pred - df$mpg[folds[[i]]])^2)
}
print(paste("Average correlation is ", round(mean(test_cor), 2)))
print(paste("range is ", range(test_cor)))
print(paste("Average mse is ", round(mean(test_mse), 2)))
print(paste("range is ", range(test_mse)))
```

```
[1] "Average correlation is  0.93"
[1] "range is  0.90883537818507"  "range is  0.946753085315825"
```

```
[1] "Average mse is  0.15"
[1] "range is  0.111756182643287" "range is  0.201818162667268"
```

You can see that the average correlation and mse are good and also that there is a wide range in both vectors. And this is with holding k steady at 3. This is a confirmation that kNN has high variance with a low value of k. Using the technique of running cross validation and averaging the results gives us a more complete picture of kNN performance on this data. Let's explore results if we use cross validation and vary k at the same time. This will involve rewriting the code.

12.7.3 Cross Validation with Various K

In the code section below we use sapply() to try different values of k on an anonymous function that does the 10-fold cross validation similarly to the previous code segment. The output of sapply() is stored in variable results. This will be a list consisting of the 40 output values, alternating the correlation and mse values. We'd like those separated so we coerce the list into a matrix m. Then column 1 of m will contain all the correlations and column 2 will contain all the mse values. Finally, there is code to create plots, which are shown in Figure 12.5. The graphs in the figure indicate that k=3 gives the highest correlation and the lowest mse.

Code 12.7.3 — Cross Validation. For k=1,3,5...

```
# try various values for k
k_values <- seq(1, 39, 2)
results <- sapply(k_values, function(k){
  mse_k <- rep(0, 10)
  cor_k <- rep(0, 10)
  for (i in 1:10){
    fit <- knnreg(df[-folds[[i]], 2:4], df$mpg[-folds[[i]]], k=k)
    pred <- predict(fit, df[folds[[i]], 2:4])
    cor_k[i] <- cor(pred, df$mpg[folds[[i]]])
    mse_k[i] <- mean((pred - df$mpg[folds[[i]]])^2)
  }
  list(mean(cor_k), mean(mse_k))
})
# reshape results into matrix
m <- matrix(results, nrow=20, ncol=2, byrow=TRUE)
```

Code 12.7.4 — Cross Validation. Plot Results

```
par(mfrow=c(2, 1))
plot(1:20, unlist(m[,1]), lwd=2, type="o", col='red',
     ylab="Correlation")
plot(1:20, unlist(m[,2]), lwd=2, type="o", col='blue', ylab="MSE")
```

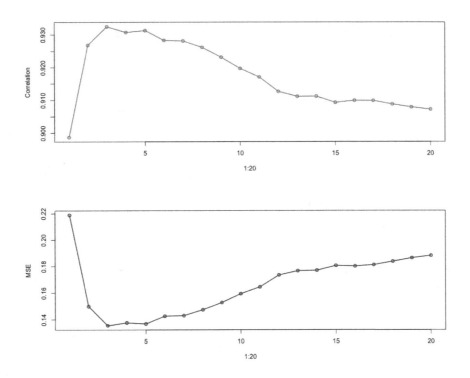

Figure 12.5: Cross Fold Validation for various K

12.7.4 Applying CV to Other Algorithms

The cross validation technique demonstrated in this section can be applied to any algorithm. However, this approach becomes significantly more time intensive with larger data. For example, if you have an algorithm on a large data set that takes 30 minutes to run, and you do 10-fold cross-validation, that will take 5 hours. The catch-22 with small data is that your small test set is likely to result in variance and yet if you put more of your limited data into the test set then you have less for training which could make your algorithm perform poorly. Cross-validation enabled us to have more confidence in our test set metrics by compensating for a relatively small data set. Researchers generally recommend values of k=5 or k=10 since these have been demonstrated empirically to create a good balance between bias and variance.

The `caret` package contains many functions related to sampling. This section had a regression example. If we are performing classification, we need to be concerned about the distribution of observations in the train and test sets. The downSample() function will randomly sample each class to be the size of the smallest class. This results in smaller data which is fine if you have a lot of data to start with. The upSample() function will randomly sample with replacement so that the smaller class becomes as large as the majority class. These are called *subsampling* techniques, and are described in the caret documentation.

12.8 Summary

The kNN algorithm is an example of an instance-based approach. It is often included in lists of clustering algorithms, although it doesn't cluster all the data, it just creates a cluster of neighbors around a test instance. The kNN algorithm is also sometimes called lazy learning because it doesn't do much until test time.

The kNN algorithm does not create a model of the data and by extension is a non-parametric algorithm. The value of k is more technically called a hyperparameter than a parameter, because it is a parameter of the algorithm, not a parameter associated with the data. Choosing k is important. If k is small, the algorithm tends towards low bias and high variance. As k gets larger, the algorithm tends towards high bias and low variance. Advantages:

- Makes no assumptions about the shape of the data
- Performs well in low dimensions
- Can be used for classification or regression

Disadvantages:

- Bogs down in high dimensions
- K must be chosen
- Data should be scaled for best performance
- Difficult to interpret

12.8.1 Quick Reference

Reference 12.8.1 kNN Classification
```
library(class)
predictions <- knn(train, test, cl=trainLabels, k=3)
```

Reference 12.8.2 kNN Regression
```
library(caret)
fit <- knnreg(train, labels, k=3)
predictions <- knnreg(fit, test)
```

Reference 12.8.3 Scaling and Unscaling, Method 1
```
scaled <- scale(df) # scale is built-in
# unscaled in package DMwR
unscaled_predictions <- unscale(predictions, scaled)
```

Reference 12.8.4 Scaling, Method 2
```
# train and test contain just predictors
means <- sapply(train, mean)
stdvs <- sapply(train, sd)
train <- scale(train, center=means, scale=stdvs)
test <- scale(test, center=means, scale=stdvs)
```

12.8.2 Lab

Problem 12.1 — Practice on the Abalone Data - kNN Regression. Try the following:

1. Download the Abalone data from the UCI Machine Learning Repository, `http://archive.ics.uci.edu/ml/datasets/Abalone`.
2. The data does not have column names so you will have to create them. Use meaningful names based on your reading about the data on the UCI site.
3. Check if there are missing values.
4. Divide the data into 80-20 train-test, setting a seed for reproducibility.
5. Normalize the data.
6. Perform knn regression with k=3. What is the cor and mse? Are these good results? Why or why not?
7. Try a range of k values to find the best k. Did the metrics improve?

Problem 12.2 — Practice on the Abalone Data - kNN Classification. Start with the same Abalone data as the previous problem, but add a size column as we did in an earlier lab.

1. Examine the rings column with range(), median(), and hist() to determine where you would like to split the data into two classes: large and small.
2. Create a new factor column for binary large/small based on the rings column and your cut-off decision.
3. Divide the data into 80-20 train-test, setting a seed for reproducibility.
4. Normalize the data.
5. Perform knn classification with all predictors except rings, using k=3. What is the accuracy of the model? Do you think these are good results? Why or why not?
6. Try a range of k values to find the best k. Did the accuracy improve?

Problem 12.3 — Practice on the Heart Data. Try the following:

1. Download the Heart data from the UCI Machine Learning Repository, `http://archive.ics.uci.edu/ml/datasets/Heart+Disease`.
2. The data does not have column names so you will have to create them. Use meaningful names based on your reading about the data on the UCI site.
3. Make sure class is a factor and that all the other columns are numeric or integer.
4. Remove columns with large numbers of NAs because the knn algorithm can't handle them.
5. After removing those columns (slope, ca, and thal), reduce the heart data to only complete cases.
6. Divide the data into 80-20 train-test, setting a seed for reproducibility.
7. Normalize the predictor data.
8. Run knn() with k=3 to create predictions on the test data. What is the accuracy? Do you think this is a good result? Why or why not?
9. Try a range of k values to find the best k. What is the accuracy?

12.8.3 Exploring Concepts

Problem 12.4 Based on your experience with the knn algorithm in R, does removing predictors necessarily improve performance? Discuss possible reasons for your answer.

Problem 12.5 If you found that for a kNN regression problem, the optimal value for k using mse differed from the optimal value using cor. Which one would you prefer? Justify your answer.

Problem 12.6 As k increases, do you think the fit to the data is more or less flexible? Justify your answer.

Problem 12.7 As k increases, do you think the fit to the data tends toward higher bias or higher variance? Justify your answer.

12.8.4 Going Further

The kNN algorithm has wide application. Here is an interesting paper that uses kNN.

Li, Fang, et. al use a modified kNN algorithm for network anomaly detection. Their paper was published by the ACM in 2007 as is available here: `https://www.cs.bgu.ac.il/~seproj/2007-2008/radami/docs/Network_Anomaly_Detection_Based_on_TCM-KNN_Algorithm.2007.pdf`

13. Clustering

Clustering is *unsupervised* learning because we either do not have labels or choose to ignore them for the purpose of learning more about the data. The goal of clustering is to find groups within the data that share common features. Figure 13.1 shows the iris data plotted using Petal.Length and Petal.Width. The goal in clustering is to group them into homogeneous clusters.

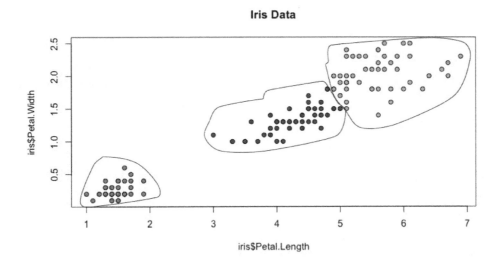

Figure 13.1: Clustering the Iris Data

13.1 Overview

There are numerous clustering algorithms, but in this chapter we focus on two of the most popular:

- k-means clustering - identifies k centers (aka centroids), and groups other observations based on nearness to the closest centroid
- hierarchical clustering - uses a distance measure to combine observations into clusters that are organized in a hierarchy

The notion of distance is central to clustering. What do we mean by distance? We can think of this as Euclidean distance but it may be optimized to be some type of variance measure. How are the clustering algorithms discussed in this chapter different from kNN? The kNN algorithm does not cluster all the observations into clusters, it simply looks for nearby observations given a test observation. The kNN algorithm is also different in that it is a supervised algorithm whereas the clustering algorithms discussed in this chapter are unsupervised.

Clustering problems have a typical workflow:

1. preprocess data
2. determine a similarity measure
3. cluster the observations
4. analyze the results
5. repeat from 2 until the clusters are meaningful

Scaling is very important in clustering because we are measuring distance (or variance). Imagine that we are clustering people by their physical characteristics, if they are 2 pounds different in weight we would consider them similar but not if they were 2 feet different in height. The number 2 has no meaning in isolation and will make sense for distance calculations only if scaled within its column. We will use R's scale() function to put all our columns in similar ranges.

13.2 Clustering in R with k-Means

The k-means algorithm is an iterative approach that starts with a random assignment. The algorithm is as follows:

1. random assignment
2. assign each observation to its closest centroid
3. recalculate the centroids
4. repeat from 2 until convergence

There are many variations on k-means. The most important variation is how step 1 is conducted. One approach is to randomly choose k observations to be the means. Another approach is to randomly assign each observation to one of k groups.

The kmeans() function is in R, we don't need to load a package. The first argument specifies the data you want to cluster. Here we are only considering Petal.Length and Petal.Width. The second argument specifies that we want 3 clusters. In the case of the iris data we know there are 3 classes so this is an unusual advantage here. Normally determining the optimal number of clusters is done experimentally. The third argument is the number of starts. Because the algorithm starts with a random assignment, the algorithm is usually run several times with different random assignments. The kmeans() algorithm will select the best one of the 20 starts we requested. We set a seed for reproducible results but the algorithm will have 20 random starts.

Code 13.2.1 — k-Means Clustering. Iris Data.

```
set.seed(1234)
irisCluster <- kmeans(iris[, 3:4], 3, nstart=20)
irisCluster
```

The results are stored in an object named irisCluster. By typing its name at the console you get the following information.

```
K-means clustering with 3 clusters of sizes 50, 48, 52
Cluster means:
  Petal.Length Petal.Width
1     1.462000    0.246000
2     5.595833    2.037500
3     4.269231    1.342308
Clustering vector:
  [1] 1 1 1 1 1 1 1 1 1 1 1 1 1 1 1 1 1 1 1 1 1 1 1 1 1 1 1 1 1 1
      1 1 1 1 1 1 1 1 1 1 1 1 1 1 1 1 1 1 1 1
 [51] 3 3 3 3 3 3 3 3 3 3 3 3 3 3 3 3 3 3 3 3 3 3 3 3 3 3 3 2 3 3
      3 3 3 2 3 3 3 3 3 3 3 3 3 3 3 3 3 3 3 3
[101] 2 2 2 2 2 3 2 2 2 2 2 2 2 2 2 2 2 3 2 2 2 2 2 3 2 2 2
      2 2 2 2 2 2 3 2 2 2 2 2 2 2 2 2 2
Within cluster sum of squares by cluster:
[1]  2.02200 16.29167 13.05769
 (between_SS / total_SS =  94.3 %)
Available components:
[1] "cluster"      "centers"      "totss"        "withinss"
    "tot.withinss" "betweenss"
[7] "size"         "iter"         "ifault"
```

Notice the 3 clusters it found were 50, 48, 52 so we know that at least 2 observations ended up clustered with a different species than they truly are. That is a moot point because clustering does not have the same goal as classifying. The output also shows the cluster means. We did not scale the iris data because Petal.Length and Petal.Width, our two features, are in the same units. The within-cluster sum of squares measures the variance of the observations within each cluster. A smaller sum of squares indicates a more compact cluster. Notice that the first cluster has a very small value of 2.022. This is the compact red cluster visualized in Figure 13.1. The other clusters are more spread out as indicated by their higher sum of squares numbers of 16 and 13.

Finally, the output shows the components you can look at within the irisCluster object. For example to see the size, type `irisCluster$size` at the console. Most of this information was already supplied in the output.

13.3 Metrics

In most clustering problems we are clustering without knowing what the "true" clustering should be, or if there even is a "true" clustering. How will you know if you have a good clustering or not? Let's first look more precisely at what a cluster is. A cluster is a set of observations that satisfies the following two properties:

- Each of the n observations belongs to one of the clusters: $C_1 \cup C_2 \cup ... \cup C_k = 1, 2, ...n$
- No observation belongs in more than one cluster: $C_i \cap C_j = \emptyset$ for all i, j

One indication that we have a reasonably good clustering is if items within a cluster are homogeneous. One way to measure this is by nearness using a distance metric like Euclidean distance. That is, we average over all k clusters, the distance between every pair of points in the cluster for all features p. We want this average distance to be minimal.

$$\sum_k \frac{1}{|C_k|} \sum_{i,j \in C_K} \sum_P (x_{ip} - x_{jp})^2 \tag{13.1}$$

The term *distance* that is commonly used in connection with k-means is intuitive because we can easily visualize it from our everyday experiences. Perhaps a more mathematically convenient term would be *variance*. We want to know the variance of a point from its assigned centroid. For point x_i, we want to quantify its variance from the mean of each centroid. Each centroid has its own mean, so the squared variance from a centroid is:

$$(x_i - \bar{\mu})^2 \tag{13.2}$$

The quantity we seek to minimize is called the **within sum of squares**. This quantity can be output from the results by typing `results$withinss` at the console. This will output the within-ss for all the clusters so if you want an overall withinss, place sum() around the expression. The within-ss indicates how compact clusters are while the between-ss indicates how well separated the clusters are.

13.4 Algorithmic Foundations of k-means

Since there would be k^n ways to divide n observations into k clusters, a direct mathematical approach would be np-complete. It could not be solved in polynomial time. Further, a loss function for k-means woud be non-convex. For this reason we use an approximation algorithm. The k-means heuristic approach will give a good result but it is not guaranteed to be a global optimum. This is why we use several starts of the algorithm. By finding many local optima we hope to get close to a global optimum.

The two iterative steps of the k-means algorithm can be viewed in a more general sense as an example of the Expectation-Maximization algorithm which estimates parameters from data. The Expectation step computes the probability of the data given the parameters. The Maximization step then computes a better estimate of the parameters. The EM steps are repeated until convergence. The k-means algorithm as viewed from the EM perspective:

1. E step: each observation is assigned to the closest centroid, the most likely cluster
2. M step: the centroids are recomputed

The EM algorithm is widely used in machine learning in cases where parameters cannot be directly calculated.

> **Exercise 13.1 — k-means.** Using the Wine Data.
> Try the following:
> - Load the wine_all.csv file from the github.
> - Make sure type and other columns are numeric.
> - Normalize the data.
> - Perform k-means clustering with k=2.
> - What is the correlation between the clusters and the wine type?
> - Plot the data with the following code. The graph would be crowded if we used all the data so first we randomly sample 250 observations. We use pH and alcohol for the x, y axis to spread the data out. We use a golden color for the white wine and a reddish color for the red wine. The clusters are identified by triangles and circles.
> - Keep in mind we are only plotting on two dimensions in the graph. The data is of what dimension? What does the clustering tell you about white and red wines in n-dimensional space?
>
> ```
> j <- sample(1:nrow(wine), 250, replace=FALSE)
> plot(pH[j], alcohol[j], pch=wine_clust$cluster[j],
>     col=c("brown3","goldenrod1")[wine$type[j]+1],
>     xlab="alcohol", ylab="pH")
> ```

13.5 Finding k

In unsupervised clustering, we do not know beforehand what the optimal value of k will be. We have to find it experimentally. The notebook in github provides an example of finding k using synthetic data. The rnorm() function was used to create 60 points, in 3 distributions with centers (10, 3), (27, 2) and (41, 5). These are the "true" clusters but the regions overlap a little. We plot the unclustered data with different shapes for each distribution. Then we try clustering with different values of k. Figure 13.2 shows the results of kmeans() with k=3. The shapes represent the "true" distributions. We see one purple square between the orange and purple clusters and 3 green circles between the purple and green. The bottom graph shows the results when k=4. The overlap between the purple and green in the top figure has become its own cluster.

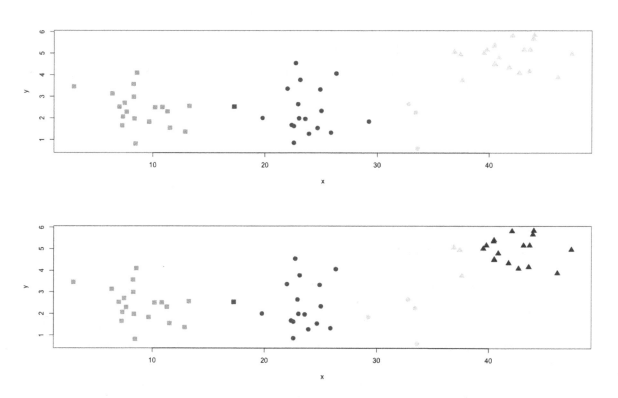

Figure 13.2: Clustering with k-means with k=3 (top) and k=4 (bottom)

We know we created the data from 3 distributions but they are not perfectly separated clusters. In the online notebook we tried k=2, 3, 4, and 5, and printed the withinss:

```
[1] "k=2:   2530.74905628694"
[1] "k=3:   611.695448018061"
[1] "k=4:   373.0421592289"
[1] "k=5:   284.426492959912"
```

It seems there is a dramatic drop from k=2 to k=3 then it gradually decreases. It makes sense that the larger the number of clusters, the smaller the within-ss. After all, if k=n (each observation in its own cluster) then within-ss would be 0.

Rerunning the algorithm with various values of k is tedious, let's do that in a function to try k = 2 to 9. The function below reruns kmeans() with each value of k in 2:9, keeping track of the sum of the within-ss from the results. The plot is shown in Figure 13.3. Notice that within-ss is decreasing but that there is an "elbow" at k=3. The value of k at the elbow is chosen for k because k values higher than that are just reflecting the observation that larger numbers of clusters result in smaller clusters and consequently lower within-ss.

Code 13.5.1 — **Finding k.** Using a Function.

```
plot_withinss <- function(df, max_clusters){
  withinss <- rep(0, max_clusters-1)
  for (i in 2:max_clusters){
    set.seed(1234)
    withinss[i] <- sum(kmeans(df, i)$withinss)
  }
  plot(2:max_clusters, withinss[2:max_clusters], type="o",
      xlab="K", ylab="Within Sum Squares")
}
plot_withinss(df, 9)
```

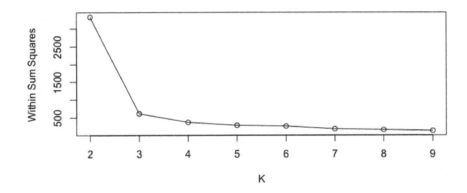

Figure 13.3: Finding K

13.5.1 NbClust

We wrote a simple function above to help us determine the best value for k. There is a very sophisticated function in package NbClust that provides information on over 30 indices. The online notebook uses NbClust to confirm that the best k is 3. Figure 13.4 shows that k=3 was selected by the majority of the criteria.

There are dozens of clustering metrics and that topic is beyond the scope of this book. We will briefly discuss one clustering metric that is available via the NbClust package. The *Rand index* is a measure of cluster purity that ranges from -1 to +1. Rand Index close to 0 means that the clustering was random. The Rand Index for k=3 was very high, 0.92 which is another indication that k= 3 is the best choice.

The graph in Figure 13.4 is a bar graph that indicates how many metrics vote k=n as the best clustering, out of dozens of metrics. The fact that the bar at k=3 is several times taller

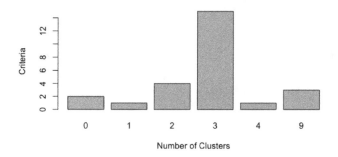

Figure 13.4: Finding K with 30 Indices in NbClust

than the other bars does not mean that a clustering with k=3 will be several times better than other values for k. It simply means that more metrics indicating that k=3 was the best choice.

13.6 Hierarchical Clustering

As we have seen, one of the difficulties of using k-means is that we have to specify k beforehand and it takes quite a bit of exploration to find the optimal k. Hierarchical clustering is a very different type of clustering. We do not have to specify how many clusters we have before running it. Another unique thing about hierarchical clustering is that it creates a dendogram of the clustering, which you can see in Figure 13.5.

A notebook in the github provides an example of hierarchical clustering with the nutrient data set in package `flexclust`. This data set lists the energy, protein, fat, calcium and iron for 27 prepackaged foods. Since the 5 variables are in different units, they are scaled first. R has a built-in dist() function that calculates Euclidean distance by default for a matrix. Once we have the distance, we input this into the hclust() function, built into R. Then the dendogram is plotted.

Code 13.6.1 — **Hierarchical Clustering.** Nutrient Data.

```
d <- dist(nutrient.scaled)
fit.average <- hclust(d, method="average")
plot(fit.average, hang=-1, cex=.8,
     main="Hierarchical Clustering")
```

13.6.1 The Algorithm

There are many variations of hierarchical clustering, here is the "bottom-up" version:
1. Place each observation in its own cluster
2. Calculate the distance between each cluster and every other cluster
3. Combine the two closest clusters

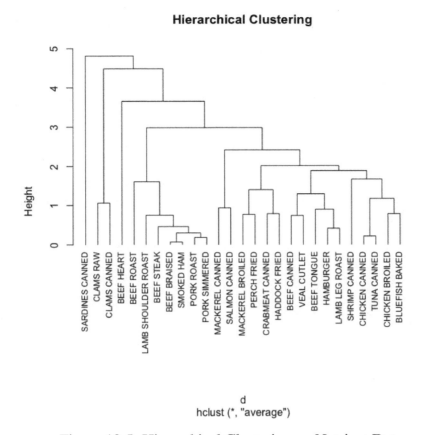

Figure 13.5: Hierarchical Clustering on Nutrient Data

4. Repeat steps 2 and 3 until all clusters merge into one cluster

How do you measure distance between clusters? There are 3 different types of measurements, called linkage, that we can use in hierarchical clustering:

1. single linkage: the shortest distance between any points in the clusters; tends to create elongated clusters

2. complete linkage: the longest distance between any points in the clusters; more compact but sensitive to outliers

3. average linkage: the average distance between points in the clusters

13.6.2 Cutting the Dendogram

Figure 13.6 shows the dendogram with 3 possible cuts in colored lines. The blue (topmost) line would result in two clusters, while the red and green lines would result in 3 and 5 clusters, respectively. The built-in cutree() function can be used to cut a tree created by hclust(). The red (middle) line cut in Figure 13.6 could be created by command cutree(fit.average, 3), where fit.average is the hierarchical clustering and 3 is the number of clusters to retrieve. The cutree() function returns a vector of indices of the cluster to which each observation belongs.

The online notebook for hierarchical clustering shows how to loop through possible cuts and evaluate the clusters. After visually inspecting the clusters to see if they make sense for the task at hand, you might consider printing tables of the clusters as shown in the online notebook. Another option is to use some kind of clustering metric.

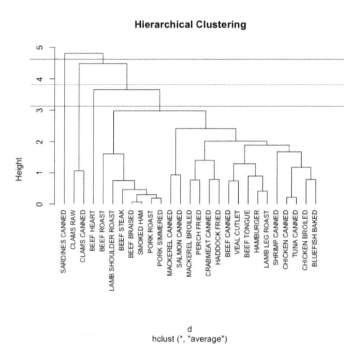

Figure 13.6: Cutting a Dendogram

13.6.3   Advantages and Disadvantages of Hierarchical Clustering

Hierarchical clustering tends to bog down with a lot of data. Another potential disadvantage is that it is a greedy algorithm. Once an observation is in a cluster, it is stuck there. The algorithm does not try several starts as k-means does.

So when should you use hierarchical clustering, also called hierarchical agglomerative clustering? If you suspect there is some hierarchical structure in data, then this algorithm may find it.

> **Exercise 13.2 — Hierarchical Clustering.** Using the same normalized wine data as above, try the following:
> - Perform hierarchical clustering on the entire wine data. Describe the dendogram.
> - Randomly sample 10 observations and perform hierarchical clustering. Compare observations that were clustered together to identify any patterns.

13.7 Summary

Although data exploration is an important first step in any machine learning approach, it is vitally important in clustering. You have to get to know your data before you can begin to select features for clustering and in the end to evaluate your results. Otherwise you are just seeing elephants in clouds.

The algorithms explored in this chapter are examples of unsupervised machine learning, specifically clustering algorithms. How are these techniques used? Clustering is helpful when a lot of data is available but it is not labeled. Clustering can find patterns in the data that would be difficult for humans to find. Use case examples include: finding customer clusters for marketing, finding clusters of home types and values for city planning, clustering species in biology, identifying high crime areas in police work, and much more.

13.7.1 Quick Reference

Reference 13.7.1 kmeans
```
# scale df first if necessary
# specify k=3 and  nstart=25
results <- kmeans(df, 3, nstart=25)
# examine results
results
```

Reference 13.7.2 Hierarchical
```
# scale df first if necessary
d <- dist(df)
fit.average <- hclust(d, method="average")
# plot the dendogram
plot(fit.average, hang=-1, cex=.8,
    main="Hierarchical Clustering")
```

13.7.2 Lab

Problem 13.1 — **Practice k-means on the Wine Data.** Try the following:
1. Use the wine data referenced in this chapter, which is available on the github.
2. We saw in the chapter how the wine type, which is a factor being treated as an integer, pulled the data into two clusters. This is not helpful in learning more about the data. For this exercise, remove the red/white type column.
3. Normalize the data.
4. Create a plot of within-ss to help determine the best k.
5. Perform k-means with this value.

Problem 13.2 — **Practice Clustering on the Glass Data.** Try the following:
- Load the Glass data set from package mlbench. Research this data set and write a brief description of the columns.
- Run kNN with k=7 on the unscaled data to predict glass type from the other columns.

Machine Learning Handbook with R and Python © Karen Mazidi 2020

- Now scale the data and see if your performance improves or not.
- Try different values of k to see if you find higher accuracy.
- Run the k-means algorithm with k=7. Comment on the result of the clustering. Make a table of values like this: `table(df$Type, glass_cluster$cluster)` and comment on any patterns you see.
- Visually check how homogenous the clusters are by printing the clusters and types of glass in each cluster.
- Use the plot_withinss function from this chapter to find the best cluster on the data.
- Use the NbClust() function to find the suggested value of k. Cluster with this value.
- Compare the Rand index values for different clusterings that you have tried.
- Perform hierarchical clustering on the data. Try cuts at 3, 4, 5, and 6, comparing the Rand index at each.
- Comment on which cut you think is best, and why.

13.7.3 Exploring Concepts

Problem 13.3 How is the kNN algorithm different from k-means?

Problem 13.4 Contrast the meaning of "k" in kNN, k-means, and k-fold cross validation.

Problem 13.5 Is the k-means algorithm guaranteed to find the optimal clustering? Why or why not?

Problem 13.6 Earlier it was stated that hierarchical clustering is a greedy algorithm. What does this mean, and why is it a potential disadvantage?

13.7.4 Going Further

The book *Practical Guide to Cluster Analysis in R* by A. Kassambara is partially available here: http://www.sthda.com/

The site also has a page devoted to hierarchical clustering: `http://www.sthda.com/english/wiki/print.php?id=237`

14. Decision Trees, Random Forests

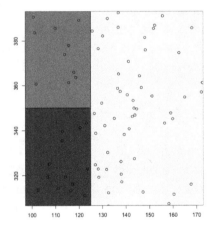

Figure 14.1: Decision Regions

14.1   Overview

Decision trees recursively split the input observations into partitions until the observations in a given partition are uniform. These regions will be rectangular in two dimensions as seen in Figure 14.1 and cuboid in higher dimensions. Notice that the decision boundaries are linear, and aligned with the axes. The algorithm is greedy and does not go back and reconsider earlier splits. Once the vertical split at about 125 is made in the figure below, the only considerations at that point is whether or not to further divide the regions to the right and to the left. Decision trees have been around since the 80s and can be used for either classification or regression. They are not among the best performing algorithms but have the advantage that they are highly interpretable and give insight into the data.

14.2   Decision Trees in R

There are several packages with decision tree functions in R, among them rpart and tree. The latter seems to be a little more robust and prints better trees so we will use that for our examples. However, the online example uses both rpart and tree so you can compare. Figure 14.2 shows the output decision tree, which has 6 leaf nodes.

Code 14.2.1 — **Decision Tree.** Iris Data

```
library(tree)
tree_iris2 <- tree(Species~., data=iris)
plot(tree_iris2)
text(tree_iris2, cex=0.5, pretty=0)
```

If you type the tree name at the console you get a tree representing branches by indendation. This also includes the split data at each level. The summary() function on the model also gives some additional information. In the online notebook we also ran the algorithm with the same train set we have used before with iris and got 3 misclassified observations for a mean accuracy of 94%, but then we know that is typical for the Iris data set, having run it through many algorithms.

Exercise 14.1 — **Decision Tree.** Using the Wine Data.
Try the following:
- Load the wine_all.csv data and divide it into 80-20 train and test.
- Perform logistic regression to predict type from all other predictors.
- Perform knn on a scaled version of the data, again predicting type.
- Create a decision tree and evaluate its results. Note the Quick Reference at the end of the chapter which shows how to use predict() for decision trees.
- Print your tree.
- Compare the results of the 3 algorithms and consider the advantage and disadvantages of each.

14.3   The Algorithm

Since decision trees can be used for regression or classification we will look at these separately, beginning with regression. Both create recursive binary splits.

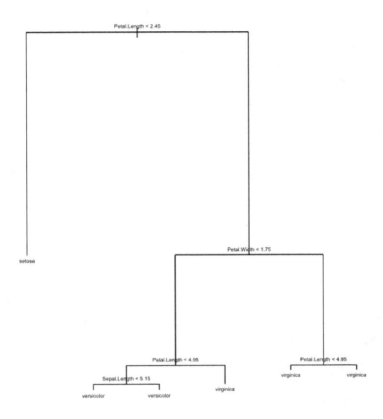

Figure 14.2: Decision Tree for Iris

14.3.1 Regression

In linear regression our goal was to minimize RSS over all the data. In decision trees, we want to minimize RSS within each region, where $\hat{y}_r$ is the mean response for the training observation in region r.

$$\sum_{r=1}^{R} \sum_{i \in r} (y_i - \hat{y}_r)^2 \qquad (14.1)$$

This is computationally infeasible in part because the data space could be divided into virtually infinite regions. Instead, a top-down, greedy approach is used to partition the data. To start, all predictors are examined to see if they make good splits in the data, and for each predictor the numerical value at which to split must be determined. Our first split will divide the data into regions r1 and r2. We will consider predictor X_1 which has a split value $split_1$, such that observations in r1 are less than the split value and other observations are in r2.

$$RSS_{X_1} = \sum_{i \in r_1}(y_i - \hat{y}_{r1}) + \sum_{i \in r_2}(y_i - \hat{y}_{r2}) \qquad (14.2)$$

This splitting process is repeated until a stopping threshold is reached.

14.3.2 Classification

The same recurvise, top-down, greedy algorithm is used for classification except that RSS is replaced by counts of classes in regions. A measure such as accuracy is not sufficient for splitting regions so other measures such as entropy or the Gini index are used. These are discussed in the mathematical foundations section. The goal of either metric is to measure the purity of the regions, how homogenous they are.

14.3.3 Qualitative data

The discussion of the algorithm for regression and classification assumed quantitative data. When splitting qualitative data, a binary feature would make a natural split between the two values. Features with more than 2 values would assign one or more values to one branch and the remaining ones to the other. Decision trees can handle qualitative data without having to create dummy variables.

14.4 Mathematical Foundations

In this section we give further information about entropy, information gain, and the Gini index. We start with entropy, which measures uncertainty in the data, and information gain, which measures reduction in entropy.

14.4.1 Entropy

First we are going to talk about entropy, a measure of uncertainty in the data. The formula for entropy is given below. H() is the traditonal symbol for entropy. Notice that the probability is multiplied by the log of the probability for each class. These are summed and then negated.

$$H(data) = -\sum_{c \in C} p_c log_2 p_c \qquad (14.3)$$

The probability of a class is just the fraction of data observations in that class. Let's look at the tennis data set as a simple example for these calculations.

The entropy of the entire data set is determined by counting 9/14 days when we did play and 5/14 when we did not:

$$H(tennis) = -\frac{9}{14} \times log_2 \frac{9}{14} - \frac{5}{14} \times log_2 \frac{5}{14} = .94 \qquad (14.4)$$

day	outlook	temp	humidity	wind	play
D1	Sunny	Hot	High	Weak	No
D2	Sunny	Hot	High	Strong	No
D3	Overcast	Hot	High	Weak	Yes
D4	Rain	Mild	High	Weak	Yes
D5	Rain	Cool	Normal	Weak	Yes
D6	Rain	Cool	Normal	Strong	No
D7	Overcast	Cool	Normal	Strong	Yes
D8	Sunny	Mild	High	Weak	No
D9	Sunny	Cool	Normal	Weak	Yes
D10	Rain	Mild	Normal	Weak	Yes
D11	Sunny	Mild	Normal	Strong	Yes
D12	Overcast	Mild	High	Strong	Yes
D13	Overcast	Hot	Normal	Weak	Yes
D14	Rain	Mild	High	Strong	No

Figure 14.3: Tennis Data Set

How do we interpret entropy? The x-axis in Figure 14.4 indicates the probability. At .5 probability, entropy is maximized. There is a lot of confusion in the data, it is the opposite of homogenous. At higher or lower probabilities, we see that entropy is lower. Lower entropy means the data is more homogenous. The probability of play in the tennis data is 0.64 and our entropy was .94, very high.

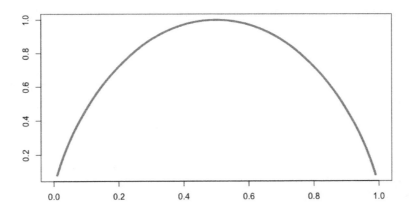

Figure 14.4: Entropy

Now let's say we want to split on wind. Wind has two levels: weak and strong. When wind is weak we have 6 examples where we play and 2 where we do not. Let's compute the entropy.

$$H(wind = weak) = -\frac{6}{8} \times log_2\frac{6}{8} - \frac{2}{8} \times log_2\frac{2}{8} = .811 \qquad (14.5)$$

What is the entropy of wind=strong? Since we have an even split play=3 and not-play=3 we know our entropy is 1. In order to compute the entropy of wind we need to combine the entropy of wind=weak and of wind=strong in a formula that weights it by the relative size of these two groups, 6/8 and 2/8.

14.4.2 Information Gain

Information gain is the reduction in uncertainty we would have, given a certain choice. It is the starting entropy minus the entropy of the split. In our case, it is the entropy of the entire data set (.94) minus the weighted entropy of wind. The formula is shown below, where f represents each value of a feature and N is the total count of items.

$$IG(split) = H(data) - \sum_f \frac{|f|}{N} H(split_f) \tag{14.6}$$

$$IG(split_{wind}) = .94 - 8/14 * .811 - 6/14 * 1 = 0.048 \tag{14.7}$$

Running similar IG statistics reveals that IG(outlook) = 0.246, IG(humidity) = 0.151, and IG(temperature) = 0.029. It turns out that outlook has the highest IG, so we would choose outlook for the decision tree split.

14.4.3 Gini index

For a given region, for each class in the region, Gini measures homogeneity. There are many variations of this formula, here is one:

$$Gini = 1 - \sum_{k \in K} p_k^2 \tag{14.8}$$

$Gini(tennis) = 1 - (9/14)^2 - (5/14)^2 = 0.459$
The maximum Gini index is 1.0. Let's look at the Gini index for wind.
$Gini(wind = strong) = 1 - (3/6)^2 - (3/6)^2 = 0.5$
$Gini(wind = weak) = 1 - (6/8)^2 (2/8)^2 = .375$
$Gini(wind) = 6/14 * 0.5 + 8/14 * .375 = .43$
We weight by the proportion of observations in each class to get a Gini for wind of 0.43, not that great. The Gini index will give comparable results to information gain, but we want a minimal Gini and a maximum IG.

14.5 Tree Pruning

Decision trees are highly sensitive to variations in the data. For this reason if we grow decision trees out fully on a training set they are likely to overfit. One strategy to reduce overfitting is to grow the tree all the way out, then prune it back to get a subtree. T_0 represents the fully grown tree. There are $|T|$ subtrees in which some internal node has been collapsed to combine its children into one region. Let Q represent the criterion for tree building for either regression or classification. Then subtrees can be indexed by lambda:

$$Subtree_t = Q + \lambda|T| \tag{14.9}$$

The optimal subtree can be found by cross validation or using a held out validation set. If lambda = 0 our subtree is the original tree. As lambda increases, the subtree is smaller and less tuned to the training data.

There is no guarantee that a pruned tree will generalize better to new data for improved performance. However the pruned tree may be more interpretable since it should have fewer branches.

The code below shows how to use cv.tree() to try various trees. We plot the deviance by tree size. It looks like the best tree is 5. Deviance is lower at a size of 8 but we are concerned that this may overfit the data. After performing cross validation, we can prune it with the prune.tree() function, and print the pruned tree.

Code 14.5.1 — **Decision Tree.** Cross validation.

```
cv_tree <- cv.tree(tree1)
plot(cv_tree$size, cv_tree$dev, type='b')
tree_pruned <- prune.tree(tree1, best=5)
plot(tree_pruned)
text(tree_pruned, pretty=0)
```

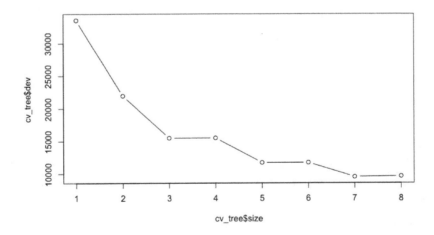

Figure 14.5: Cross Validation on Decision Tree

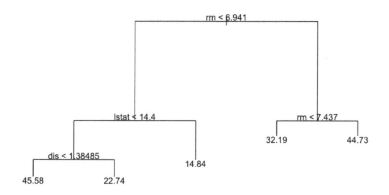

Figure 14.6: Pruned Decision Tree

Exercise 14.2 — **Pruning a Decision Tree.** Using the Wine Data.
Try the following:
- Using the cross-validation technique demonstrated in this chapter, prune the decision tree you created for the wine data.
- Print the tree.
- Evaluate your results on the same test data as before.
- How does accuracy compare with the unpruned tree? Which tree do you prefer, and why?

14.6 Random Forests

The term bootstrap means to repeatedly sample from a data set. Bagging is short for bootstrap aggregation and the main idea is to repeatedly sample the data to overcome the variance in a technique. As we have discussed, decision trees have high variance. The random forest builds on the idea of bagging but the trees are de-correlated as follows. At each split, a random subset of predictors is selected from all the predictors and one is chosen. A typical size of the subset is the square root of the number of predictors. Suppose there is a strong predictor that many bagged trees would choose first. The random forest approach prevents trees from chosing the same predictors in the same order. This allows new trees to be discovered that may outperform trees choosing the strongest predictor first. In effect, the down side of the greedy algorithm is mitigated by restricting the choice of predictors.

14.7 Cross validation, Bagging, Random Forests in R

In the github is an example of a regression tree on the Boston housing market. For comparison purposes we first built a linear regression model using all predictors. The correlation of the predicted versus the test median home value was .8 and the root mean squared error was 5.36, meaning that the home price was off by about $5,360. Running the tree algorithm on the same train/test data had a correlation of .88 and an rmse of 4.2. The decision tree got better results than linear regression. The following code example shows how to perform cross validation on the tree. The output graph in Figure 14.5 indicates that a tree size of 5 should give good results, perhaps without overfitting. Next the code shows that we prune the tree. The pruned tree is shown in Figure 14.6. The pruned tree has 5 leaf nodes compared to 8 in the unpruned tree which you can view online. The pruned tree had a correlation of 0.81 and an rmse of 5.27. This shows a reduced performance but has the advantage of being more interpretable with fewer leaf nodes.

Next we try bagging and random Forest on the same data. The parameter importance tells the random Forest algorithm to consider predictor importance. The parameter mtry specifies the number of variables to sample at each split. The default value for classification is sqrt(p) and for regression is p/3, where p is the number of predictors. If mtry is set to the number of predictors, then bagging is performed instead of the Random Forest. In the code block below, a Random Forest is created because mtry is left to the default values.

We see in the output, shown below the code example, that 500 trees were created, trying 4 variables at each split. The test correlation on the bagged trees jumped to 0.93 and the rmse decreased to 3.4, meaning that we were off on the home price by only an average of $3,400.

Code 14.7.1 — Random Forest. Let mtry use default settings.

```
library(randomForest)
set.seed(1234)
rf <- randomForest(medv~., data=train, importance=TRUE)
```

```
Call:
 randomForest(formula = medv ~ ., data = train, importance = TRUE)
               Type of random forest: regression
                     Number of trees: 500
No. of variables tried at each split: 4

        Mean of squared residuals: 10.66999
                  % Var explained: 87.5
```

In the online notebook you can see that we also tried bagging by setting the number of variables to the maximum. The results were very similar. Recall that the difference between bagging and Random Forest is that the Random Forest is discouraged from predicting the strongest predictor first so that the trees are more unique. In the Boston data, rm was the strongest predictor on all the models so it seems that choosing this as the first split is the best choice. The strongest predictor may not always be the best initial split, however.

Exercise 14.3 — **Bagging and Random Forest.** Using the Wine Data.

Try the following:
- Using the unpruned decision tree you created earlier, try bagging.
- How many trees were created?
- The results from bagging talk about an OOB estimate of error. Research what that means and write a 1-2 sentence explanation.
- Now try random forest.
- Compare the output of the bagging and the random forest. What do you observe?
- Compare the results of bagging and random Forest to your earlier results in terms of accuracy.
- Besides accuracy, what other considerations would cause you to prefer one algorithm over the others?

14.8 Summary

As you can see in the Boston example online, linear regression and the regression tree got fairly similar results. Linear regression will typically outperform decision trees when the underlying function is linear. However if the relationship between the predictors and the target is not linear and complex, decision trees will probably perform better. In the Check Your Understanding examples, you observed that decision trees can perform similarly to logistic regression, particularly with bagging or random forests.

Decision trees are considered to be non-parametric algorithms. Decision trees have an advantage in being easily interpretable. Decison trees have low bias and high variance. Decision trees are sensitive to the distribution of predictors so slightly different data can result in very different trees. This high variance can be overcome with bagging or random forests. Pruning the tree may help it generalize to new data by holding back from overfitting but this is no guarantee of improving performance.

14.8.1 Quick Reference

Reference 14.8.1 Build Decision Tree
```
library(tree)
tree1 <- tree(y~., data=df)
plot(tree1)
text(tree1, cex=0.5, pretty=0)
```

Reference 14.8.2 Evaluate Decision Tree
```
# remove type="class" for regression
tree_pred <- predict(tree1, newdata=test, type="class")
table(tree_pred, test$type)
mean(tree_pred == test$type)
```

Reference 14.8.3 Cross Validation and Pruning
```
# cross validate to find  best
cv_tree <- cv.tree(tree1)
plot(cv_tree$size, cv_tree$dev, type='b')

# prune to best
tree_pruned <- prune.tree(tree1, best=5)
```

Reference 14.8.4 Bagging or Random Forest
```
library(randomForest)
set.seed(..)
# importance=TRUE considers variable importance
# mtry=p (number of predictors)
#      will perform bagging instead of random forest
tree_bag <- randomForest(y~., data=df, importance=TRUE, mtry=13)
random_forest <- randomForest(y~., data=df, importance=TRUE)
```

14.8.2 Lab

Problem 14.1 — Practice Decision Trees on the Abalone Data. Try the following:

1. Use the abalone data available on the github. Load the data, providing names as done in the labs for Chapter 4.
2. Divide the data into train and test sets.
3. Perform linear regression and evaluate correlation and mse on the test set.
4. Perform knn regression and compute correlation and mse. You will need to convert sex from a factor to integer before scaling. Copy your train and test sets to a new name so the original train and test are preserved.
5. Create a decision tree, print the tree, and evaluate on the test data.
6. Try bagging and compute your metrics on the test data.
7. Compare the results on all models and discuss why you think the best model was able to outperform the others.

Problem 14.2 — Classification on the Heart Data. Try the following:

- Load the processed.hungardian.data.csv from the git hub. Make sure class is a factor.
- Remove columns 11:13 because they have too many NAs, and use complete.cases() to get rid of remaining NAs.
- Split the data into 80-20 train and test.
- Create a logistic regression model on the data and evaluate its accuracy on the test data.
- Create an additional train and test set that are normalized for knn.
- Run knn with k=10 and evaluate its performance on the test data.
- Create a decision tree, print it, and evaluate its performance.
- Try the random forest algorithm and evaluate its performance.
- Comment on which algorithm performed best.

Problem 14.3 — **Classification on the Glass Data.** Try the following:

- Load the Glass data set from package mlbench. Research this data set and write a brief description of the columns.
- Divide the data into 80-20 train-test.
- Create scaled versions of the train and test data for kNN. Try various values for k and see how accurate the algorithm can get.
- Create a decision tree, print it, and evaluate its accuracy on the test data.
- Try random forest on the data and evaluate its accuracy.
- Comment on which cut you think is best, and why.
- Discuss what we would have to do with the data to use logistic regression.

14.8.3 Exploring Concepts

Problem 14.4 Compare how linear regression makes predictions compared to decision trees.

Problem 14.5 Compare how kNN makes predictions compared to decision trees.

Problem 14.6 Explain why linear regression has high bias and decision trees have high variance.

14.8.4 Going Further

Professor Lior Rokach from Tel-Aviv University has shared his overview of decision trees here: `http://www.ise.bgu.ac.il/faculty/liorr/hbchap9.pdf`

15. The Craft 4: Feature Engineering

15.1 Feature Engineering

Feature engineering involves changing the data in some way to improve performance on the algorithm. Let's say we have a date field and we know that our target variable has different values for weekdays versus weekends. Some algorithms may be able to work with such data but other algorithms may perform better if we change the date field as a binary weekday/weekend factor. If we have columns in the data that are highly correlated with each other, we might consider deleting all but one of the correlated variables to reduce the total number of columns fed into the algorithm.

15.1.1 Principal Components Analysis

Principal Components Analysis (PCA) is a data reduction technique that can help you reduce the dimensions of your data. PCA transforms the data into a new coordinate space while reducing the number of axes. Each axis of the reduced space represents a principal component. The first PC represents the dimension of greatest variance, and the other PCs represent decreasing variance. An intuitive explanation is to visualize n-dimensional space reduced to a k-dimensional elliptical space where k is smaller than n. This is a data reduction technique, we are losing data and may correspondingly lose accuracy in any models.

We are going to take a quick look at PCA on the iris data. In the notebook in github, we first divide the iris data into train and test, 100 and 50 observations respectively. Then the preProcess() function from caret is used to find the principal components.

Code 15.1.1 — **PCA.** Iris data.

```
pca_out <- preProcess(train[,1:4],method=c("center","scale","pca"))
pca_out
```

```
> pca_out
Created from 100 samples and 4 variables

Pre-processing:
  - centered (4)
  - ignored (0)
  - principal component signal extraction (4)
  - scaled (4)

PCA needed 2 components to capture 95 percent of the variance
```

We see that PCA reduced the 4 variables to 2 principal components. These two components capture 95% of the variance in the data. Let's plot the two components PC1 and PC2 and color the points according to the true class. We see that we have one class that is separate from the other two, shown in red. And we see that the blue and green are fairly well seperated but that there is some overlap. This suggests that classification will be possible but challenging.

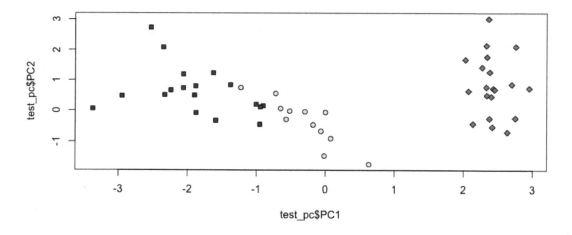

Figure 15.1: Principal Components for the Iris Data

In the online notebook, we tried kNN and got a mean accuracy of .94. Although this is lower than the 98% accuracy we got in Chapter 9 using knn on all 4 predictors, it is a confirmation that PCA is capturing something important in the data. We also ran a decision tree on the PCA data and got a little lower accuracy of .92. The tree is shown below.

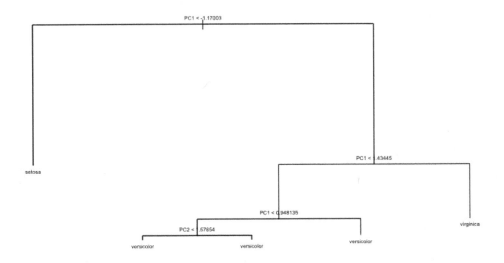

lda

Figure 15.2: Principal Components Decision Tree

15.1.2 Linear Discriminant Analysis

PCA is applied to data without regard to class and such is used like other unsupervised methods for data analysis. Linear Discriminant Analysis, LDA, does consider the class. LDA seeks to find a linear combination of the predictors that will maximize the separation of the classes while minimizing the within-class standard deviation. There is an lda() function in package MASS which we use on the same data as PCA above.

Code 15.1.2 — Linear Discriminant Analysis. Iris Data.

```
library(MASS)
lda1 <- lda(Species~., data=train)
lda1$means
```

	Sepal.Length	Sepal.Width	Petal.Length	Petal.Width
setosa	4.943333	3.350000	1.470000	0.2633333
versicolor	5.973684	2.752632	4.268421	1.3315789
virginica	6.515625	2.925000	5.493750	1.9750000

We see that the LDA analysis has identified means for all variables by class. When we used the lda1 model for prediction in the online notebook, we got an accuracy of 98%. Further when we plot the lda predictions by class using the two linear discriminants returned by the model, we see a nice separation. The color of the points indicates the true class while the shape indicates the predicted class.

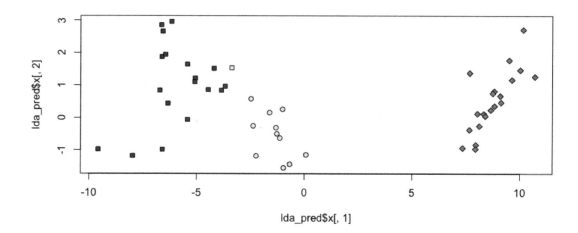

Figure 15.3: Linear Discriminant Analysis, Iris Data

In comparing PCA and LDA, the most significant difference is that PCA is unsupervised and LDA is supervised. Both can be used for dimensionality reduction. In this example, both reduced the 4 iris predictors to two predictors. LDA will have an advantage over PCA when the class is known.

Part Five: Kernel Methods and Ensemble Methods

Preface to Part Five

Part Five explores kernel methods and ensemble methods, two extensions of machine learning algorithms that increase computational complexity but have the potential to increase accuracy as well.

- Chapter 16 looks at SVM, support vector machines. SVM is a powerful algorithm due to the kernel transformations that it can perform on data to get the best results.
- Chapter 17 gives an overview of ensemble methods, which combine many learners into a better learner. Particular emphasis is given to the popular XGBoost algorithm.
- Chapter 18 examines the foundations of learning theory.

16. Support Vector Machines

Whereas most of the algorithms discussed so far arose out of statistics, the support vector machine is an invention from computer science. Vladimir Vapnik developed the ideas for the support vector machine in his PhD thesis in the 1960s in his native Russia. Unfortunately, the computing power was not present there at that time to implement the algorithm. Later Vapnik emigrated to the U.S. to work for Bell Labs. He submitted several papers to top conferences including NIPS but his papers were rejected. Vapnik's persistence paid off, he went on to win numerous awards including in 2017 the IEEE von Neumann Medal. As of this writing he has over 180K citations on Google Scholar.

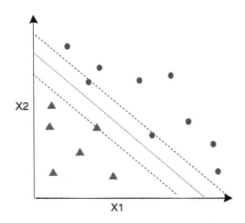

Figure 16.1: Separating Hyperplane

16.1 Overview

SVM is a very popular algorithm because it performs well in a variety of scenarios. The most common scenario is binary classification but it can also be extended to multiclass classification and even regression. The key ideas are summarized in Figure 16.1 where we see two classes, represented by red triangles and blue dots, divided by a separating hyperplane, represented by the orange line. Although visualized in 2 dimensions representing two predictors for illustrative purposes, we should think of the separating line as being a hyperplane in multidimensional space for the more common occurence of having multiple predictors. Notice that the separating line has margins on either side, in green. The goal is to find a margin that separates the classes which is not any wider or narrower than necessary. We see instances actually on the margin, these are called the *support vectors* from which the algorithm gets its name. As we see later, classification is simply a matter of determining which side of the margin an instance falls on, designated by class +1 and class −1.

16.2 SVM in R

One of the nice things about SVM is that it does multi-class classification. On the iris data set, we were able to do multiclass classification as shown below, with 95% accuracy. Notice the confusion matrix that was output by the table() function. Most of the observations are on the diagonal, only 4 observations out of the test set were misclassified. The implementation we are using in the example below is from the e1071 package.

```
Code 16.2.1 — SVM. Iris Data Set

library(e1071)

svm1 <- svm(Species~., data=train, kernel="linear",
        cost=10, scale=TRUE)

pred <- predict(svm1, newdata=test)
table(pred, test$Species)
pred          setosa versicolor virginica
  setosa         27         0         0
  versicolor      0        22         0
  virginica       0         5        24
mean(pred==test$Species)
[1] 0.9367089

# plot the support vectors
plot(svm3, test, Petal.Width ~ Petal.Length,
     slice = list(Sepal.Width = 3, Sepal.Length = 4))
```

Figure 16.2 shows a plot for the test data, but similar results would be seen using the train

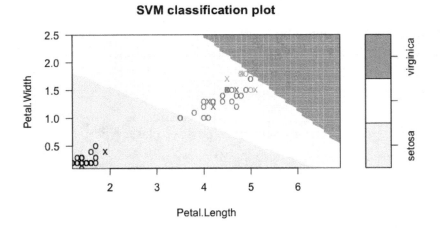

Figure 16.2: SVM Plot

data or on the entire data set. The plot is a nice feature of the svm function. Note the color coding for the 3 classes. The limitations of this type of svm plot are that you can only plot 2 dimensions and the data must be quantitative.

16.3 The Algorithm

The standard svm uses a linear decision boundary defined by:

$$\mathbf{w}^T\mathbf{x} + b \tag{16.1}$$

To classify new observations, data will be assigned to the +1 class on one side of the decision boundary and to the −1 class on the other.

$$\hat{y} = sign(\mathbf{w}^T\mathbf{x}_{new} + b) \tag{16.2}$$

The decision bounary is defined by the orthogonal vector **w**. For binary classifiers, w is assumed to point toward the positive class. The margin is the perpendicular distance from the decision boundary to the closest points (support vectors) on either side. The classification rule will be:

$$if\ (\mathbf{w}^T\mathbf{x}_{new} + b) > 0\ then\ y = +1 \qquad if\ (\mathbf{w}^T\mathbf{x}_{new} + b) < 0\ then\ y = -1 \tag{16.3}$$

Taking advantage of the fact that y will be +1 or −1 we can rewrite the two equations above as one:

$$y_i(\mathbf{w} \cdot \mathbf{x}_{new} + b) - 1 \geq 0 \tag{16.4}$$

Note that in the above, the equation will be equal to zero for support vectors.

We can visualize this solution geometrically. For a new point x_{new} we can visualize a vector from the origin to this point which we will call u. Is u on the positive or negative side? We can project u onto w to get the direction and length, and then classify according to this decision rule:

$$w \cdot u + b \geq 0 \tag{16.5}$$

If the above is true, it will be classified as the positive class, otherwise it will be classified as the negative class.

16.4 Mathematical Foundations

The goal is to learn the hyperplane from the training data, making the margin as wide as it can be, given the data. The width of the margin is the difference of two support vectors, one on each margin, normalized by the unit vector of w:

$$(x_+ - x_-) \cdot \frac{w}{\|w\|} \tag{16.6}$$

The positive support vector has width 1-b while the negative support vector has width 1+b. Adding these gives 2, so the quantity to optimize is:

$$max \; \frac{2}{\|w\|} \equiv max \; \frac{1}{\|w\|} \equiv min \; \|w\| \equiv min \; \frac{1}{2}\|w\|^2 \tag{16.7}$$

with the final step above selected for mathematical convenience. The quantity to minimize is constrained by the support vectors:

$$y_i(w \cdot x_i + b) - 1 = 0 \tag{16.8}$$

The above notation for the support vectors takes advantage of the fact that y is either positive or negative 1.

Lagrangian multipliers, denoted by alpha below, allow us to put together our optimization expression with the constraints:

$$L = \frac{1}{2}\|w\|^2 - \sum_i \alpha_i [y_i(w \cdot x_i + b) - 1] \tag{16.9}$$

To find w, we take the partial derivative with respect to w and set to zero:

$$\frac{\partial L}{\partial w} = w - \sum_i \alpha_i y_i x_i = 0 \qquad \Rightarrow \qquad w = \sum_i \alpha_i y_i x_i \tag{16.10}$$

The equation for w above tells us that w is a linear sum of all the samples. For most samples, alpha will be 0. Alpha will be non-zero only for those on the margin. Next we need to find b by taking the partial derivative of the Lagrangian equation with respect to b.

$$\frac{\partial L}{\partial b} = -\sum_i \alpha_i y_i = 0 \qquad \Rightarrow \qquad b = -\sum_i \alpha_i y_i \qquad (16.11)$$

Now plug in the solution for w back into equation 7.9:

$$L = \frac{1}{2}(\sum_i \alpha_i y_i x_i)(\sum_j \alpha_j y_j x_j) - (\sum_i \alpha_i y_i x_i)(\sum_j \alpha_j y_j x_j) - \sum_i \alpha_i y_i b + \sum_i \alpha_i \qquad (16.12)$$

We can simplify the above by combining terms and eliminating the next-to-last term because b is a constant and the alphas will be zero.

$$L = \sum_i \alpha_i - \frac{1}{2}\sum_i \sum_j \alpha_i \alpha_j y_i y_j (x_i \cdot x_j) \qquad (16.13)$$

As we see above, the optimization depends on the dot product of pairs of samples. This turns out to be a quadratic optimization problem which is solved by existing software solutions.

16.4.1 Slack Variables and the C Hyperparameter

If the data cannot be neatly separated by the margins, it may be possible to get good results by letting a few observations fall on the wrong side of the margin. These are called **slack variables**. The term C controls how much impact slack variables are allowed to have on the determination of the optimal w. Larger values of C result in larger margins and more support vectors. Smaller values of C will have lower bias, higher variance than larger values.

$$\epsilon_i \geq 0, \sum_n \epsilon_i \leq C \qquad (16.14)$$

Allowing for slack variables can also generalize better to test data because it will not overfit the training data. It is always better to perform a little worse on the training data if performance on test data can be improved. Previously we defined support vectors as instances on the margin. When we allow for slack variables, the support vectors become instances either on the margin or on the wrong side of the margin given their class. C is the "cost" hyperparameter that can be optimized experimentally as shown in the following Check Your Understanding. The SVM algorithm has some hyperparameters to tune so we need to set aside data for that. For a linear SVM we need to specify the cost parameter. The optimal hyperparameters are usually found by experimenting on a validation data set that is separate from the test set. The following code shows how to divide data into 3 sets, train, test, and validation. After setting a seed as usual, we set up a variable, groups, to hold the percent of data we want in each group. Then we sample using the cut() function. We have not used this function before; cut(x) divides the range of x into intervals and codes the values in x according to which interval they fall. The leftmost interval corresponds to level one, the next leftmost to level two and so on. We also see the use of the cumsum(), cumulative sum function, which returns a vector whose elements are the cumulative sums.

```
# train-test-validate split
set.seed(1234)
groups <- c(train=.6, test=.2, validate=.2)
i <- sample(cut(1:nrow(df),
              nrow(df)*cumsum(c(0,groups)), labels=names(groups)))
train <- df[i=="train",]
test <- df[i=="test",]
vald <- df[i=="validate",]
```

Exercise 16.1 — SVM on the Titanic Data. Try the following:
- Load the titanic3.csv data (available on the github) into variable df.
- Subset the data to only columns pclass, survived, sex, age. Make sure that survived and pclass are factors.
- Check for NAs. Replace NAs in the age column with the average age. Use complete.cases() to get rid of remaining NAs.
- Divide into 60% train, 20% test, and 20% validation as shown in the code above.

Now let's try SVM:
- Build an SVM model on the train set using cost=10 and kernel="linear".
- Evaluate on the test set. What is your accuracy?
- The cost parameter is a hyperparameter that determines how much impact slack variables are allowed to have. Larger values of cost result in larger margins. Smaller values for cost will make the model move toward lower bias, higher variance. Try various values for cost as shown in the code below.

```
# experiment with cost hyperparameter
set.seed(1234)
tune.out <- tune(svm, survived~., data=vald, kernel="linear",
          ranges=list(cost=c(0.001, 0.01, 0.1, 1, 5, 10, 100)))
summary(tune.out)
best_model <- tune.out$best.model
summary(best_model)
pred <- predict(best_model, newdata=test)
acc_svm2 <- mean(pred==test$survived)
```

Some explanation of the code above:
- Look at the summary of tune.out. It tells you the best cost was 0.01.
- Notice that you don't have to rerun the model with this best cost. The algorithm will extract the best model for you.
- This best model is then used to make predictions on the test data. The results should be a little better than the first svm.
- Note that we tuned the hyperparameters on the validation set. If we tuned it on the training set, we would probably overfit that data and not do well on the test data. If we tuned it on the entire data set that would be against good principles because we are letting the algorithm see test data. By tuning on a validation set we avoid these problems. We had about 260 observations for the validation set. If we had more data we would have more confidence in our hyperparameters.

16.5 Kernel Methods and the Gamma Hyperparameter

The discussion above assumed a linear decision boundary. However, data is often not linearly separable. Kernel functions can be used to map the linear function to another form so that the data is linearly separable. The first line of Figure 16.3 shows data that is not linearly separable. The bottom part of the figure illustrates the mapping of the data to a higher dimension so that it is now linearly separable. This visualizes a polynomial kernel.

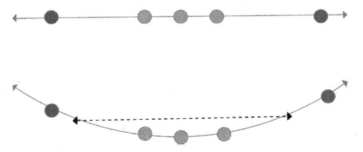

Figure 16.3: Mapping to a Polynomial Kernel

Figure 16.4 illustrates a radial kernel in which the decision boundary is roughly circular. Points are classified according to whether they are inside or outside this radial boundary.

Recall that our linear svm relied on the inner product of observations $x_i \cdot x_j$. This can be combined with a non-linear kernel function $K(x_i \cdot x_j)$. The two most common kernels are the polynomial kernel: $(x_i \cdot x_j)^d$ and the radial kernel: $exp(-\gamma(x_i \cdot x_j)^2)$. The gamma parameter controls the bias-variance tradeoff. A larger gamma can overfit, having low bias and high variance. A smaller gamma could have higher bias and lower variance.

16.6 SVM Regression

SVM linear, polynomial, and radial kernels can be used for classification or regression. The first example in this chapter was for classification, now we turn our attention to a regression

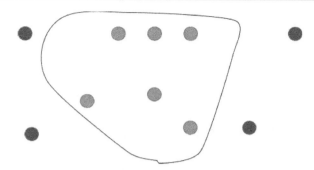

Figure 16.4: Mapping to a Radial Kernel

problem. The full notebook online shows the Boston housing data set in the MASS package. We want to predict median home value for a neighborhood given various parameters such as the number of rooms, and indicators of the nature of the neighborhood. First we perform linear regression and get an rmse=5.09, meaning that it is off on the median house estimate by about 5,090 dollars. Correlation of the predicted versus target values is 0.8.

Next we try SVM regression on the same train and test data, shown in the code below. The svm() function looks similar to other R functions with some additional parameters. Recall from the discussion about slack variables, that the C variable controls how much we will allow variables to violate the decision boundary. The value C can set or the algorithm default to cost=1. Later we will discuss a cross-validation technique to find the best C. In the svm() call below we selected a linear kernel and chose not to scale the data. When should you scale the data? If you have one predictor with very large values compared to the other predictors, it will dominate calculating the distance between the separating hyperplane and the support vectors. The data may perform better with scale=TRUE, but it depends on the data. The online notebook shows svm being performed on a subset of important predictors, using the predictors identified as significant by the linear regression model. Since SVM is performing dot product of training examples, having fewer predictors can lessen the complexity and improve run time. The linear regression model slightly outperformed the SVM model in the online notebook, and the lm() model also has the advantage of being highly interpretable.

Code 16.6.1 — **SVM Regression.** Boston Housing.

```
library(e1071)
svm_fit1 <- svm(medv~., data=train, kernel="linear", cost=10,
    scale=FALSE)
summary(svm_fit1)
svm_pred1 <- predict(svm_fit1, newdata=test)
cor(svm_pred1, test$medv)
mse_svm1 <- mean((svm_pred1 - test$medv)^2)
```

In the code above we just arbitrarily picked a cost=10 value. There is a tune() function in R that tries to find optimal hyperparameters for the svm using a grid search. This involves trying all the suggested vaues for the hyperparameters in a cross-validation scheme. The output of summary() is shown below the code. Look down the column to find the lowest error. It seems to be at cost=0.1.

Code 16.6.2 — Tuning Hyperparameters. Finding the best C.

```
tune_svm1 <- tune(svm, medv~., data=train, kernel="linear",
        ranges=list(cost=c(0.001, 0.01, 0.1, 1, 5, 10, 100)))
summary(tune_svm1)
```

```
Parameter tuning of 'svm':
- sampling method: 10-fold cross validation
- best parameters:
 cost
  0.1
- best performance: 28.22127

- Detailed performance results:
   cost      error dispersion
1 1e-03 45.37743   28.59339
2 1e-02 29.26508   18.06280
3 1e-01 28.22127   16.40897
4 1e+00 28.42638   16.52989
5 5e+00 28.42807   16.52849
6 1e+01 28.43127   16.53240
7 1e+02 28.43401   16.55991
```

Notice in the output that there really is not much difference in the error from cost=0.1 to cost=100. The best model can be extracted with `tuned$best.model`. When the best model was run in the online notebook, the results were slightly worse and still not as good as linear regression.

Cost is a hyperparameter. What is a hyperparameter? Whereas the parameters of a model are internal to the model and can be estimated from data, the *hyperparameters* are external to the model and are often optimized experimentally.

16.6.1 Radial Kernel SVM

Next we try a radial kernel SVM. The radial kernel has an additional hyperparameter, gamma, which controls the shape of the hyperplane boundary. Smaller gammas give sharper peaks in higher dimensions whereas larger gammas give more rounded peaks. Higher gammas allow the decision point to be influenced highly by points close to the decision boundary, making peaks and valleys in the decision bounary. Higher gammas may overfit. This suggests that smaller gammas tend toward lower bias and higher variance and that larger gammas increase bias and lower variance.

Code 16.6.3 — **SVM Regression.** Radial Kernel.

```
svm_fit2 <- svm(medv~., data=train, kernel="radial",
      cost=1, gamma=1, scale=FALSE)
svm_pred2 <- predict(svm_fit2, newdata=test)
cor(svm_pred2, test$medv)
mse_svm2 <- mean((svm_pred2 - test$medv)^2)
```

The online notebook demonstrates trying the tune() function again to get the best hyperparameters. One limitation in this example is that the hyperparameters were tuned on a small validation set of about 100 observations. Nevertheless, the radial kernel SVM significanty out-performed the linear regression model, achieving a correlation of 0.899 and an rmse of 3.927.

Exercise 16.2 — **Kernel Methods on the Titanic Data.** Try the following:
- Continuing with the same data as Check Your Understanding 7.1, build a model with kernel="polynomial", gamma=1, and cost=1.
- Evaluate on the test data and compare to the linear model.
- Build a model with kernel="radial", gamma=1 and cost=1.
- Evaluate on the test data and compare to the linear and polynomial models.
- Try variations of parameters on the validation data, as shown in the code below.
- Evaluate on the test data, using the best model, and compare to the earlier models.

```
set.seed(1234)
tune.out <- tune(svm, survived~., data=vald, kernel="radial",
              ranges=list(cost=c(0.1,1,10,100,1000),
                          gamma=c(0.5,1,2,3,4)))
```

16.7 Summary

Because only a few instances determine the margins, SVM is robust to observations that are far from the hyperplane. SVM classifiers share this in common with logistic regression. For points away from the hyperplane, the loss function is zero in SVM and very small for logistic regression. This is why logistic regression and SVM often give similar results. When classes are well separated, SVM tends to perform better than logistic regression. When the classes overlap, logistic regression may perform better. SVM can be used for both regression and classification. Furthermore, either SVM regression or SVM classification can use linear, polynomial, or radial kernels. This makes SVM a highly versatile algorithm that will perform well in a variety of applications.

16.7.1 New Terminology in this Chapter

The new terminology in this chapter mainly involves aspects of the SVM algorithm:

- separating hyperplane
- margins
- support vectors
- slack variables
- kernels: linear, polynomial, radial
- hyperparameters

16.7.2 Quick Reference

The e1071 package provides the implementation of SVM we used in this chapter. The svm() function performs classification if the target is a factor and regression otherwise. The kernel can be linear, polynomial, or radial. We can also choose to scale the data or not with the SCALE parameter.

Reference 16.7.1 SVM Classification or Regression
```
# classification or regression depends on target type
svm_model <- svm(formula, data=train, kernel="linear",
    cost=10, scale=TRUE)
```

Reference 16.7.2 Divide into Train/Test/Validation Sets
```
set.seed(1234)
groups <- c(train=.6, test=.2, validate=.2)
i <- sample(cut(1:nrow(df),
                nrow(df)*cumsum(c(0,groups)), labels=names(groups)))
train <- df[i=="train",]
test <- df[i=="test",]
vald <- df[i=="validate",]
```

Reference 16.7.3 SVM Tuning
```
set.seed(1234)
# tuning a linear svm
tune_svm1 <- tune(svm, medv~., data=vald, kernel="linear",
          ranges=list(cost=c(0.001, 0.01, 0.1, 1, 5, 10, 100)))
summary(tune_svm1)
# tuning a radial svm
tune.out <- tune(svm, medv~., data=vald, kernel="radial",
                ranges=list(cost=c(0.1,1,10,100,1000),
                            gamma=c(0.5,1,2,3,4)))
# extract best model
tune.out$best_model
```

Machine Learning Handbook with R and Python © Karen Mazidi 2020

16.7.3 Labs

Problem 16.1 — **SVM Classification on the Glass Data.** Try the following:
- Load the glass data from package mlbench.
- Check for NAs and run str() on the data.
- Divide the data into 60/20/20 train/test/validate data.
- Run naive Bayes on the training data and evaluate on the test data.
- Run an SVM linear model on the training data and evaluate on the test data.
- Tune the hyperparameters on the validation set, and evaluate on the best model.
- Run an SVM polynomial model on the training data and evaluate on the test data.
- Run an SVM radial model on the training data and evaluate on the test data.
- Tune the hyperparameters on the validation set, and evaluate on the best model.
- Compare all the models you created in terms of accuracy on the test data.

Problem 16.2 — **SVM Advantages and Disadvantages.** A friend is comparing a naive Bayes model and a logistic regression model and getting fairly good results. Would you recommend SVM? What questions would you ask about the data before making your recommendation?

16.7.4 Going Further

This chapter used the svm() function in package e1071. This function is an interface into the well-known C++ implementation by Chang and Lin called libsvm. Read more about their work here: https://www.csie.ntu.edu.tw/~cjlin/libsvm/

An in-depth tutorial on SVM for pattern recognition by Burges and Burges from the *Data Mining and Knowledge Discovery* journal is available here: https://www.microsoft.com/en-us/research/

17. Ensemble Methods

Ensemble methods combine weak learners into a strong learner. The random forest and boosting methods described in the decision tree chapter are ensemble learners. Other algorithms besides decision trees can be combined for ensemble learning as well.

17.1 Approaches

Ensemble techniques typically combine weak learners either sequentially or in parallel. The sequential approach involves using weak learners one after the other, each time more heavily weighting the mislabeled observations as they are input into the next learner. The parallel approach uses many weak learners that are created at the same time and aggregates the results. An example of the parallel approach is a Random Forest. Ensemble approaches can use any machine learning algorithm as base learners. However, ensemble approaches will achieve greater improvements with low-bias, high-variance learners.

In this chapter we try four different ensemble methods on a phishing data set:

- boosting (library adabag)
- random Forest
- adaboost (library fastAdaboost)
- xgboost

In the online notebook, a phishing data set from the UCI Repository is converted from Weka format to an R data frame, then split into train and test sets. The data set has 11K rows and 30 predictors for the Result target, which is a binary variable indicating phishing or not. The target column is fairly well balanced, with 56% of observations in one class and 44% in the other class.

Logistic regression was run as a baseline and received an accuracy of 94%. In addition the Matthew's correlation coefficient was calculated as 87%. Matthew's correlation coefficient, mcc, can be used as a binary classification metric, and ranges between -1 and +1 where +1 is perfect agreement, -1 is perfect disagreement, and 0 is random agreement. The mcc metric is considered a better metric than accuracy because mcc accounts for differences in class distribution. The formula for mcc is:

$$mcc = \frac{TP \times TN - FP \times FN}{\sqrt{(TP+FP)(TP+FN)(TN+FP)(TN+FN}} \qquad (17.1)$$

17.2 Bagging and Random Forest

Bagging (bootstrap aggregation) helps overcome variance in models. A Random Forest for example trains multiple trees on subsets of the data. This makes each tree independent of the others. The results are averaged for regression and majority vote is used for classification. The Random Forest algorithm uses a different data sample and different subsets of features for each tree, thereby allowing a significant reduction in variance. Bagging is a special case of the Random Forest algorithm with the full set of predictors used for each tree instead of a subset. In the online notebook, random forest achieved one of the highest accuracy scores, 96%, and one of the highest mcc scores, 93%.

17.3 Boosting

Whereas bagging uses subsets of the data, boosting uses the entire training data. Another key difference is that bagging builds learners in parallel, boosting builds them sequentially. The boosting approach learns more slowly than the bagging approach. When using decision trees as learners, the trees that are built are small with just a few nodes. Each subsequent tree that is built is added to the function in order to update the parameters. As each new learner is built, the data is weighted according to the mispredictions of previous learners. Observations with larger errors are given larger weights so that the next learner can overcome this deficiency.

17.3.1 AdaBoost

The AdaBoost (adaptive boosting) algorithm is a variation of boosting that is commonly used. The algorithm trains a given number of learners, one at a time. For the first iteration, the weights for training examples are equal, $1/N$, where N is the number of observations. In each subsequent iteration, the weights for observations with large errors are increased, while those that are correct are decreased. As each learner is trained, its weighted error is recorded. After iterating over all learners, these weighted errors are used to weight the learners themselves, so that more accurate learners are given higher weights. There are many boosting implementations in R.

17.3.2 Package adabag

The adabag package implements Freund and Schapire's Adaboost.M1 algorithm[1], the SAMME algorithm[2] by Zhu, as well as Breiman's Bagging algorithm[3] using classification trees. AdaBoost.M1 and SAMME are generalizations of AdaBoost for more than two classes. The boosting() function uses classification trees and single classifiers. The package also has a bagging() function.

The code block below first shows how to run the algorithm. The first argument to boosting() is a typical R formula, the second is the data. The third argument is boos=TRUE which indicates that a bootstrap sample of the training data should be used; if FALSE, the entire data is used. The mfinal parameter is the number of iterations in boosting or the number of trees; the default is 100. The coeflearn parameter controls the algorithm selected and the alpha parameter which is a weight for each tree in the ensemble.

Code 17.3.1 — Boosting in R. Package adabag

```
library(adabag)
adab1 <- boosting(Result~., data=train, boos=TRUE, mfinal=20,
      coeflearn='Breiman')
summary(adab1)

pred <- predict(adab1, newdata=test, type="response")
acc_adabag <- mean(pred$class==test$Result)
mcc_adabag <- mcc(factor(pred$class), test$Result)

print(paste("accuracy=", acc_adabag))
print(paste("mcc=", mcc_adabag))
```

Notice in the code above that the predictions need to be extracted with $class. The above run got an accuracy of 95% and an mcc score of 90%.

17.3.3 Package fastAdaboost

The fastAdaboost implementation uses C++ code to run about 100 times faster than native R-based libraries, according to the package documentation. As of this writing, it worked only for binary classification problems, whereas the adabag package has been extended for multiclass classification. The implementation uses Freund and Schapire's Adaboost.M1 algorithm, and Zhu's SAMME algorithm.

The code below got an accuracy of 96% and an mcc score of 93%.

---

[1]http://citeseerx.ist.psu.edu/viewdoc/download?doi=10.1.1.51.6252&rep=rep1&type=pdf

[2]http://ww.web.stanford.edu/~hastie/Papers/SII-2-3-A8-Zhu.pdf

[3]https://www.stat.berkeley.edu/users/breiman/adaptbag99.pdf

---

Code 17.3.2 — **Boosting in R.** Package fastAdaboost

```
library(fastAdaboost)
set.seed(1234)
fadab <- adaboost(Result~., train, 10)
summary(fadab)

pred <- predict(fadab, newdata=test, type="response")

# pred$class holds the classification
acc_fadab <- mean(pred$class==test$Result)
mcc_fadab <- mcc(pred$class, test$Result)
print(paste("accuracy=", acc_fadab))
print(paste("mcc=", mcc_fadab))
```

17.4 XGBoost

In the Decision Trees chapter, advanced tree methods of Random Forest and Boosting were described. These advanced trees work by building hundreds of trees which are then aggregated. A more robust algorithm, XGBoost, is described in this section.

The XGBoost (Extreme Gradient Boosting) algorithm was developed by Tianqi Chen and presented in the 2016 KDD Conference. The chief improvements in the algorithm over earlier tree boosting methods result in extreme scalability, running up to 10 times faster than earlier algorithms. The R implementation of the XGBoost algorithm (xgboost) won the 2016 John M. Chambers Statistical Software Award. The award is well-deserved since this package runs faster than Python sklearn's version and another R version, gbm. The computational part of the package is written in C++ and can take advantage of multithreading on a single machine.

Before running XGBoost, the training data needed to be convered into a numeric matrix, and the training labels converted from +1/-1 encoding to 0/1 integers. The same processing is done to the test data before predictions can be made. In the initial run, the nrounds=5 setting was used. This got slightly lower results that the other algorithms in the notebook. However when nrounds was bumped up to 100, it got the best performance and runs amazingly fast.

```
train_label <- ifelse(train$Result==1, 1, 0)
train_matrix <- data.matrix(train[, -31])

test_label <- ifelse(test$Result==1, 1, 0)
test_matrix <- data.matrix(test[, -31])
```

```
Code 17.4.1 — Boosting in R. Package fastAdaboost

library(xgboost)

model <- xgboost(data=train_matrix, label=train_label,
                 nrounds=100, objective='binary:logistic')

probs <- predict(model, test_matrix)
pred <- ifelse(probs>0.5, 1, 0)

acc_xg <- mean(pred==test_label)
mcc_xg <- mcc(pred, test_label)
print(paste("accuracy=", acc_xg))
print(paste("mcc=", mcc_xg))
```

Keep in mind that the train and test data has to be processed in just the right way before XGBoost will run. The accuracy was 96% and the mcc score was 93%. This example shows why XGBoost has become very popular. Next we explore this algorithm on a built-in data set and demonstrate the package vizualization features.

17.4.1 XGBoost and Visualization

The `xgboost1` notebook in the GitHub shows an example using the algorithm on a mushroom data set included in the xgboost package. The next code block shows how to train the algorithm. The first two arguments are the features and labels. The number of rounds of training is set to 2 in this example, and the objective function is binary. Read about other parameters by typing `?xgboost()` at the console.

```
Code 17.4.2 — XGBoost. Train the algorithm

model <- xgboost(data=train$data, label=train$label,
                 nrounds=2, objective='binary:logistic')
```

As shown in the online notebook, the predict() function can be used on the model just as for other algorithms. Also, the predictions can be transformed to binary 0/1 results in the same way as was done for logistic regression. The online notebook also shows how to perform cross validation. The following code chunk creates a plot of the model, shown in Figure 17.1.

```
Code 17.4.3 — XGBoost. Plot the results

xgb.plot.tree(feature_names = agaricus.train$data@Dimnames[[2]],
    model=model)
```

The plot above is difficult to read without zooming in. A simpler model could be created by modifying the max.depth parameter when the model was built. The model built and plotted above created only two trees due to the parameter nround=2. If more trees are built, the output

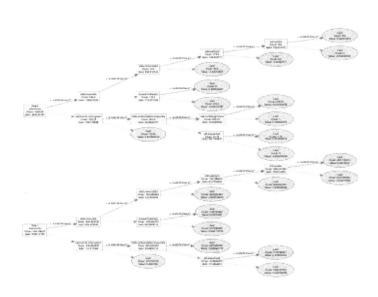

Figure 17.1: Plot the Model

will be even more difficult to interpret. The XGBoost package has a solution for that. The following code chunk shows how to ensemble 30 trees together into one plot.

Code 17.4.4 — **XGBoost.** Build 30 trees and combine the plot

```
bst <- xgboost(data = train$data, label = train$label,
               max.depth = 15, eta = 1, nthread = 2, nround = 30,
               objective = "binary:logistic",
               min_child_weight = 50)
xgb.plot.multi.trees(model = bst,
        feature_names = agaricus.train$data@Dimnames[[2]],
        features.keep = 3)
```

As with decision trees, an important consideration is depth. The XGBoost package contains a function to plot results based on varying depth in order to pick an optimal depth. Recall

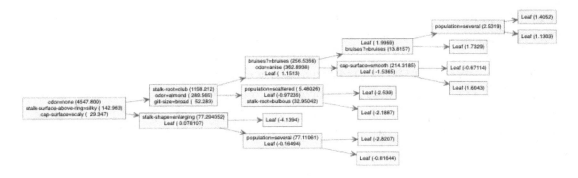

Figure 17.2: Ensemble Plot

from the decision tree chapter that deeper trees are likely to overfit. Additionally, feature importance can be plotted, as demonstrated in the online notebook.

17.4.2 The Algorithm

As discussed in other supervised learning algorithms, a loss function with regularization is needed for training. The training loss measures how well the model fits the training data. Regularization controls the complexity of the model. A given loss function with regularization could be expressed as follows:

$$\mathcal{L} = \frac{1}{N}\sum_{i=1}^{n}(\mathbf{y}_i - \mathbf{w}^T\mathbf{x}_i)^2 + \lambda\|\mathbf{w}\|^2 \tag{17.2}$$

There is a trade-off between these two components. Optimizing training loss is helpful for making models that predict well on future unseen data. Optimizing regularization is helpful for making simpler models, which are more stable and less likely to overfit.

Since the space of all possible trees is unlimited, decision tree algorithms are built around heuristics such as the following:

- Recursively split on the features with the highest information gain until some stopping threshold of leaf node similarity
- Prune the tree to avoid overfitting
- Set a maximum depth to constrain the function space and avoid overfitting
- Use smoothing for leaf weights

In contrast, the additive training (aka boosting) approach starts with a stump tree and repeatedly adds functions (trees).

$$\hat{y}_0 = 0 \tag{17.3}$$
$$\hat{y}_1 = f_1(x) = \hat{y}_0 + f_1(x) \tag{17.4}$$
$$... \tag{17.5}$$
$$\hat{y}_t = f_1(x) = \hat{y}_0 + f_1(x) + ... + f_t(x) \tag{17.6}$$

At each iteration, a new function is added. This new function can correct for errors of the previous functions in order to incrementally reduce error. Misclassified instances from previous iterations will receive higher weights to try to correct these misclassifications in the current iteration. For computational reason, a Taylor expansion is used for the loss function.

In the XGBoost algorithm, the definition of the tree is refined to be vectors of leaf scores, with a leaf index mapping function to map each instance to its leaf. Now the tree complexity can be defined as a combination of the number of leaf nodes and the L2 norm of the leaf scores.

17.5 XGBoost Parameters

The parameters for XGBoost fall into three categories: general model parameters, booster parameters, and learning parameters. Each will be discussed next. More details can be found in the documentation

17.5.1 General Parameters

Most of these parameters deal with run-time issues such as number of threads, how much output is desired during training (verbosity), and other features which are optimized internally and don't need to be set by the user. The most important general option is which booster to use. The default is gbtree, which can be used for classification or regression. Other options are gblinear or dart. The dart booster drops trees to mitigate overfitting. Regression can use any of the three options. Classification can use the default gbtree or dart.

Another general parameter is nrounds, which has a default of 100. This is the number of iterations of the algorithm. The larger the value, the longer training will take. To avoid overfitting, this parameter can be tuned with the cross validation function, as demonstrated in the online notebook.

17.5.2 Tree Booster Parameters

There are numerous parameters. The following is a short description of the most important parameters.

- eta - the learning rate; default=0.3, range[0,1]; the learning rate shrinks the feature weights to make the model more conservative
- gamma - minimum loss reduction for splitting; default=0, range[0, inf]; the larger the gamma value, the more conservative the algorithm will be
- max_depth - the maximum depth of a tree; default=6; deeper trees are more likely to overfit and require more memory for training
- min_child_weight - minimum sum of instance weight in child node; default=1; the larger this parameter is, the more conservative the algorithm will be, and the more instances will be in leaf nodes
- lambda - L2 regularization term on weights; default=1; making the lambda value larger will make the algorithm more conservative

17.5.3 Learning Parameters

The most important parameter in this category is the learning task and corresponding learning objective. The default is reg:squarederror, which is regression with squared loss error. Other options include:

- reg:squaredlogerror - regression with squared log loss
- reg:logistic - logistic regression
- reg:logisticraw - logistic regression for binary classification to output predictions rather than probabilities
- multi:softmax - for multiclass classification; requires num_class() to be set to the number of classes

The evaluation metric used during training will have different defaults based on the objective. The defaults can be over-ridden using rmse (root mean square error), rmsle (root mean square log error), mae (mean absolute error), and many more metrics described in the documentation.

17.5.4 XGBoost Summary

The XGBoost R implementation has many advantages:

- By default, the algorithm will run on all cores of your machine
- The package provides its own custom cross-validation function
- The package provides its own tree pruning function
- Several aspects of the model can be plotted with package functions
- Missing values are handled internally
- Can perform regression or classification
- The model can be saved to disk

17.6 Stacking

Stacking is a meta-algorithm. Step 1 trains multiple learners. Step 2 combines the output of the learners in a meta-classifier or meta-regressor. The R package SuperLearning uses this approach. A sample run in the online notebook did not give good results. To get best results from SuperLearner, hyperparameters need to be tuned with cross validation, this was not done in the online notebook.

17.7 Summary

This chapter compared several different ensemble methods. Ensemble methods often use high-variance learners such as decision trees as base learners. The ensemble techniques reduce the variance. Bagging is especially good at reducing variance, while boosting is better at decreasing bias. The stacking method is often used to improve predictions but requires a lot of fiddling that may not result in improvement over the ensemble methods covered here.

17.8 Exploring Further

Many resources for the algorithm are available online.

- Slides by Tianqi Chen, the creator of XGBoost are available here: `https://homes.cs.washington.edu/~tqchen/pdf/BoostedTree.pdf`
- A community documentation website is available: `https://xgboost.readthedocs.io/en/latest/index.html#`

18. The Craft 5: Learning Theory

Machine learning began at the intersection of mathematics and computing. From there, the computing side raced away from the mathematical foundations in its zeal to see what could be accomplished with these algorithms. Nevertheless, some computer science researchers continued to explore the theoretical foundations of machine learning. This chapter explores some of those ideas.

18.1 PAC learning

Probably Approximately Correct (PAC) learning provides a somewhat philosophical framework for reasoning about what we can theoretically learn from a machine learning algorithm on a given data set. The name "probably approximately correct" initially stuck me as hilarious, as if it is trying to formalize someone saying: *yeah, kinda, sorta*. What the name is trying to evoke is the idea that with a high probability, we can learn a good approximation of the data.

A machine learning algorithm is trying to learn a concept, C, and hopes to find a solution that closely models C. To make this more concrete, in a housing price prediction problem, C would be the market value of a home; in a credit review problem, C would be whether or not a person is a good credit risk. To keep things simple, our concept C will be restricted to binary classification problems. For a given problem, $C(x)$ is the ground truth of what we want to learn from the data. We will train a model or hypothesis, h, on training data with the hope that h will be able to generalize well to previously unseen testing data. In formal terms, we want $h(x)$ to be as close as possible to $C(x)$. The PAC model does not attempt to quantify machine learning in a theorem, or put the genie in a bottle. Rather, it seeks to provide a framework for analysis so that insights into the process of machine learning can be gathered.

18.1.1 PAC definition

Let's say we run a binary classification algorithm on randomly drawn training data. The distribution of all the data is D, so our sample is just a subset of all possible training sets. The model that our learner L learns is a hypothesis, and this is but one hypothesis out of the set of all possible hypotheses H that could explain this data D. We will let n be the size of this hypothesis space $|H|$.

We would like the error to be small, and we would like some degree of certainty in the correctness of the hypothesis. We will quantify the error bounds using epsilon, and the certainty bounds by delta. The error should be less than $\frac{1}{2}$ for a binary classification problem; otherwise, your learner didn't learn anything and you might as well have tossed a coin. Likewise, the probability of failure to meet the accuracy threshold for a hypothesis should be less than 50% or we can't call it a *probably* correct hypothesis.

$$0 \leq \epsilon \leq \frac{1}{2} \tag{18.1}$$

$$0 \leq \delta \leq \frac{1}{2} \tag{18.2}$$

The 'probably' in PAC is quantified by the delta, and the 'approximately' is quantified by the epsilon.

With these definitions behind us, we can express the PAC idea as follows:

C is PAC-learnable by learner L in hypothesis space H, if and only if learner L will, with probability $1 - \delta$, find a hypothesis h in polynomial time, that has an error less than ϵ.

On its face, this definition can be seen as nothing more than a desiderata: a wish list for our classifier. The utility of PAC learning is in answering such questions as: (1) do I have enough data to learn? and (2) can the learner learn with the desired accuracy and confidence in polynomial time?

18.1.2 Number of training examples

One of the early uses of PAC theory was to estimate how many training examples, m, would be needed for a learner to learn a good hypothesis. This is frequently quantified as:

$$m \geq \frac{1}{\epsilon}\left(ln|H| + ln\frac{1}{\delta} \right) \tag{18.3}$$

Notice that as epsilon decreases, $\frac{1}{\epsilon}$ increases, which means that the number of training examples, m, will be higher. This makes sense, more training examples can give us a more accurate classifier. The number of training examples needed also rises with the probability of a good classifier, and the size of the hypothesis space.

18.1.3 PAC example

Let's say for a binary classification problem, we want 75% accuracy with 80% certainty. How many training examples do we need if there are 4 binary predictor variables?

In order to use Equation 18.3, we need to know the possible number of hypotheses. Each binary predictor has two possible states, plus one state of 'don't care' if the learner ignores that variable. This gives us 3 possible states for 4 variables. Consequently, there are 81 possible hypotheses because $|H| = 3^4 = 81$.

Now we have the data we need to plug into Equation 18.3. For 75% accuracy with 80% certainty, we need only 23 training examples.

$$m \geq \frac{1}{0.25}\left(ln81 + ln\frac{1}{0.2}\right) \approx 23 \tag{18.4}$$

If we increase our desired accuracy to 90% and confidence to 95%, we need about 74 training examples.

$$m \geq \frac{1}{0.1}\left(ln81 + ln\frac{1}{0.05}\right) \approx 74 \tag{18.5}$$

PAC learning theory is useful when initially exploring problems and algorithms to determine if your problem has a learnable solution. PAC is not always correct, in that sometimes the theory indicates that a problem is solvable but it turns out to be intractable in practice, and sometimes the theory indicates that a problem is not solvable but a solution is found anyway.

18.2 VC dimensionality

What if the learning space $|H|$ is not finite but infinite? In this case, we cannot use Equation 18.3. We need a different way to measure the complexity of H. A well-known approach is the Vapnik-Chervonenkis dimension (VC dimension).

VC dimensionality relies on the notion of shattering instances so that each fragment of the input space contains instances of the same class. Consider a binary classification problem with two binary predictors, x_1, x_2. What is the VC dimension of the hypothisis space, VC(H)? We can shatter the observations in this input space as follows:

```
observations where x1 == 0
observations where x2 == 0
```

Since can shatter into two spaces, VC(H) == 2. In fact for conjunctions of n Boolean variables, VC(H) = n.

What about real-valued variables? Consider the VC dimensions for a learning problem with two real-valued predictors x1 and x2, which we can visualize as shown in Figure 18.1.

We can shatter a space on 3 points as you can visualize on the left. You can imagine a linear classifier that excludes A, one that excludes B, and one that excludes C. Therefore

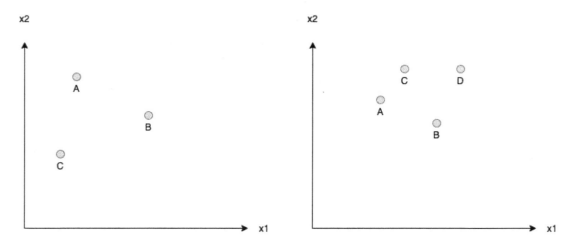

Figure 18.1: VC(H) = 3

VC(H) = 3. On the right, with 4 points, we cannot visualize a linear classifier that could exclude C but not D, for example. Therefore in this space, VC(H) = 3.

The definition of VC dimension says that if there is a set of n points that can be shattered by the classifier, and there is not a set of $n+1$ points that can be shattered, then the VC dimension is n.

An important caveat to this is that not all possible sets of n points have to be able to be shattered. Consider in Figure 18.1, that if we had 3 points on a line, these could not be shattered. This does not disprove that there exists *some* set of 3 points that can be shattered.

The reason that 4 points cannot be shattered in this example, is that in this space, at least two points will always be colinear so that they could not be shattered.

The number of training examples m that are needed in terms of VC dimensions is:

$$m \geq \frac{1}{\epsilon}\left(4log_2\frac{2}{\delta} + 8VC(H)log_2\frac{13}{\epsilon}\right)$$

(18.6)

Let's assume that we want 90% accuracy with 95% confidence for the problem in Figure 18.1.

$$m \geq \frac{1}{0.1}\left(4log_2\frac{2}{0.05} + 8*3*log_2\frac{13}{0.1}\right) \approx 1898$$

(18.7)

Plugging in 3 for VC(H) and the epsilon and delta values indicates that we need at least 1898 training examples. This is an upper bound, and does not imply that you can't create a good classifier with fewer than 1898 examples. A lower bound rule of thumb that is sometimes mentioned is ten times the VC dimension, which in this case would be 30.

18.3 **Going Further**

- Chapter 7 of Tom Mitchell's *Machine Learning* provides a thorough introduction to theoretical foundations of machine learning
- David Haussler provides a deep dive into PAC learning: `https://www.aaai.org/Papers/AAAI/1990/AAAI90-163.pdf`
- An annual conference on Learning Theory is sponsored by ACL: `https://www.learningtheory.org/`

VI Part Six: Python for Machine Learning

Preface to Part Six

Part Six introduces machine learning with Python. Python is a general-purpose language that can be used for general programming, machine learning, scientific computing, AI, web development, and any application you can think of.

R, in contrast, is designed for one thing: statistical work and visualization. Python has been edging out R in popularity measures in the past few decades, but the reality is that most organizations involved in machine learning and data science use both.

I'm writing this second edition during the Covid-19 epidemic. A surprising find on the TIOBE index and other metrics is that R has suddenly jumped in popularity. Speculation is that all the work on vaccines, therapeutics, and epidemiology have caused this surge since R is widely used in those fields.

19. Python Basics

This chapter covers enough Python to allow you to start coding projects. The first thing to do is install Python by going to https://www.python.org/downloads/. The code in this book is compatible with Python 3.8 or later. If you have Python 2.7 on your machine, you will want to upgrade to Python 3.

Once Python is installed, you should be able to open a Terminal command line on your system and type python. If your system has both Python 2 and Python 3 installed, type python3 at the console. This opens the Python interactive shell, outputs information about the version of Python installed, and provides the interactive prompt, >>>. Here is a simple interactive demo:

```
$ python3
Python 3.8.2 (v3.8.2:7b3ab5921f, Feb 24 2020, 17:52:18)
[Clang 6.0 (clang-600.0.57)] on darwin
Type "help", "copyright", "credits" or "license" for more information.

>>> name = "Karen"
>>> print("Hello", name)
Hello Karen
>>>
```

Python is an interpreted language and playing around at the console like this is a great way to learn. What did the code above do? The first line saved a string into variable name; the second line printed to the console. Python is designed to be clean, readable code, almost like reading pseudocode, so it is easy to figure out what the code does just by reading it.

Python is dynamically typed. Variable **name** was not declared, Python just figured out what type of variable it should be. Later in the code, variable **name** could change to some other type if a different type of data is assigned to it. Python will not complain. It is the programmer's responsibility to keep up with what types of data variables refer to.

There are several ways to write Python code:

- Type code in to the console; this is useful for testing out ideas and learning how Python works
- Type code into a simple text file, ending in .py; such Python scripts can then be run from the console
- Type code into an IDE; this approach is best for larger projects
- Type code into a Jupyter notebook; this approach is nice for sharing code with others

The short demo above showed how to run Python code at the terminal. To save code in a Python script, just use any simple text editor that saves plain text (ASCII) files, and make sure the file ends in **.py**. Then you can run the code from the console:

```
python myscript.py
```

or, if your system has both Python 2 and Python 3 installed:

```
python3 myscript.py
```

For larger projects, most people prefer to code in an IDE. There are many great (and free!) IDEs for Python, such as PyCharm.

19.1   JupyterLab

Somewhere between the interactive shell and the stand-alone program run in an IDE is a Jupyter notebook. Project Jupyter is an open-source project that supports interactive programming. This is a common platform for sharing code, commentary, and results for scientists, data scientists, and more. Jupyter notebooks are available on the github site for the book and you can read those online without having to install Jupyter.

JupyterLab is the latest advance in the Jupyter Notebook ecosystem. JupyterLab is backwardly compatible with Jupyter notebooks but provides much more functionality with features such as file explorers, output windows, and a console. JupyterLab brought an RStudio-type environment to Jupyter notebooks. Installing and using JupyterLab is not required to go through the material in this book. Coding in an IDE is fine. However, being able to share code in a notebook is a good skill to have. To install JupyterLab, go to `https://jupyterlab.readthedocs.io/` for installation instructions. Installation of jupyter can be completed with the usual pip install: `pip install jupyterlab`. Alternatively, you could install Anaconda which installs Python, Juypter and other packages. Be aware that Anaconda will take up a lot of space on your computer, so consider that before installing it. Throughout the book, please keep in mind that the "pip" command should be "pip3" if you have both Python 2 and 3 on your system.

Jupyter notebooks intersperse text cells and code cells very much like an RStudio notebook. Any output from code cells displays immediately below the cell. Text cells are for commentary; they can be plain text and can use Markdown for formatting. There is built-in help for Markdown in Jupyterlab.

For the remainder of the chapter we will use code that can be found in the github in a series of Jupyter notebooks. You can follow along in your own notebook, or open up a Python interactive terminal at your computer and type along.

19.2 Getting Started with Python 3

The goal of this chapter is to learn enough Python to complete projects. There are links at the end of the chapter for more in-depth Python resources. Here are a few things to keep in mind about Python:

- Python is an interpreted language
- source code is compiled into bytecode to be executed by the operating system
- there are no type declarations as in other languages, like : int i;
- types are checked dynamically as the program runs
- Python uses indents to signify code blocks, not { }
- the end of a line is the end of a statement, no need for ;
- Python is case sensitive
- comments start with #

This book focuses on Python 3. There were some significant changes between Python 2 and Python 3 that break backward compatability. The main thing you will notice when looking at code is that with Python 3, parenthesis are required around the print statement:

```
print "hello"    # Python 2
print ("hello") # Python 3
```

Another thing to keep in mind when looking around at Python code in the wild are two flame wars: spaces v. tabs, and camelCase v. underscores. Underscores are generally preferred, but the main thing is to be consistent within your own code and follow conventions of your peers when writing code with others. Regarding tabs versus spaces, PyCharm converts tabs to spaces automatically, but when writing code at the console, spaces need to be used. The authority on Python style is the PEP8 style guide: `https://www.python.org/dev/peps/pep-0008/`.

The next few sections teach the basics of Python programming:

- Python native data types and how to use them
- Python control structures to create loops, functions, if statements
- Python built-in data structures: lists, dictionaries, and more

19.3 Variables and Data Types

The native data types in Python include:

- int - non-limited length
- float - same as C double
- complex
- boolean
- string - 'single' or "double" quotes

Python also has some useful built-in constants: `True`, `False`, and `None`.

Python variables are essentially pointers to memory locations. The type of a variable is determined by its contents. Type along at the console:

```
>>> v = 5
>>> type(v)
<class 'int'>
>>> v = 'a'
>>> type(v)
<class 'str'>
>>>
```

In the code above, when 5 is assigned to v, the type of v is int. Later when 'a' is assigned to v, the type of the variable changes to string. What happened under the hood is that after the first assignment, v pointed to the integer 5, and after the second assignment, v was modified to point to the string 'a'.

Operators can have different meanings in different contexts, as shown below. The shortcut operator += means addition with integers but concatenation with strings. By the way, Python does not have the ++ or −− shortcut operators as many other languages do. The last line below will cause an error. Don't be afraid of experimenting with code and causing errors. Getting to know Python's error messages is an important part of learning the language.

```
v = 5
v += 1
print(v)    # v is now 6
v = 'a'
v += 'b'
print(v)    # v is now 'ab'
v += 1    # '++' or '--' will cause an error
```

The print() function is used to output to the console, and the input() function is used to get input from the user. Here is an example of console input and output:

```
name = input("What's your name? ")
print('Hello ', name, '!')  # notice that ',' adds spaces
print('Hello '+ name + '!') # '+' (concatenate) does not add spaces
```

The input() function reads whatever the user types as a string. To get numeric data from a user, the string input can be converted to numbers with the built-in int() and float() functions:

```
radius = input("Enter radius: ")
radius = float(radius)
area = radius * radius * 3.14
print("area = ", area)
```

19.4 Python Scripts

A Python script is just a plain text file of Python code that ends in .py. If there are no functions in the file, all the code should start at the leftmost column. Remember that indents have meaning in Python! Each line of code will be executed sequentially. The following code example shows a commonly used outline for Python scripts with a main function, and shows how to process system arguments.

Code 19.4.1 — **A Python Script.** Example with Arguments

```
import sys

def main():
    print("Hello " + sys.argv[1] + "!")

if __name__ == '__main__':  # uses double underscores (dunders)
    main()
```

In the code above, any system libraries needed are imported first. The `sys` library is used to get command-line arguments. After the import, a `main` function is defined. The main function just prints Hello to the user. Python will import sys then read in the main function definition. If we want it to actually run main, it needs to be called. The last two lines call the main function. This is a typical way of starting a program. Later we will discuss what a single underscore or double underscore signify, for now just copy this code. You can run this script as follows, assuming it is saved it as hello.py:

```
$python hello.py Karen
$Hello Karen!
```

19.5 Control Structures

The following example shows the syntax for an if, an if-else, and an if-elif-else. Notice that code blocks are defined simply by indentation. This can be tricky at first. A common error is to place statements at the wrong indentation level. Notice also that you do not need parenthesis around the condition for the if statement, but you do need the colon ending the condition. The if-else needs a colon at the end of the condition and a colon at the end of the else. The if-elif-else shows show to have multiple conditions checked in one statement. There is no case or switch statement in Python, since the if-elif-else structure can be used to implement the logic.

Code 19.5.1 — **Python IF Statements.** Note the importance of the indents.

```python
grade = 66

# simple if
if grade >= 60:
    print("passed")

# if-else
if grade >= 60:
    print('passed')
else:
    print('failed')

# if-elif-else
if grade >= 90:
    print('excellent')
elif grade >= 60:
    print('passed')
else:
    print('failed')
```

Python has built in constants True and False. Logical False can also be 0, and empty object, or the built-in constant None. Everything else is True. Let's see how that works:

```python
flag = True
if flag:
    print('flag is true')

string1 = 'abc'
if string1:
    print(string1)

string1 = ''
if not string1:
    print('Empty string)
```

The first print statment checks the value of variable flag, which is True, and prints the statement. It is not considered Pythonic to do this: `if flag == True`, because it is unnecessarily complex. Notice the second if statement above also results in True because the variable string1 is not null. The third example above prints if the string is empty.

Code 19.5.2 — **Python while Statement.** Condition must change in the loop

```
i = 3
while i > 0:
    print(i)
    i -= 1

3
2
1
```

Again, the while condition does not need parentheses around it but does need the colon at the end. The body of the while loop in indented. Here is the same logic using a for loop:

```
for i in range(3, 0, -1):
  print(i)
```

The for loop above uses the built-in range(start, stop, step) function that creates a sequence of values to iterate over. This is one way to use a traditional for loop. Typically we use the for loop to iterate over a sequential object:

Code 19.5.3 — **Python for loop.** Iterating over a list.

```
for item in ['a', 2.3, 'hello']:
    print(item)

a
2.3
hello
```

The code ['a', 2.3, 'hello'] creates a sequential structure that the for loop iterates over. This structure is a list, which is discussed later. With each iteration, the next element of the list is copied to item, and then printed.

The code example above iterated over each element in the list, but what if you also want to know their position in the list? The built-in function enumerate does that.

Code 19.5.4 — **For Loop.** Using the enumerate() construct.

```
mylist = ['apple', 'banana', 'orange']
for i, item in enumerate(mylist):
    print(i, item)

0 apple
1 banana
2 orange
```

The enumerate() function returns two things, the index and the element. In the for loop above, the variable i will contain the index, starting at 0, and the variable item will contain the element. Python functions, either built-in or user-defined, can return more than one object.

The code example below shows how to define and call a function. A function is defined with reserved word def. A function definition needs a name and optionally, arguments in parenthesis, followed by the colon. Statements within the function are indented. All the statements in the function body, including the return, are at the same level of indentation, except when you need further indentations as in the for and if statements.

Code 19.5.5 — **Functions.** Function definition and sample call.

```
def find_first(names):
    first = names[0]
    for name in names[1:]:
        if name < first:
            first = name
    return first
names = ['Jane', 'Zelda', 'Bud']
print('The first name alphabetically is ', find_first(names))

The first name alphabetically is Bud
```

The function above iterates through a list of names to find the one that is first alphabetically. There are several things that should concern you about the code: (1) the function expects variable names to be a list but the type was not checked, (2) the code assumes that names has at least one element, and (3) the function was not documented. Here is how you could rewrite the code to check variable names, and provide some documentation.

```
def find_first(names):
    """

    Finds the first item alphabetically in a list.
    Args:
        names:  a list of items to be compared
    Returns: string
        the first item, alphabetically
    Example:
        >>>find_first(['george','anne'])
        >>>'anne'
    """

    if not type(names) == list:
        return 'Error: "names" is not a list'
    if not names:
        return 'Error: "names" is an empty list'
    first = names[0]
```

```
for name in names[1:]:
    if name < first:
        first = name
return first
```

The documentation in the function above with the triple quotes is called a *docstring*. A docstring can be used for a string literal that spans multiple lines, but it is primarily used for function documentation. The docstring above might be overkill for such a simple function but it demonstrates good practices. The first line of the docstring should be a simple description of what the function does, starting with a verb. Function documentation should explain the input arguments as well as what the function returns, and finally give a sample function call.

Most of the coding examples in the book and online in the github will not demonstrate either the type checking that is essential for reliable code, or this full documentation style for functions. This is done intentially for the reader, to condense the number of lines to read. However, in actual projects, this kind of documentation is standard.

> **Exercise 19.1** Practice writing functions and calling them:
> 1. Write a function to return the average of a list of numbers. Test your function.
> 2. Write a function to check if number k evenly divides n. Return a boolean value. Print a message in the calling code. By the way, the operator % is modulus and works as in other programming languages.

19.6 Strings

Python has a built-in `str` class with many built-in functions for text processing. Strings can be enclosed in single or double quotes, as well as triple quotes for multiple lines. Python doesn't have a char type, a character is just a string of length 1. You can access the individual characters in a string with [n], where n ranges from 0 to the length of the string minus 1. The code below iterates over a string one character at a time, using i to index into the string. The output is shown below the code.

```
string1 = 'hello'
for i in range(len(string1)):
    print(i, string1[i])
```

```
0 h
1 e
2 l
3 l
4 o
```

Python also supports negative indices. That is, [-1] is the last element, [-2] is the next to last, and so on.

```
print(string1[-1])
o
print(string1[-2])
l
```

19.6.1 Slicing and Operators

Substrings can be extracted from strings in various ways with slicing:
- s[i:j] extracts from s[i] to s[j-1]
- s[i:] extracts from s[i] to the end of the string
- s[:j] extracts from the beginning to s[j-1]
- s[:] makes a copy of the entire string

Try the following at the console:

```
string_utd = 'The University of Texas at Dallas'
string_utd[18:23]
string_utd[4:]
string_utd[9:] + ", " + string[18:23]
```

There are special operators for strings:
- + for concatenation
- * for repetition
- *in* for iteration or conditional
- % for formatting

Try the following at the console:

```
print('a' + 'b')
print('a' * 3)
print('a' in string_utd)
# older form of formatting
print("Format an int: %d, a float: %2.2f, a string: %s" % (5, 5.6, 'hi'))
# newer formatting style
print("Format an int: {}, a float: {:2.2f}, a string: {}".format(5, 5.6, 'hi'))
# f-string (newest) formatting style
print(f"Format an int: {5}, a float: {5.6:2.2f}, a string: {'hi'}")
```

19.6.2 String Methods

There are dozens of built-in string methods. You can find a comprehensive list in the Python documentation. Here are some that are commonly used:
- upper() and lower() to change case
- isalpha(), isdigit(), isspace()
- startswith() and endswith()
- strip() to remove whitespace from start and end
- split() to split a string into a list of substrings

- join() to join a list of strings into one string
- find() - return index or -1
- count() - count unique occurrences
- len() - return length of string

Some of these methods return strings, some return boolean values and some return integer indices. The return type makes sense when you practice using the functions. Because they are methods they can be applied to strings as in `mystring.method()`. The first few code samples show methods that take an input string.

String methods that return a string

The methods in the following code sample, lower(), upper(), and strip(), apply to a string, and returns a modified string.

Code 19.6.1 — **Selected String Methods.** These methods return strings.

```
# upper() and lower()
string_pp = 'Pied Piper'
print(string_pp.lower(), string_pp.upper())
pied piper PIED PIPER


# strip whitespace from both ends
spacey = " hello "
not_spacey = spacey.strip()
len(not_spacey)
5
```

String methods that return a Boolean

The methods in the following code sample apply to a string and return boolean values True or False.

Code 19.6.2 — **Selected String Methods.** These methods check string content and return Boolean values.

```
# check characters
string4 = 'number = 3'
print(string4[0].isalpha())   # True
print(string4[-1].isdigit())   # True
print(string4[6].isspace()) # True


# check start and end of string
string_hello = 'hello world'
print(string_hello.startswith('hello'))   # True
print(string_hello.endswith('world'))   # True
```

String methods that return an integer

The following methods operate on a string and return integers. The find(text) function returns the index where "text" starts in the string. The count(text) function returns the number of times that "text" appears in the string. There is an index() function that works like find() but raises an exception if the text is not found in the string; the find() function will return -1.

Code 19.6.3 — **Selected String Methods.** These methods return integers.

```
string_utd = 'The University of Texas at Dallas'
i = string_utd.find('Dallas')
string_utd[i:]  # Dallas

count_a = string_utd.count('a')
print(count_a)  # 4
```

String and list methods

The next two methods convert from a string to a list or vice versa. The split() function will split a string into a list based on white space by default. The join() function take a list and joins the elements into a string with the join character (or none) specified.

Code 19.6.4 — **Selected String Methods.** Methods that work on lists and strings.

```
long_string = 'this is a lot of text in a string'
tokens = long_string.split()  # split a string into words

print(' '.join(tokens)) # separates words with a space # list to string
```

Exercise 19.2 Write the following string manipulation functions and test them on various input strings:
1. Given a string, return the first and last characters joined into a new string; if the string is less than 2 characters, return the string
2. Given a string, return the number of vowels
3. Given a string, return a string containing all found vowels, ex: 'ieaieuai....' for this sentence.
4. Given a string, return a string containing 'aeiou' if all vowels found, 'ai' if only vowels a and i were found, etc. The returned string of vowes should be in alphabetical order.
5. Given a string of phone numbers in form (555) 555-1212, return just the numbers.

19.7 **Lists, Tuples, Dicts, and Sets**

Python has several built-in data structures that organize data. These structures are called **containers** and have a fairly uniform set of methods for operating on them. We explore the most important types of Python containers in this section: lists, tuples, dicts, and sets.

19.7.1 **Lists**

A Python list is an ordered sequence of objects. These objects can be of any type, and can be other lists. Lists are mutable, meaning that we can change them in place. This is in contrast to strings. When we change a string in place, Python actually creates a new string. Follow along at the console as we show several ways to create lists from data and/or other lists. Echo each list back to the console as you go so that you understand the syntax.

Code 19.7.1 — **Lists.** Ways to create and combine lists.

```
lista = [1, 2, 3] # create a list using [ ]
listb = list(range(4, 7)) # create a list using list()
listab = lista + listb # "+" means concatenate for lists
listab += [8, 9] # "+=" is the concat shortcut
listab += [7] # we need [ ] around the 7
print('length = ', len(listab))
```

We can modify lists by adding items as shown in the next code example. Again, follow along at the console and echo back "fruits" after each command.

Code 19.7.2 — **Lists.** Ways to add list items.

```
fruits = ['apple', 'banana', 'orange']
fruits.insert(0, 'peach') # insert at the start of the list
fruits.append('pear') # insert at the end of the list
print(' '.join(fruits))
```

Items can be removed from a list with pop() and del. Removing items from the front of a Python list is slow for large lists. Sometimes it might be more efficient to sort the list first, then remove the last element.

Code 19.7.3 — **Lists.** Ways to remove list items.

```
if 'apple' in fruits:
    fruits.remove('apple')
fr = fruits.pop()   # pops last item
fr = fruits.pop(0)  # pops first item
i = fruits.index('banana')  # throws Value Error if not in list
del fruits[i] # throws Index Error if out of range
del fruits[:] # clears out a list
```

By the way, Python will let you overwrite functions. Look at the following code sequence (but don't do this!). Once the code overwrote 'list', the original function list() could not be called. If you accidentally do something like this at the console, just get out of the console and go back in to reset everything to the original state.

```
list = [1, 2, 3] # don't do this!
new_list = list(1, 2, 3)
Traceback (most recent call last):
  File "<stdin>", line 1, in <module>
TypeError: 'list' object is not callable
```

Copying a list is straightforward: list2 = list1. However, you may observe some strange behavior when you copy a list if that list contains lists. Try the following at the console:

```
# copy example 1
list1 = [1, 2, [3, 4], 5]
list2 = list1
list2[2][0] = 9
list1  # the sublist in list 1 was changed when list 2 was changed
```

In the example above we performed a shallow copy. Python copied each element and a pointer to the list within the list. The way around this is to do a deep copy:

```
from copy import deepcopy
list1 = [1, 2, [3, 4], 5]
list2 = deepcopy(list1)
list2[2][0] = 9
list1 # list1 remains unchanged
```

In Python try to avoid for loops because they are slow. Instead of looping over elements in a for loop, try to use a *list comprehension*. A list comprehension iterates over elements in an object, and creates a list of these objects. The basic syntax below just iterates over each element in the old list and makes a new list:

```
list_new = [x for x in list_old]  # don't copy a list this way
```

The real power of list comprehensions comes in adding conditions:

Code 19.7.4 — List Comprehensions.. Use list comprehensions instead of for loops.

```
friends = ['Jim', 'Hamed', 'Charlotte']
friends2 = [f.lower() for f in friends]
#friends2 = ['jim', 'hamed', 'charlotte']
friends3 = [f for f in friends if not f.startswith('C')]
# friends3 = ['Jim', 'Hamed']
```

Exercise 19.3 Practice with lists:
1. Make a list from the individual words in a sentence.
2. Print only tokens that start with a given letter or group of letters.
3. Print only tokens that end with a given letter or group of letters.
4. Use a list comprehension to create a list of only words greater than 2 characters long.

19.7.2 Tuples

A tuple is a sequence of objects, just like a list. The difference is that tuples are immutable and use parenthesis instead of square brackets to easily distinguish them. Why do we need tuples? There are situations that arise where you want something like a list but immutable. For example, a key for a dictionary can be a tuple, but not a list, because the tuple is immutable. You can convert between tuples and lists with the list() and tuple() functions. The first line of code below created tuple t1 by specifying a comma separated list on the right side of the assignment operator. The second line of code created a tuple with the tuple() function. Unpacking a tuple involves copying each element to a variable. This can be a useful way to return multiple values from a function.

Code 19.7.5 — **Tuples.** Create and Unpack Tuples.

```
# create a tuple in 2 different ways
t1 = 'a', 3, 5.6 # create a tuple
t2 = tuple(range(1:4))

# tuple unpacking
astring, adigit, afloat = t
print("%d %s %f" % (adigit, astring, afloat))
```

19.7.3 Sets

A set is an unordered container object that does not allow duplicates. Sets are immutable in that you cannot change a set element in place but sets have other methods such as union(), intersection(), and difference().

Code 19.7.6 — **Sets.** Set Creation.

```
# create a set
set1 = {'apple', 'banana', 'orange'}
# create a set from a list
list1 = [1, 2, 3, 4, 3, 2, 1]
set1 = set(list1)
print(set1)
{1, 2, 3, 4}
```

Exercise 19.4 Practice with Tuples and Sets:
1. Create a tuple from the letters of a word using the split() function. Print the tuple in a loop.
2. Create a set from the tuple. Print the set.

19.7.4 Dicts

Python dictionaries contain unordered key:value pairs. Order is not maintained in dicts so if you want them in a particular order for processing, you must sort them as shown in the following code example. The sorted() function will return a sorted list of key:value pairs. Key types can be anything that is immutable, like strings or tuples. Dictionary values can be any Python type.

```
Code 19.7.7 — Dictionaries. Creating and Using Dicts.

# create dict in two ways
fruits = {'a':'apple', 'b':'banana', 'p':'pear'}   # one way
# another way:
fruits = {}   # create an empty dict
fruits['a'] = 'apple'
fruits['b'] = 'banana'
fruits['p'] = 'pear'

print(fruits['p'])
fruits['p'] = 'peach'  # change 'p' value
print(fruits['p'])

if 'c' in fruits:       # check for 'c' to avoid key error
    print(fruits['c'])
else:
    print("There is no fruit c")

# iterate over dict
for k, v in sorted(fruit.items()):
    print(k, v)
```

In the code above we used 'in' to check if an item was in the dictionary in order to avoid key errors. Another way is to use get() as shown below:

```
# use .get() to avoid key error
print("fruit c = ", fruits.get('c'))
```

We can delete dict items using their key values as in del fruits['p'].

19.7.5   Operations on Container Objects

We can iterate over container objects (and strings) with the for-in loop and test for membership with in as well. We demonstrate these methods with a tuple below, but they work on other containers as well.

Code 19.7.8 — Container Methods. Loops and Membership Check

```
friends = ('Jim', 'Hamed', 'Charlotte')

for friend in friends:
    print('Hello', friend)

if 'Charlotte' in friends:
    print('Hello Charlotte')
```

There are functions for sorting containers as well. Use sorted() when you want a new list returned and sort() or reverse() to modify the list in place. The slicing techniques we discussed in strings above work the same on lists. Keep in mind that if a container is unordered, like sets and dicts, what sorted() returns is a sorted list.

Code 19.7.9 — Container Methods. Sorting.

```
friends = ['Jim', 'Hamed', 'Charlotte']
for friend in sorted(friends):
    print(friend)

print('after sorted():',' '.join(friends))
friends.sort()
print('after sort():', ' '.join(friends))
friends.reverse()
print('after reverse():', ' '.join(friends))
# slicing
print('after reverse():', ' '.join(friends[1:]))
```

Exercise 19.5 Try the following:
1. Create a long text string.
2. Create a set of unique tokens in the string.
3. Create a dictionary of vocabulary counts by iterating over the set of words.
4. Print the dictionary counts in alphabetical order.

280 of 392 Chapter 19. Python Basics

19.8   More Python

There is much more to Python than has been covered so far. The best way to learn more is to start coding. Python is a versatile language that you can use for either traditional, object-oriented, or functional programming. You can refer to the Python notebooks on the github for how to create and use classes, read from and wrie to files, handle exceptions, and use regular expressions. For now, we have covered enough to get started with the rest of the material.

19.9   Summary

This has been a whirlwind tour of Python. As you develop your Python skills you will need more detailed resources. Here are a few recommended resources:

- Dive into Python `http://www.diveintopython.net/index.html`
- The Hitchhiker's Guide to Python `https://docs.python-guide.org/`
- The Python Documentation `https://docs.python.org/3/index.html`
- PEP 8 Style Guide `https://www.python.org/dev/peps/pep-0008/`

20. Python ML Libraries

This chapter is an introduction to the major packages used for machine learning in Python. Here are some of the most commonly used libraries in Python machine learning:

- NumPy - numerical array processing
- pandas - data manipulation
- Scikit-Learn - machine learning algorithms
- Seaborn - plotting

The SciKit-learn library is updated every 3 months and so your code can quickly become out of date. NumPy and pandas are part of the SciPy ecosystem. SciPy is also frequently updated but not as often as SciKit-learn. A later chapter will look at machine learning algorithms in the Keras package.

The package manager `pip` is installed with python. After installation, pip is used to install or upgrade packages. As of this writing, the latest version of pip is 20. See `pip.pypa.io` for more information.

If you have a Mac or other computer with Python 2 installed, your pip for Python 3 will be pip3 instead of just pip. If you want to upgrade your pip, type the following at the command line:

```
python -m pip install --upgrade pip
python3 -m pip install --upgrade pip   # Python 3
```

The examples below show different uses of pip/pip3. All of the following commands are run from the command line, not from within Python.

Code 20.0.1 — **pip.** Using pip/pip3 package manager.

```
pip install x            # install package x
pip install x==2.01      # install x version 2.01
pip install x>=2.01      # install at least x version 2.01
pip install --upgrade x  # update package x
pip uninstall x           # uninstall package x
pip --version            # find your version
```

20.1   NumPy

NumPy is a library for scientific computing. NumPy is designed to work efficiently with multidimensional arrays. The key data structure in NumPy is the array, which is a multi-dimensional object where elements must be of the same type. NumPy arrays are more efficient in terms of storage and computation than native Python lists. The *rank* of the array is the number of dimensions (called *axes*) and the *shape* is specified by a tuple of integers of the length of each dimension. Let's see how to create a numpy array from a Python list.

Code 20.1.1 — **numpy.** Create a 1d numpy array.

```
import numpy as np
a = np.array([1,2,3,4,5], float)
print(a[2])
3.0
```

In the code above, we first imported NumPy and associated it with the identifier 'np'. Then we used the `np.array()` function to create a numpy array from a Python list, making each element of type float. Notice that we index a NumPy array the same as a list. The array that was created is one-dimensional. Let's look at a two-dimensional array. It will create two rows, each a 3-column list.

Code 20.1.2 — **NumPy.** Create a 2d numpy array.

```
b = np.array([[1,2,3], [4,5,6]], int)
b[1,1]
5
```

NumPy arrays can be reshaped, and there are built-in functions to retrieve information about the array. The output of this code block is shown immediately below the code. The code first fills a 1d array with 0-9. Then these 10 elements are reshaped to be a 5x2 array. Notice that len() returns the length of the first axis.

Code 20.1.3 — NumPy. Shape and rank.

```
c = np.array(range(10), float)
print("c originally: ", c)
c = c.reshape(5, 2)
print("c with the new shape: \n", c)
print("The new shape is: ", c.shape)
print("Length = ", len(c))
```

```
c originally:  [ 0.  1.  2.  3.  4.  5.  6.  7.  8.  9.]
c with the new shape:
 [[ 0.  1.]
 [ 2.  3.]
 [ 4.  5.]
 [ 6.  7.]
 [ 8.  9.]]
The new shape is:  (5, 2)
Length =  5
```

Code 20.1.4 — NumPy. Create and initialize arrays.

```
c.fill(0) # c is overwritten with zeros
d = np.zeros((2,3)) # d is a 2x3 array of zeros
```

You can use Python mathematical operators like + and - on NumPy arrays, and they will work on an element-by-element basis. Some NumPy functions are applied to the entire array. In the code below we see examples of sum(), mean(), min() and max(). Notice in the last example that we can apply these functions to only one axis, or to the entire array.

Code 20.1.5 — NumPy. Operations on arrays.

```
np.sum(array1)  # sum all elements
np.mean(array1) # find the average of all elements
range = np.max(array1) - np.min(array1) # find the range
f = np.array(range(10), float).reshape(5,2)
print(f)
[[ 0.  1.]
 [ 2.  3.]
 [ 4.  5.]
 [ 6.  7.]
 [ 8.  9.]]
print(f.mean(axis=0)) # find mean of columns
 [ 4.,  5.]
```

NumPy can generate random numbers, as shown below. Set a seed to get reproducible results. Notice that the next-to-last line of code below used a boolean selection criterion for indexing of the array. In the last line of code the array is sorted. The sort was performed on rows by default.

```
np.random.seed(17)
rand_array = np.random.rand(2,3)
print(rand_array)
[[ 0.6375209   0.57560289  0.03906292]
 [ 0.3578136   0.94568319  0.06004468]]

# boolean indexing
print(rand_array[rand_array>.2])
[ 0.6375209   0.57560289  0.3578136   0.94568319]

# sort
print(np.sort(rand_array))
[[ 0.03906292  0.57560289  0.6375209 ]
 [ 0.06004468  0.3578136   0.94568319]]
```

There is much more to NumPy, including dot products and matrix operations. There are several NumPy cheat sheets available on the web.

20.2 Pandas

The pandas library is a powerful data analysis toolkit for structured data. A pandas **series** handles one-dimensional data while a pandas **data frame** handles two-dimensional data. Pandas is often used for reading in data frames such as csv files, as shown below. To follow along, download Heart.csv from the github. Notice that we specify which column serves as the row identifier. The head() function displays the first 5 rows by default.

Code 20.2.1 — **Pandas.** Read in Data.

```
import pandas as pd
df = pd.read_csv('Heart.csv', index_col='ID')
print(df.head())
```

There are many ways to access elements, as shown next. We see two ways to access the first row of the Age column.

Code 20.2.2 — **Pandas.** Access data elements.

```
print(df['Age'][1])  # bracket notation
print(df.Age[1])     # dot notation
```

Pandas has a couple of accessors, `loc` which uses labels, and `iloc` which uses index positions. Both specify the indices in row, col order. Both of the following retrieve the same element.

Code 20.2.3 — **Pandas.** Accessors loc and iloc.

```
print(df.loc[1, 'Age']) # '1' because using row ID
print(df.iloc[0, 0])
```

The following examples demonstrate subsetting and slicing data frames. Slicing works the same as for Python lists.

Code 20.2.4 — **Pandas.** Subsetting and Slicing.

```
df_new = df[['Sex', 'Age']]
print(df_new.head())
print(df['Age'][:5])
```

When a single column of a pandas data frame is selected, it will be a series by default. To force it to be a data frame, surround the selection with double brackets. This is important to keep in mind because many algorithms accept only a data frame as input, not a series.

Code 20.2.5 — **Pandas.** Subsetting and Slicing.

```
df_not = df['Sex']     # not a data frame
df_new = df[['Sex']] # is a data frame
```

Additional examples can be found in the GitHub notebooks.

20.3   Scikit-Learn

The Scikit-Learn project began in 2007 and made its first public release in 2010. Scikit-Learn is an open-source project, supported by an international team of developers, releasing new versions about every 3 months. The community also has some great tutorials.

This section presents a simple example to show basic sklearn usage. The example uses the built-in iris dataset. The built-in data sets are objects that have a `.data` member variable which holds the data array which is of size n_samples, n_features. If it is a supervised learning data set it will have response variables stored in the `.target` member. In sklearn, a bunch is like a dictionary with key-value pairs.

First we look at some data loading and exploration on the built-in iris data set. The output of each print statement is shown immediately below that statement.

Code 20.3.1 — **Scikit-Learn.** Data Exploration.

```
from sklearn import datasets

iris = datasets.load_iris()
print(iris.data[:5])  # first 5 rows of data
[[ 5.1  3.5  1.4  0.2]
 [ 4.9  3.   1.4  0.2]
 [ 4.7  3.2  1.3  0.2]
 [ 4.6  3.1  1.5  0.2]
 [ 5.   3.6  1.4  0.2]]

print(iris.target[:5]) # first 5 labels
[0 0 0 0 0]

print('iris shape is ', iris.data.shape)  # get the data's shape
iris shape is  (150, 4)

print(type(iris))
<class 'sklearn.utils.Bunch'>

print(type(iris.data))  # features and target are NumPy arrays
print(type(iris.target))

<class 'numpy.ndarray'>
<class 'numpy.ndarray'>
```

To get set up for supervised machine learning, variable **X** will represent a data frame of predictor variables, and **y** will represent the target variable. There is a nice synergy between Pandas and Scikit-Learn so that it is easy to convert data between the libraries as shown in below.

Code 20.3.2 — **Scikit-Learn.** Set Up Data.

```
X = iris.data
y = iris.target

import pandas as pd
df = pd.DataFrame(X, columns=iris.feature_names)
df.head()
```

The next code block demos the k-nearest neighbors algorithm in sklearn, here used to classify iris species. The data is divided into a train and test set using an sklearn function.

Code 20.3.3 — **Scikit-Learn.** kNN.

```
from sklearn.neighbors import KNeighborsClassifier
from sklearn.model_selection import train_test_split
X_train, X_test, y_train, y_test =
        train_test_split(X, y, test_size=0.3, random_state=21,
        stratify=y)
knn = KNeighborsClassifier(n_neighbors=7)
knn.fit(X_train, y_train)
y_pred = knn.predict(X_test)
knn.score(X_test, y_test)
0.9555555555555556
```

20.4 Seaborn

Many Python packages exist for plotting, but Seaborn is quite simple to use and so it is explored in this chapter. The online notebook gives a few examples of plotting on the iris data. The X data is converted to a data frame as shown in the last section. The plot code below assumes that the data is in data frames which will normally be the case. Converting the iris data to data frames is shown below.

```
# load iris
iris = datasets.load_iris()
X = iris.data
y = iris.target

# convert to data frames
df = pd.DataFrame(X, columns=iris.feature_names)
df_y = pd.DataFrame(y, columns=["species"])
```

20.4.1 Plotting a quantitative array

The code block below shows how to plot the distribution of a quantitative array. The parameter kde=True draws the curve and rug=True makes the tick marks across the bottom, indicating observations. The plot is shown in Figure 20.1.

Code 20.4.1 — **Seaborn.** Distribution Plot

```
sb.distplot(df["petal length (cm)"], kde=True, rug=True)
```

20.4.2 Plotting two quantitative arrays

The next code block shows how to create a relation plot for two quantitative variables. To add more information, the color and shape of the dots varies by class of the target variable y. The plot is shown in Figure 20.2.

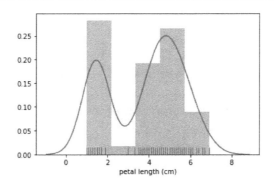

Figure 20.1: Distribution Plot

Code 20.4.2 — **Seaborn.** Relation Plot

```
sb.relplot(x="petal length (cm)", y="petal width (cm)",
        data=df, hue=df_y.species, style=df_y.species)
```

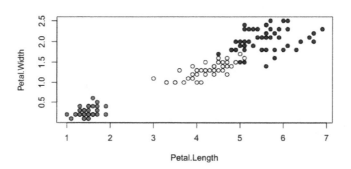

Figure 20.2: Relation Plot

20.4.3 Plotting a Categorical array

The following code block and plot show the distribution of the target, species. The distribution is even across the 3 classes.

Code 20.4.3 — **Seaborn.** Category Plot

```
sb.catplot(x="species", kind="count", data=df_y)
```

The following code block and figure plot a categorical value, species, on the x axis, and a quantitative array, petal length, on the y axis. The first line of code below is a big ugly and needs explanation. Normally, all of our data would be read in from a csv file into one data frame and we could easily create a plot like this with one line of code. However, we had the X

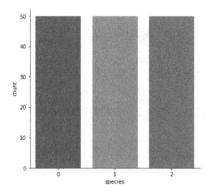

Figure 20.3: Category Plot

and y in different data frames and they needed to be combined with pandas concat() function. When this was done with this line of code the species column contained NaN. This was because the indexes were not aligned properly in the concat, and so with the added parameters, everything joined nicely.

```
df_temp = pd.concat([df, df_y])
```

```
Code 20.4.4 — Seaborn. df_temp = pd.concat([df.reset_index(drop=True),
        df_y.reset_index(drop=True)], axis=1)
sb.catplot(x="species", y="petal length (cm)", data=df_temp)
```

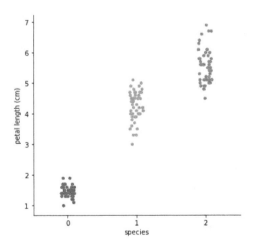

Figure 20.4: Category and Petal Length Plot

20.5 Data cleaning

The online notebook gives an example of reading in a diabetes data set and performing data cleaning operations. A few of those data cleaning operations are discussed next.

20.5.1   Remove Columns

If only a subset of columns is needed, these columns can be selected during the read:

```
df = pd.read_csv('diabetes.csv', usecols=['glucose', 'diabetes'])
```

The next code block assumes that all columns were read and two columns, row and pedigree, are to be removed.

Code 20.5.1 — Data Cleaning. Removing Columns

```
# remove "row" and "pedigree" columns

df = df.drop(columns=['row', 'pedigree'])
print(df.head())
```

	pregnant	glucose	pressure	triceps	insulin	mass	age	diabetes
0	6	148.0	72.0	35.0	NaN	33.6	50	pos
1	1	85.0	66.0	29.0	NaN	26.6	31	neg
2	8	183.0	64.0	NaN	NaN	23.3	32	pos
3	1	89.0	66.0	23.0	94.0	28.1	21	neg
4	0	137.0	40.0	35.0	168.0	43.1	33	pos

20.5.2   Dealing with NAs

The first step in dealing with missing values is to find out how many NAs are present.

Code 20.5.2 — Data Cleaning. Check for NAs

```
# check for NAs

df.isnull().sum()

pregnant     0
glucose      5
pressure     35
triceps      227
insulin      374
mass         11
age          0
diabetes     0
```

Since the triceps and insulin columns have many NAs, they will be filled with the averages for those columns. As discussed in a previous chapter, filling almost half of a column's values with a mean or median value will significantly dilute the column's predictive utility.

Code 20.5.3 — **Data Cleaning.** Replace NAs with mean()

```
# fill triceps and insulin with average
import numpy as np

tri_mean = np.mean(df.triceps)
df.triceps.fillna(tri_mean, inplace=True)

insulin_mean = np.mean(df.insulin)
df.insulin.fillna(insulin_mean, inplace=True)

df.isnull().sum()

pregnant     0
glucose      5
pressure    35
triceps      0
insulin      0
mass        11
age          0
diabetes     0
```

Since there are only a handful of remaining NAs, the next code block drops all rows that contain missing values.

Code 20.5.4 — **Data Cleaning.** Drop Rows with NAs

```
df = df.dropna()
print('\nDimensions of data frame:', df.shape)

Dimensions of data frame: (724, 8)
```

20.5.3 Converting categorical data

First, check the data types. All of the predictors in this data set are numeric, but the target column is categorical.

Code 20.5.5 — **Data Cleaning.** Check data types

```
df.dtypes
```

```
pregnant      int64
glucose     float64
pressure    float64
triceps     float64
insulin     float64
```

```
mass         float64
age            int64
diabetes      object
```

The diabetes column contains 'yes' or 'no' strings, which will be of type 'object'. These need to be converted to categorical data. The next two code blocks show two ways to convert data to a categorical (factor) column.

> Code 20.5.6 — **Data Cleaning.** Make Factor
>
> ```
> # convert diabetes to categorical data type
>
> df.diabetes = df.diabetes.astype('category')
> ```

As shown in the online notebook, the data type for diabetes is now 'category' instead of 'object' and will display as 'yes' or 'no'.

> Code 20.5.7 — **Data Cleaning.** Make Factor Codes
>
> ```
> # convert diabetes to numeric factor codes
>
> df.diabetes = df.diabetes.astype('category').cat.codes
> ```

As shown in the online notebook, the data type for diabetes is now 'int8' and displays as 1 or 0.

The online notebook gives an example of one-hot encoding, in which a single column with n category levels is converted into n columns in which each row has one "1" value and the rest are 0s.

20.6 Summary

This chapter demonstrated how to use NumPy, pandas, sklearn, and Seaborn in machine learning problems. Familiarity with these libraries will become second nature with experience.

21. Python ML Examples

This chapter will briefly show Python examples of the supervised machine learning algorithms previously discussed in the R chapters. All of the examples are available as Jupyter notebooks in the GitHub. The examples use the Titanic and Boston housing data sets.

21.1 Linear Regression

The Boston data set is one of the data sets provided in sklearn. However, to show how to import a csv file, this first example uses the Boston data downloaded from a site that provides all R data sets as csv files. The link to the site is in the online notebook.

21.1.1 Reading and examining data

The pandas library is the most popular Python library for data manipulation. The code section below shows how to read a csv file into a pandas data frame, print the first few rows, and get some general information about the data such as the dimensions. There is a `df.head()` command demonstrated in the online notebook but not here due to space limitations.

Code 21.1.1 — **Read a csv.** Initial data examination

```
import pandas as pd
df = pd.read_csv('data/Boston.csv')
print('\nDimensions of data frame:', df.shape)
print('\nDescribe rm and medv:\n',
        df.loc[:, ['rm', 'medv']].describe())
```

The describe() function works well with quantitative data, providing similar information as R's summary() function. The output is shown below:

```
Dimensions of data frame: (506, 15)

Describe rm and medv:
               rm          medv
count  506.000000  506.000000
mean     6.284634   22.532806
std      0.702617    9.197104
min      3.561000    5.000000
25%      5.885500   17.025000
50%      6.208500   21.200000
75%      6.623500   25.000000
max      8.780000   50.000000
```

The plot below shows the relationship between the number of rooms on the x axis and the median home value on the y axis. There does seem to be a linear trend: the more rooms a house has, the more expensive it is. However, a number of observations have 50 for the median home value, shown as a horizontal row of dots across the top of the graph. This data set used "50" to represent 50 and higher. These observations could be removed as outliers but they are left in for this example.

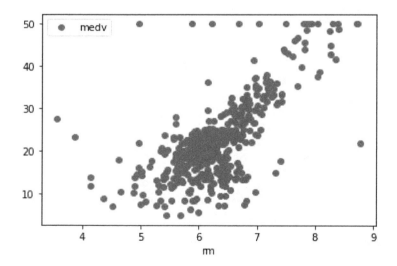

Figure 21.1: Boston housing data

21.1.2 Train test split

The next code block shows how to make a random train-test split in sklearn, using the built-in function. Before splitting, X is set up as the predictor data frame and y is a series of target values. The X predictors and y targets are the first two arguments to the train-test function. The next argument shown in the code below means that 20% of the data will be placed in test, with a random seed of 1234.

 This function returns a tuple of 4 items which will populate the variables X_train, X_test, y_train, and y_test. The code shows that the train data frame has 404 rows and test test data frame has 102 rows.

Code 21.1.2 — Linear Regression. Train-test split

```
# train test split
from sklearn.model_selection import train_test_split

X = df.iloc[:, 0:13]
y = df.iloc[:, 14]

X_train, X_test, y_train, y_test = train_test_split(X, y,
    test_size=0.2, random_state=1234)

print('train size:', X_train.shape)
print('test size:', X_test.shape)

train size: (404, 13)
test size: (102, 13)
```

21.1.3 Train the model

To train a model, the LinearRegression module needs to be imported first. Then an instance of the LinearRegression object is saved in variable `linreg`. The 'fit' method is applied for training, using the training predictors and target. The fit method echoes out the parameters it used in fitting the data. More information can be found about these parameters in the sklearn documentation.

Code 21.1.3 — Linear regression. Training

```
# train the algorithm
from sklearn.linear_model import LinearRegression

linreg = LinearRegression()
linreg.fit(X_train, y_train)

# output from fit method:
LinearRegression(copy_X=True, fit_intercept=True,
    n_jobs=None, normalize=False)
```

21.1.4   **Testing and evaluation**

The code blocks below shows how to test and evaluate.

Code 21.1.4 — **Linear regression.** Testing

```
# make predictions
y_pred = linreg.predict(X_test)
```

Code 21.1.5 — **Linear regression.** Evaluation

```
# calculate mse and r-squared
from sklearn.metrics import mean_squared_error, r2_score
print('mse=', metrics.mean_squared_error(y_test, y_pred))
print('correlation=', r2_score(y_test, y_pred))
```

The following code produces a correlation plot of the graph. There is a strong positive correlation between the predictions and test values, however most points are not that close to the line. The blue shaded regions shows that values in the middle range are closer to line than values at either end. At the far right, the values of "50" contributed to the higher residuals at that end.

Code 21.1.6 — **Linear regression.** Plot the test data

```
# plot correlation between test and predictions

sb.regplot(x=y_test, y=y_pred)
```

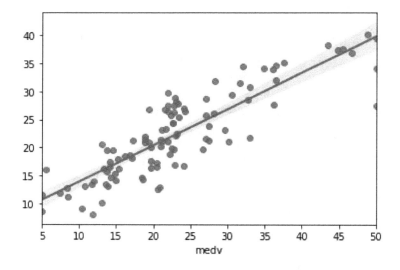

Figure 21.2: Fit to Test Data

21.1.5 Comparison with R Linear Regression

One of the benefits of R machine learning is that help is provided on any function within the RStudio environment. With sklearn, you have to find the right page in the documentation.

The summary() of the R linear regression model outputs coefficients and evaluation statistics, residual statistics, as well as statics about the model. The online notebook shows how to output the coefficients of the model in sklearn, but there is no comprehensive evaluation function comparable to R.

Further the four plots of the model that R can produce are much more informative than the regplot demonstrated here.

Overall, we conclude that the R environment for linear regression is more comprehensive than sklearn.

21.2 Logistic Regression

This section demonstrates logistic regression in Python on the Titanic data set. The full notebook is in the GitHub.

21.2.1 Read the data

The pandas library is used to read in the csv file. This example shows how to import only certain columns.

Code 21.2.1 — **Logistic regression.** Read csv

```
### load the data
import pandas as pd
df = pd.read_csv('data/titanic3.csv',
    usecols=['pclass', 'survived', 'sex', 'age'])
```

21.2.2 Data Cleaning

The first code block shows how to convert the survived, pclass, and sex columns to factors.

Code 21.2.2 — **Logistic regression.** Factors

```
# convert columns to factors
df.survived = df.survived.astype('category').cat.codes
df.pclass = df.pclass.astype('category').cat.codes
df.sex = df.sex.astype('category').cat.codes
```

The next code block shows how to replace NAs in the age column with the mean of the column.

Code 21.2.3 — **Logistic regression.** Dealing with NAs

```
# fill missing values
import numpy as np

age_mean = np.mean(df.age)
df.age.fillna(age_mean, inplace=True)
```

21.2.3 Train

After the 80/20 train/test split, the training data has 1047 examples and the test data has 262 examples, as shown in the online notebook. The code below fits a logistic regression model to the training data. The code also shows how to extract a score of the fit to the training data. The score is an accuracy metric.

The code used all the default settings for the many parameters that can be found in the online documentation (see: `https://scikit-learn.org/stable/modules/generated/sklearn.linear_model.LogisticRegression.html`). One of the more important options is to chooks the optimization algorithm, or 'solver'. The default is 'lbfgs' which is a limited-memory bfgs solver, where bfgs stand for the names of the algorithm developers. The sklearn documentation recommends some of the solvers for small versus large data sets, and others for multinomial problems.

Code 21.2.4 — **Logistic regression.** Train

```
from sklearn.linear_model import LogisticRegression

clf = LogisticRegression()
clf.fit(X_train, y_train)
clf.score(X_train, y_train)

# output
0.7831900668576887
```

21.2.4 Test and Evaluate

The code blocks below shows how to generate predictions and evaluate with accuracy, precision, recall, and f1, as well as how to generate a confusion matrix. The output of the test and evaluate code is as follows:

```
accuracy score:  0.7977099236641222
precision score:  0.7901234567901234
recall score:  0.64
f1 score:  0.7071823204419889
```

Code 21.2.5 — **Logistic regression.** Test and Evaluate

```
# make predictions
pred = clf.predict(X_test)

# evaluate
from sklearn.metrics import accuracy_score, precision_score,
      recall_score, f1_score

print('accuracy score: ', accuracy_score(y_test, pred))
print('precision score: ', precision_score(y_test, pred))
print('recall score: ', recall_score(y_test, pred))
print('f1 score: ', f1_score(y_test, pred))
```

Code 21.2.6 — **Logistic regression.** Confusion matrix

```
from sklearn.metrics import confusion_matrix

confusion_matrix(y_test, pred)

# output:
array([[145,  17],
       [ 36,  64]])
```

The online notebook experimented with the option: `class_weight = 'balanaced'`, which automatically adjusts the weights inversely proportional to the class distribution. Using the balanced class parameter did not improve the accuracy but the sensitivity and specificity were more evenly balanced.

21.2.5 Comparison with R Logistic Regression

The R logistic regression could handle missing values in age but errors are thrown for missing values in sklearn.

As with linear regression, the summary of the logistic regression model in R has no comparable functionality in sklearn. Most statisticians and data scientists would probably prefer R for both linear regression and logistic regression because of the wealth of statistical analysis that R provides.

On the plus side, the wealth of parameters in the sklearn LogisticRegression module makes it a good choice for many applications.

21.3 Naive Bayes

This section applies the Naive Bayes algorithm to the Titanic data. The data preprocessing steps are identical to the steps in the Logistic Regression example.

21.3.1 Train

By default, the algorithm will per form Laplace smoothing for zero probabilities, just as R does. The training accuracy for Naive Bayes is about 0.73 whereas the training accuracy for logistic regression was 0.78.

Code 21.3.1 — **Logistic regression.** Train

```python
from sklearn.naive_bayes import MultinomialNB

clf = MultinomialNB()
clf.fit(X_train, y_train)
clf.score(X_train, y_train)


# output:
0.7277936962750716
```

21.3.2 Test and Evaluate

The code block below shows a different evaluation available in sklearn: the classification report. The report is shown below the code block.

In the report, the precision, recall, and f1 scores are broken down by class. Recall from earlier chapters that precision is the true positives divided by (true positives plus false positives). The recall is the true positives divided by (true positives plus false negatives). The f1 metric is the harmonic mean between precision and recall. The support column gives the number of samples with that label.

The macro average will find the mean of each label and average those together, whereas the weighted average considers considers frequencies for each class. For multi-class classification, a micro-average will also be included in the classification report. The micro-average uses the total true positives, false negatives and false positives regardless of the labels. For binary classification, the micro-average will be the same as accuracy.

Code 21.3.2 — **Logistic regression.** Test and Evaluate

```python
# make predictions
pred = clf.predict(X_test)

from sklearn.metrics import classification_report
print(classification_report(y_test, pred))
```

	precision	recall	f1-score	support
0	0.67	0.88	0.76	162
1	0.62	0.31	0.41	100

accuracy			0.66	262
macro avg	0.65	0.60	0.59	262
weighted avg	0.65	0.66	0.63	262

21.3.3 Different NB algorithms

The online notebook showed that improved results are achieved using the BernoulliNB model over the MultinomialNB model used above. Accuracy improved from 0.65 to 0.78, which is just slightly lower than the logistic regression accuracy of 0.79. The sklearn documentation describes a few variations of the Naive Bayes algorithm, including:

- BernoulliNB - best for binary predictors
- MultinomialNB - best for discrete predictors with multiple levels
- GaussianNB - best for quantitative predictors

Note that any of these algorithms can handle predictors of all types. The Bernoulli model binarizes predictors. The sex predictor is already binary, pclass has 3 levels but would be binarized by the training algorithm. The age predictor would also be binarized into above/below an age.

Determining beforehand which algorithm to use is difficult, which is why two different algorithms were tried in the notebook. Besides the handling of data, the two algorithms are conceptually different. MultinomialNB considers counts for multiple features whereas BernoulliNB cares about the presence or the absence of a feature.

21.3.4 Comparison with R Naive Bayes

Again, the R version of Naive Bayes makes it easy to extract the learned probabilities from the model whereas sklearn does not. On the plus side, the sklearn makes it easier to try different algorithms and parameter settings.

Just as in R, the sklearn NB implementation can extract class probabilities instead of class predcitons:

```
# get predictions
pred = clf.predict(X\_test)

# get probabilities
probs = clf.predict\_proba(X\_test)
```

21.4 kNN

This section runs the Titanic data through the kNN algorithm for a classification demo, then runs the Boston housing data through kNN for a regression demo.

21.4.1 kNN for Classification

The code block below shows how to train the kNN classifier. A k value of 5 was arbitrarily chosen.

Code 21.4.1 — **kNN.** Train

```python
from sklearn.neighbors import KNeighborsClassifier

clf = KNeighborsClassifier(n_neighbors = 5)
clf.fit(X_train, y_train)

# output:
KNeighborsClassifier(algorithm='auto', leaf_size=30,
        metric='minkowski', metric_params=None, n_jobs=None,
        n_neighbors=5, p=2, weights='uniform')
```

The classification report for kNN can be seen in the online notebook. Accuracy was close to logistic regression, but slightly lower.

21.4.2 kNN for Regression

The code block below shows how to train the kNN regression algorithm. Values of k= 5 and 7 and finally 3 were tried, with k=3 giving the best results.

Code 21.4.2 — **kNN.** Train

```python
# train the algorithm
from sklearn.neighbors import KNeighborsRegressor
regressor = KNeighborsRegressor(n_neighbors=3)
regressor.fit(X_train, y_train)
```

The mse was considerably higher at 35.7 than the mse for linear regression of 27.85. The correlation was much lower. Different values of k=5 and k=7 resulted in worse performance.

Code 21.4.3 — **kNN.** Scaling the data

```python
from sklearn import preprocessing

X_train_scaled = preprocessing.scale(X_train)
X_test_scaled = preprocessing.scale(X_test)
```

As shown in the online notebook, after scaling the data and running kNN with k=3 on the scaled data, the mse dropped to 21.7 and the correlation jumped to 0.79. Not only is this significantly better than when the data was not scaled, it also outperforms linear regression.

21.4.3 Comparison with R kNN

An advantage of the R kNN system is the ease of performing cross-validation to determine the best k. A later discussion in this chapter about creating a pipeline would be one way to try various values of k in an efficient manner.

Scaling the data is equally straightforward in both R and sklearn.

21.5 Decision Trees

This section runs the Titanic data through the Decision Tree algorithm for a classification demo.

21.5.1 Training a Decision Tree

The following code demonstrates training a decision tree with the default settings. The output below the training code in the online notebook shows these default settings.

> **Code 21.5.1 — Decision Tree.** Train
>
> ```
> from sklearn.tree import DecisionTreeClassifier
>
> clf = DecisionTreeClassifier()
> clf.fit(X_train, y_train)
> ```

The results were similar to the regression tree algorithm.

21.5.2 Comparison with R Decision Tree

Running the decision tree algorithm in R and sklearn is equally straightforward. The advantage of R is the ease of visualization of the decision trees. There are visualization options using libraries such as GraphViz but getting them to work is problematic across Windows, Mac, and Linux computers. For this reason, examples are not included here.

21.5.3 Random Forests

> **Code 21.5.2 — Random Forest.** Train
>
> ```
> from sklearn.ensemble import RandomForestClassifier
>
> # train
> clf2 = RandomForestClassifier(max_depth=4, random_state=1234)
> clf2.fit(X_train, y_train)
> ```

The results from the classification report show similar results to the decision tree in terms of accuracy, but with higher precision and lower recall. This is surprising since in R the random forest always significantly outperformed the decision tree. More exploration could answer the question if the sklearn decision tree is better or if the sklearn random forest is worse compared to R.

21.6 Summary

As discussed for each algorithm, there are some advantages in R for some algorithms, particularly linear and logistic regression. One overall advantage of sklearn over R is that in R we used different functions created by different groups over decades which requires learning the syntax for each function. In contrast, sklearn is a unified library, so that the syntax for the different algorithms is largely the same, albeit with different parameters for each algorithm.

Hopefully, this chapter has demonstrated that having both R and Python machine learning in your toolkit is better than having just one ecosystem. Algorithms are coded up and optimized by people with different approaches. Having a variety of implementations to choose from is ideal.

The sklearn ecosystem of course consists of much more than was explored in this chapter. The sklearn documentation on `scikit-learn.org` is divided into main sections: classification, regression, clustering, dimensionality reduction, model selection, and preprocessing. The model selection section includes documentation for cross-validation, grid search, and more. Another useful module is the Pipeline which allows sequential data transformations, following by a get method. The pipeline is often used in machine learning for text data which requires much preprocessing.

22. The Craft 6: Data Wrangling 2

This chapter looks at common techniques for data wrangling with Python. An enormous amount of time in a machine learning project can be spent on data cleaning. We gave a brief overview of data cleaning with Python in Chapter 20. We will repeat some of that code here, so that you have one place to look for reference. The first thing you may want to do is remove some columns, in this case the name and idk columns:

```
df = df.drop(columns=['name', 'idk'])
```

22.1 Missing values

We can check for missing values as follows:

```
df.isnull().sum()
```

The code above outputs a list of each column in the data, along with the number of NAs in that column. One technique to get rid of NAs is to just remove all rows which contain an NA in any column:

```
df.dropna()
```

You may end up losing too much data, especially in smaller data sets. Another option is to use the pandas fillna() function:

```
df.fillna(value)
```

The value may be zero, or the mean of the column, the median of the column, or any other statistical measure that makes sense for a given data set.

The sklearn imputer() function can be used to fill NAs with the mean or other values. The code follows the usual sklearn fit-transform flow:

```
from sklearn.impute import SimpleImputer
imputer = SimpleImputer()

data = imputer.fit_transform(data)
```

22.2   Parsing dates

Dates in a data set may be in text form such as '12/01/2020'. For machine learning, converting the text data to a standard date format. This example converts a string to a date/time object.

```
d = pd.to_datetime('05/20/2020', format='%m/%d/%Y')

Timestamp('2020-05-20 00:00:00')

type(d)
<class 'pandas._libs.tslibs.timestamps.Timestamp'>
```

To convert a column, you can follow this pattern:

```
df['Date'] = pd.to_datetime(df['Date'], format='%m%d$Y')
```

See the pandas documentation for more examples: `https://pandas.pydata.org/pandas-docs/stable/user_guide/timeseries.html`

22.3   Character encoding

There are many different ways to encode text data to binary/hex. Python works well with UTF-8, so try to stick to that encoding whenever possible. The Python encode() and decode() functions can be used to change the encoding, in this case from UTF-8 to ASCII:

```
newString = (originalString.encode('ascii', 'ignore')).decode('utf-8')
```

You can specify the encoding when you read in data:

```
df = pd.read_csv('data.csv', encoding='Windows-1252')
```

If you don't know the encoding, you can find out as shown below. The example uses the chardet library.

```
import chardet

with open(file.csv', 'rb') as raw:
    print(chardet.detect(raw.read(100000)))
```

Read much more about chardet and character encoding here: `https://chardet.readthedocs.io/en/latest/index.html`

22.4 Inconsistent data

What if your data set relied on users typing in data, and some of them use different spelling or words? You can use basic Python to find all matches and update them. In the teams list, we see that there are many variations of 'Dallas Cowboys'. These variations are extracted into a variable called teams_dallas. These are then used to replace any of the variations with a standard form.

```
teams = ['Dallas Cowboys', 'Cowboys', 'Green Bay', 'boys']
teams_dallas = [s for s in teams if 'boys' in s.lower()]

teams_dallas
['Dallas Cowboys', 'Cowboys', 'boys']

 clean_teams = ['Dallas Cowboys'
      if team in teams_dallas else team
      for team in teams]
 clean_teams
['Dallas Cowboys', 'Dallas Cowboys', 'Green Bay', 'Dallas Cowboys']
```

Another Python package, fuzzywuzzy, to the rescue! This package will do a fuzzy match on strings using Levenshtein Distance, a measure of how many characters apart two strings are. The following example is from the fuzzywuzzy page. We have a list of NFL teams entered by users, called 'choices'. The process.extract() function extracts fuzzy matches to 'new york jets' from choices.

```
from fuzzywuzzy import process

choices = ["Atlanta Falcons", "New York Jets", "New York Giants"]
process.extract("new york jets", choices)
    [('New York Jets', 100), ('New York Giants', 78)]
```

Read much more about fuzzywuzzy here: `https://pypi.org/project/fuzzywuzzy/`

22.5   Scaling data

In a future chapter we will discuss neural networks which perform better on scaled data, data which fits a predetermined range, usually 0 to 1. One way to scale the data is shown below:

```python
from sklearn import preprocessing

scaler = preprocessing.StandardScaler().fit(X_train)

X_train = scaler.transform(X_train)
X_test = scaler. transform(X_test_
```

The scaler is fit to the training data only, then used to transform the training data and the test data. This is considered a best practice so that the test data remains independent of the training data.

22.6   Summary

This chapter highlighted a few things you might encounter in data wrangling. There is no way to prepare for everything you might encounter in data. Keep in mind that if you have a problem, someone else may have already solved it, so search for packages that fit your situation. This can save you hours and hours of time.

VII Part Seven: Neural Networks

Preface to Part Seven

In Part Seven we look at neural networks. The foundational concepts of neural networks have been around since the 1950s but in the past few years, researchers have pushed boundaries far beyond earlier results. There are two reasons for the renewed interest in neural networks: (1) processing power has increased, and (2) big data is commonly available. A deep neural network is just a network with more hidden layers.

The human brain has about 100 billion neurons, and each neuron is connected to 1000 or more other neurons. Each neuron has multiple inputs that receive signals from other neurons. When the combined inputs reach a certain threshold, the neuron fires, sending signals out to connected neurons.

To say that neural networks or even deep neural networks act like the human brain is a gross overreach. We don't fully understand how the human brain works. Further, we don't have the massive parallel architecture of artificial neurons on the scale of the human brain. Nonetheless, we shall see that these are very powerful algorithms.

23. Neural Networks

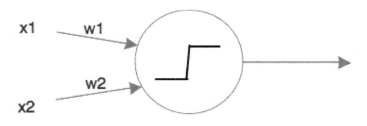

Figure 23.1: Perceptron

The idea for neural networks, also called artificial neural networks (ANNs), was originally inspired by biological neural networks in mammals. Frank Rosenblatt is credited with developing the perceptron for pattern recognition in the late 1950s. A *perceptron*, as illustrated in Figure 23.1, takes several input values and produces an output signal. In this example, there are two inputs x_1 and x_2 and these are multiplied by their respective weights and sent through the *activation function*. The activation function, here illustrated as a step function, will output +1 if the combined inputs reaches a certain threshold, and −1 otherwise. The total input to the perceptron is: $\sum_i w_i x_i$

The perceptron was overhyped by its proponents and the press as has often been the case in advances throughout the history of AI. A backlash came in 1969 with a book by Minsky and Papert[1] that described limitations of the single-layer perceptron, for example, that it could not learn the XOR function. Although it was demonstrated soon thereafter that combining

---

[1] Minsky, Marvin, and Seymour Papert. "Perceptrons: An Introduction to Computational Geometry." (1969).

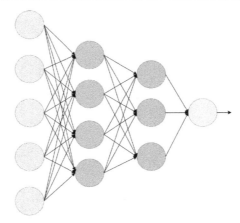

Figure 23.2: Neural Network with 2 Hidden Layers

perceptrons in multiple layers could learn XOR, the negative perception persisted for decades. In fact, a network of these perceptrons can learn any function that can be expressed with step functions. Further improvements were made by replacing the step function as the activation function with smoother functions such as the sigmoid. Having a sigmoid activation function allows the network to do regression as well as classification. A neural network, then is the evolution of the perceptron to include multiple neurons in a network with the sigmoid or other flexible activation function. This is typically called a *feed-forward network* because the variables and weights are calculated left to right, going forward through the network.

A neural network is illustrated conceptually in Figure 23.2. Reading forward through the network, left to right, we see 5 input nodes in yellow. There are two hidden layers illustrated with green nodes, 4 in the first hidden layer and 3 in the second hidden layer. Finally the output layer in blue gives the output of the network. In a feed forward network such as this, each node's output is an input to the next layer. Further, each connection in the illustration has a weight value that is multiplied by the output of the source node to compute the input to the destination node. Each of the green and blue nodes will have an activation function such as the sigmoid which determines its output. Each individual node (neuron) in the hidden layers can learn something different, essentially learning different things from the input so that the network is essentially a composition of functions. A "deep" neural network as discussed in the next chapter is a network with many hidden layers.

23.1   Neural Network Regression Example

This section builds a neural network for regression in sklearn, using the Boston data set to predict median home value from all predictors. The online notebook shows that the data is divided into 80% train 20% test. Then the notebook runs the linear regression algorithm as a baseline.

Neural networks tend to converge faster and perform better on scaled data. The online notebook shows two ways to normalize the data: using Python and pandas functionality, as well as the code shown below that uses the scaler() from sklearn. With the default settings as shown below, the data will be normalized. Normalizing is transforming the data to fit a normal distribution whereas scaling keeps whatever skew the data has and fits it to a predetermined range, like 0 to 1.

Code 23.1.1 — **Neural Network.** Scale the Data

```
# scale the data using sklearn functionality
from sklearn import preprocessing

scaler = preprocessing.StandardScaler().fit(X_train)

X_train = scaler.transform(X_train)
X_test = scaler.transform(X_test)
```

Notice that the sklearn scalar was fit to the training data only, and then applied to both train and test sets. This approach is considered the best practice for scaling so that information from the train set does not leak to the test set.

The next code block shows how to train the neural network. The regressor is instantiated to have 6 nodes in the first hidden layer and 3 in the second. The max iterations argument is sometimes needed if the algorithm didn't coverge with the default 200 iterations. Notice that a seed is given for reproducibility. The neural network will initialize the weights randomly (unless we specify initial weights). This random state will produce slightly different results each run if the random state parameter is omitted.

Code 23.1.2 — **Neural Network.** Train

```
# train the algorithm
from sklearn.neural_network import MLPRegressor

regr = MLPRegressor(hidden_layer_sizes=(6, 3), max_iter=500,
          random_state=1234)
regr.fit(X_train, y_train)
```

The network has been trained. The next code block shows how to predict and evaluate.

Code 23.1.3 — **Neural Network.** Predict and evaluate

```
# make predictions
y_pred = regr.predict(X_test)

# evaluation
from sklearn.metrics import mean_squared_error, r2_score
print('mse=', mean_squared_error(y_test, y_pred))
print('correlation=', r2_score(y_test, y_pred))
```

The first network that was built got worse performance than the linear regression model, as shown in the table below. For the second neural network, the solver was changed to lbfgs and the max interations was changed to 1500. The lbfgs solver tends to work better than the default adam solver on small data.

	Linear Regression	**Neural Network 1**	**Neural Network 2**
correlation	0.73	0.71	0.89
mse	27.44	29.31	11.56

Table 23.1: Results on the Boston Housing Data

We got improved results with the neural network over linear regression; however, there is a bit of trial and error and luck involved. On a small data set, linear regression is likely to outperform a neural network. Plus, the linear regression model is easy to fit and highly interpretable. Neural networks can learn complex relationships that simple algorithms like linear regression cannot but a neural network is not necessarily the best choice. Another distinction between the two algorithms is that linear regression will find the optimal parameters whereas a neural network may find a local optima and there is no guarantee that it is the best you can do. Unfortunately there is a lot of trial and error involved in working with neural networks. For example, several larger network sizes were tried but they received worse results. When designing the network, it is best to start out with a simple network and then try more complex networks. A more complex network may overfit because it is learning noise in the data.

The neural network visualization tools aren't as good as the plot in the R neuralnet() function, so the R plot is included in Figure 23.3 just for illustration purposes. The sklearn network will be different but similar. Notice that the predictors are shown in the leftmost layer, the input layer. The two hidden layers (6, 3) are shown next, and finally on the right is the one output layer. Each node's value is calculated by multiplying all predictors and the intercept by their weights, and then summing these values. The weights for the intercepts are shown in blue.

23.1.1 Hidden Nodes and Layers

The most important decision when building a neural network is its architecture, or topology. The input and output layers should be fairly intuitive for a given problem but designing the hidden layers is challenging. How many hidden layers? How many nodes in the hidden layers? Having too few hidden nodes may result in underfitting while having two many can result in overfitting. There are a few rules of thumb to find the number of hidden nodes:
- between 1 and the number of predictors
- two-thirds of the input layer size plus the size of the output layer
- < twice the input layer size

Following these very general guidelines for the Boston data with 13 predictors, the suggestions are: (1) 1 - 13, (2) 9, and (3) < 26. We tried 9 hidden nodes and arranged them in two layers.

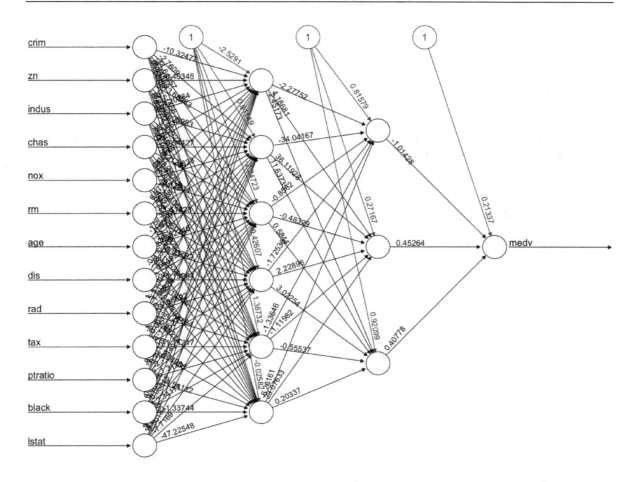

Figure 23.3: Neural Network for the Boston Data

Are there any advantages in having two layers rather than 1? In this particular problem, the results were dramatically worse than linear regression when we tried one hidden layer with 9 nodes rather than spreading the nodes into two layers. If the mapping of the inputs to the outputs is smooth, one layer should be enough. Having two layers can capture a more complex relationship, at the cost of extra training time. A potential downside of more layers is that you may overfit if you have a small training set. A simpler architecture is usually recommended for small data.

23.2 The Algorithm

In Figure 23.3 you can see that each neuron has its own bias term and weight, drawn in blue. Every neuron in the hidden and output layers will have a bias term, as you can see in the neural net plot above. The bias is like the intercept term in a linear regression or logistic regression model, it is always 1, and multiplied by its weight. In a feed forward neural network, each input including the bias term is multiplied by its weight to get a sum of inputs. This is just basic matrix multiplication which is optimized in modern computers to be very fast. Once a neuron or node receives its sum of weighted inputs, the activation function kicks in. In a simple activation function, if the sum is over a certain threshold, the output will be 1 otherwise it will be 0.

So far we have not described any learning. We have just described the feed forward mechanism. The weights are initialized randomly so the first output of the feed-forward mechanism is just a random guess. So how does it learn? Like any supervised algorithm, a neural network learns from labeled data. So on the first pass through the network with its random guess, the network will know whether the output is close to the labeled target or not. The network improves by adjusting the weights using *back propagation*, and efficient methods of computing gradients. Weights are adjusted by assigning blame backwards so that these neurons' weights are adjusted. The error is the difference between the output and the true label. Ideally we would like this error to be zero. If we had a single input we could adjust that input's weight using the slope, (the derivative). However we will have many inputs each with their own weights. The derivatives will be in matrix form and give us the gradient matrix. We want to move down that error surface simultaneously for all inputs. Each input node's weights are adjusted according to its own gradient. Visualize this as n skiers, one for each input, skiing down different mountain slopes simultaneously where some slopes are steeper than others. We will update the previous hidden layer, then the next, all the way back to the input layer. Training, then, is just a series of forward and backward passes until convergence, meaning that the error is under some threshold value.

23.3   Mathematical Foundations

Training a neural network is an optimization problem, as is the case for many algorithms we have explored. These problems need a loss function. For both regression and classification neural networks, the mean squared error can be used:

$$\mathcal{L} = \frac{1}{2N} \sum_{i=1}^{n} \|(y_i - f(x_i))\|^2 \tag{23.1}$$

where $\|x\| := \sqrt{x_1^2 + \ldots + x_n^2}$

The error term helps with the credit assignment problem, determining how much blame for the error to assign to each input weight. We will take the derivative of the cost function to find the gradients, the rate of change of the cost function with respect to the neuron's output.

$$\nabla E = \left(\frac{\partial E}{\partial w_1}, \ldots, \frac{\partial E}{\partial w_n} \right) \tag{23.2}$$

The gradients are computed for each training example. Then they are aggregated to modify the weights by this difference between the old values and the new values multiplied by a parameter, alpha, the learning rate.

$$\triangle w_i = -\alpha \frac{\partial E}{\partial w_i} \qquad (23.3)$$

Each forward and backard pass through the network is called an *epoch*. If the alpha is too small it may take too long to converge, but if it is too large you may overcorrect. The error surface may not be perfectly convex but be bumpy and may have local minima.

The gradient descent approach described above is sometimes called *batch gradient descent* because we update the gradients for all examples in one batch. An alternative is *stochastic gradient descent*, in which the weights are updated after each example. The error surface for different examples will look different so this prevents us from getting stuck in a local minima, at the cost of greater computation time. A good compromise is *mini-batch descent* in which works like batch descent but on a subset of the full data at a time.

23.4 Neural Network Classification Example

Next we look at a classification example on the PimaIndiansDiabetes2 data set that was exported from R package `mlbench`. As shown in the online notebook, some data cleaning was done to handle NA values. The target column, diabetes, needs to be converted to a categorical data type. Two options are shown below. The first uses the pandas astype() function to convert the diabetes column to categorical data with the quality that when you print the data it will how as text 'pos' or 'neg'. The second example adds the cat.codes option to convert the categorical data and display it as integers.

Code 23.4.1 — **Convert target.** Categorical data

```
# convert diabetes to categorical data type, representing as text
df.diabetes = df.diabetes.astype('category')

# convert diabetes to categorical, representing as integers
df.diabetes = df.diabetes.astype('category').cat.codes
```

In the online notebook, the data is divided into train/test. Then we perform logistic regression with diabetes as the target and all other columns as predictors. The logistic regression classifer got .86 accuracy on the test data.

23.4.1 Neural Network Classification

In the online notebook, two different neural networks were created. The first one used hidden layers (5, 2), and the lbfgs solver on scaled data. This network performed worse than logistic regression, getting an accuracy of 0.85. The code below shows how to train the model. The predict and metric code is the same as code shown in the previous chapter's classification example, so it is not repeated here.

Code 23.4.2 — **Build the Neural Network.** Diabetes Data.

```
# train
from sklearn.neural_network import MLPClassifier

clf = MLPClassifier(solver='lbfgs', hidden_layer_sizes=(5, 2),
    max_iter=500, random_state=1234)

clf.fit(X_train_scaled, y_train)
```

A second neural network was built in the online notebook, using a simpler architecture of only 3 hidden nodes. This model achieved the same accuracy as the logistic regression model. Several more complex models were built but the more complex the model, the worse the performance. On small data sets, a simpler model is usually the best approach because more complex models will learn noise in the data.

23.4.2 Training

The more complex the architecture (the number of hidden layers and nodes), the longer training will take. The algorithm may reach its predefined maximum number of iteration steps before it converges below the specified threshold. Both the number of steps and the threshold are adjustable parameters. It's unlikely that you will get lucky and specify an architecture that performs optimally by chance. Creating the network is an iterative trial-and-error process. If your data is very large, you might want to go through this trial-and-error phase with a subset of the training data, like 10K observations or less and a validation set.

One of the default parameters in sklearn is tol, the tolerance for optimization. The algorithm will stop training when the loss function score is not improved by this amount. If a model fails to converge this tolerance can be increased from its default 1e-4 value. Recall that the derivatives give the slope and the minimum error will be when the derivates are near 0 in the gradient descent algorithm.

> Exercise 23.1 — **Classification on the Wine Data.** The data set "wine_all.csv" is available on the github. It was created by combining a red data set and a white data set from the UCI repository.
> Try the following:
> - Load the data and examine it with str().
> - Divide into 80-20 train and test.
> - Normalize the train and test predictors, leaving out the type column, our target.
> - Train a neural network with 16 hidden nodes, act.fct="logistic", linear.output=FALSE.
> - What is your accuracy on the test data?
> As we will see in the next chapter, using Keras gives us a lot more flexibility in designing an architecture and we will use this same data set again with much better results. ▪

23.5 Summary

Neural networks are primarily defined by these properties:
- the network architecture or topology - the number of neurons in the model and the number of layers
- the activation function which transforms the inputs to an output; the sigmoid function is commonly used

Neural networks can learn complex functions from data. Generally they will not outperform simpler models for small data but truly shine when the amount of data is large and the function to learn is complex.

In this chapter we focused on the sklearn package for neural networks. In the next chapter we focus on Keras, which vastly outperforms neuralnet() in terms of accuracy and speed for neural networks of any depth. Unfortunately for Windows users, Keras can run on Windows but it's not really recommended. If you want to run Keras, it is recommended to first set up a dual-boot Ubuntu or virtual machine, and run Keras from there.

23.5.1 New Terminology

- backpropagation
- epoch
- neuron or node
- perceptron
- activation function

23.5.2 Quick Reference

Reference 23.5.1 Convert target to categorical
```
# convert target to categorical data type

df.target = df.target.astype('category')
or:
df.target = df.target.astype('category').cat.codes
```

When scaling or normalizing data, determine the parameters only from the training data to avoid leaking information to the test data.

Reference 23.5.2 Scale the Data
```
# normalize the data
from sklearn import preprocessing

scaler = preprocessing.StandardScaler().fit(X_train)

X_train_scaled = scaler.transform(X_train)
X_test_scaled = scaler.transform(X_test)
```

Reference 23.5.3 Neural Network for Regression

```
# train the algorithm
from sklearn.neural_network import MLPRegressor

regr = MLPRegressor(hidden_layer_sizes=(6, 3), max_iter=500,
          random_state=1234)
regr.fit(X_train, y_train)
```

Reference 23.5.4 Neural Network for Classificaiton

```
# train
from sklearn.neural_network import MLPClassifier

clf = MLPClassifier(solver='lbfgs', hidden_layer_sizes=(5, 2),
          max_iter=500, random_state=1234)
clf.fit(X_train_scaled, y_train)
```

23.5.3 Going Further

The heart of neural networks is the propagation algorithm. An entire chapter devoted to backprop can be found here: `http://page.mi.fu-berlin.de/rojas/neural/chapter/K7.pdf`. The chapter is from Raul Rojas's *Neural Networks - A Systematic Introduction*.

24. Deep Learning

Simply put, deep learning involves neural networks with many hidden layers. Deep learning was made possible by increased computing power and availability of more data. Deep learning became a hot trend because it improved performance on many hard-to-solve problems involving pattern recognition with big data. Another reason that deep-learning became popular is that it automated feature engineering. In previous chapters we discussed a few techniques for shaping raw data into features that are useful for machine learning algorithms. With deep learning, the algorithm itself can learn features from the inputs at the same time it is learning the target function for the data.

24.1 Keras

In this chapter we will focus on Keras running on top of Tensorflow. Keras was designed primarily by Francois Chollet from Google. Keras is an interface that makes building a deep network relatively painless. The website `https://keras.io` provides a wealth of resources on Keras, including installation instructions. The code samples in this chapter use Keras 2. Rather than provide installation instructions for different systems, this chapter will demonstrate using Keras in Google Colab.

24.1.1 Google Colab

Google Colab provides a Jupyter notebook environment to run machine learning on a virtual machine in the cloud. To get started, go to `https://colab.research.google.com` and log into your google account. You will also specify a folder in your Google drive where notebooks you create in Google Colab are stored.

When you go to the colab url, you will see an environment similar to Figure 24.1. This pop-up overlay shows the first option is a Welcome to Colaboratory page that gives an overview of the service. When you have created notebooks, you will see them listed here. You can click on them to open them, or click on the Google Drive folder icon to see where they stored. On the bottom right is a link to create a New Notebook. The notebooks for code in this chapter are available on the GitHub. Notice in the bar at the top of the pop-up is a link to GitHub where you can Upload a notebook or link directly to one in a GitHub.

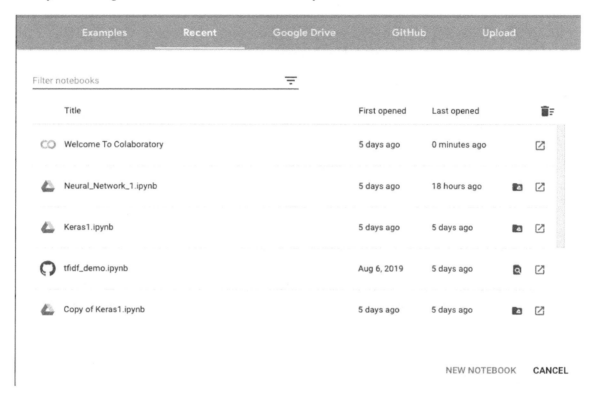

Figure 24.1: Google Colab Landing Page

24.2   Data Representation in TensorFlow

The fundamental data representation in TensorFlow is a *tensor*, which is a generalization of vectors and matrices to an arbitrary number of dimensions, called axes. In an R context, a 1D tensor is like a vector, a 2D tensor is like a matrix and an nD matrix is like an array. The n is sometimes called its rank, but the terminology can be inconsistently used. A tensor is defined by:

- Rank - the number of axes
- Shape - in n dimensions
- Type - integer or double

For data similar to a data frame, 2D tensors of shape (samples, features) are sufficient. Time series or sequential data requires 3D tensors of shape (samples, timesteps, features).

Images require 4D tensors of shape (samples, height, width, channels) or some variation, where channel is 1 for greyscale and 3 for RGB data. Video will require 5D tensors with the 5th axis for frames and the others similar to images.

24.3 Keras in Google Colaboratory Example

The website https://keras.io has learning resources, reference material and examples. This section looks at an example of a simple Sequenatial model on the MNIST data set. The MNIST data set is a collection of handwritten digits normalized to fit into a 28x28 grid of pixels. The task is to classify which of the 10 digits each example represents. This first example provides cursory examples of the code and terminology just to get some experience and context. Later sections discuss the terminology in more detail.

Since Keras 2, Keras is now part of TensorFlow. This means there are two parallel APIs, one for Keras and one for Tensorflow Keras. The code samples in this chapter will use Tensorflow Keras.

This first code block imports tensorflow and sets up some parameters. The neural network model will be a Sequential model, which is just a feed-forward network like we built in sklearn in the previous chapter. The hidden layers of the neural network will be Dense, which is like the hidden layers discussed in the previous chapter, and Dropout, which randomly drops some neuron's outputs by setting them to 0 to avoid overfitting. The learning will happen with rmsprop, a back-propagation algorithm. The training data has 60K observations, but training will select batches of 128 examples at a time. The target, the digit 0-9, has 10 classes. The number of epochs is limited to 20, so training will stop after 20 forward and backward passes.

Code 24.3.1 — Imports and Constants. Import TensorFlow

```
import tensorflow as tf

batch_size = 128
num_classes = 10
epochs = 20
```

The work to be done is divided into 3 phases: (1) prepare the data, (2) build the model, and (3) train and evaluate. First, data preparation.

24.3.1 Data Preparation

The MNIST handwriting recognition data set is built into the Keras package and is already randomly divided into train and test sets. The data will take a minute to load on the first run. Each observation is a representation of a handwritten digit in a 28x28 grid of pixels.

Code 24.3.2 — Data Preparation. Load the MNIST Data

```
(x_train, y_train), (x_test, y_test) =
      tf.keras.datasets.mnist.load_data()
```

The train and test arrays are of dimension 60Kx28x28 and 10Kx28x28. The 28x28 represents the original handwritten images transformed into this grid. The values in the original data were greyscale values from 0 to 255. These are divided by 255 to transform the data into floating-point data.

The y_test and y_train variables are NumPy 1D arrays of length 10K and 60K, with values representing the true digit label. These are converted to categorical data using a built-in tf.keras function.

Code 24.3.3 — **Data Preparation.** MNIST Data preparation

```
x_train, x_test = x_train / 255.0, x_test / 255.0

# convert class vectors to binary class matrices
y_train = tf.keras.utils.to_categorical(y_train, num_classes)
y_test = tf.keras.utils.to_categorical(y_test, num_classes)
```

24.3.2 Build the Model

Before training can start, we have to design the network and then compile it. The following code starts with a sequential model and adds 2 hidden layers with 512 nodes each, and a final output layer with 10 nodes, one for each possible digit classification. The hidden layers have relu activation function and the output layer has softmax. These terms are described in detail below.

The compile step specifies the loss function, the optimizer and the metrics used to evaluate. The loss function is categorical crossentropy, a good choice for labels that must fit in one class only. The optimizer chosen is root mean squared back propagation, and the metric using in training is accuracy.

Code 24.3.4 — **Build the Model.** Compile and Summary

```
model = tf.keras.models.Sequential([
  tf.keras.layers.Flatten(input_shape=(28, 28)),
  tf.keras.layers.Dense(512, activation='relu'),
  tf.keras.layers.Dropout(0.2),
  tf.keras.layers.Dense(512, activation='relu'),
  tf.keras.layers.Dropout(0.2),
  tf.keras.layers.Dense(num_classes, activation='softmax'),
])

model.summary()

model.compile(loss='categorical_crossentropy',
              optimizer='rmsprop',
              metrics=['accuracy'])
```

24.3.3 Train and Evaluate

The fit() method trains the model with the data and parameters that have been previously specified. We requested 20 epochs with verbose output and a batch size of 128. The fit method evaluates itself as it goes through each epoch using 20% of the training data as held-out validation data. The history variable is keeping track of information we can examine later. This process took about 2 minutes on Google Colaboratory, and about the same on a Mac mini with Keras/Tensorflow running on the CPU.

Code 24.3.5 — Train and Evaluate. MNIST Data.

```
history = model.fit(x_train, y_train,
                    batch_size=batch_size,
                    epochs=epochs,
                    verbose=1,
                    validation_data=(x_test, y_test))

score = model.evaluate(x_test, y_test, verbose=0)
print('Test loss:', score[0])
print('Test accuracy:', score[1])
# output
Test loss: 0.13159886472393972
Test accuracy: 0.9825
```

The model.evaluate() function returns scores, which is a list in which the first element is the test loss and the second element is test accuracy.

Notice that the training above stored the training results in a variable named 'history'. Typing `history.history.keys()` at the console reveals the training metrics that an be retrieved. We can plot these metrics as shown in the next code block which plots the validation accuracy on the training data with the accuracy on the held-out validation test data. The labels 'train' and 'test' both refer to portions of the data set. The plot is shown in Figure 24.2.

Code 24.3.6 — Training History. Visualization

```
import matplotlib.pyplot as plt

# Plot training & validation accuracy values
plt.plot(history.history['val_acc'])
plt.plot(history.history['acc'])
plt.title('Model accuracy')
plt.ylabel('Accuracy')
plt.xlabel('Epoch')
plt.legend(['Train', 'Test'], loc='upper left')
plt.show()
```

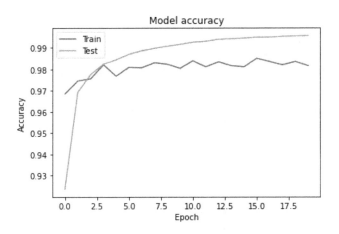

Figure 24.2: Progress Plot while Training on MNIST Data

Notice in the figure that epochs 0 - 20 are represented across the x axis. The training accuracy is the jagged line. The line jumps up and down because in the batch processing of 128 examples will get different training accuracy results. The test accuracy quickly jumps up to the high 90s range and appears to not level off. The more training epochs you have, the more you can increased the accuracy on the validation data but on the otherhand, could also overfit the data.

24.4 Deep Learning Basics

Now that we have run through an example of building a network, training, and evaluating, let's step back and discuss some of the terminology that we just used. We have only used a couple of layers in our examples, so we could call this shallow learning instead of deep learning, but the principles and terminology remain the same as we add more layers. The basic algorithm is the same as discussed in the previous chapter on neural networks: the data feeds forward through the network, at each layer being multiplied by the weights, until the output value is calculated. The output has an error which we measure with a loss function, also called the objective function. This acts as a feedback signal to modify the weights. This modification is done by the optimizer, typically some variation of the back propagation algorithm. Training proceeds forward and backward through iterations, epochs. Evaluation is done at the end of each epoch. Training stops when the error is below a certain threshold. When a batch size is given, that number of samples are processed independently but in parallel in one epoch. Larger batch sizes will train faster but may run into memory issues.

So what advantages do deep networks have over shallow ones? The most obvious answer to that is that many layers help learn more complex functions. Beyond that, deep architectures help with feature engineering. In a shallow network the input data must already have been manually manipulated into a good representation for the network. Deep learning can partially automate this by learning features as it learns the function in many layers. According to Challot in his book *Deep Learning with Python*, these are the two key principles that make deep learning unique and powerful:

1. increasingly complex representations are learned layer by layer over many iterations
2. the intermediate representations are learned jointly so that as one feature changes, all the others are adjusted automatically

Deep architectures have a lot of moving parts: activation functions, optimization schemes, metrics, and more, discussed below.

24.4.1 Layers and Units

Designing the optimum number of layers, and units within layers, is not yet a science but more of a trial-and-error approach that you will develop intuitions for as you gain experience. A few guidelines are:

- You want the number of units in an intermediate layer to be greater than or equal to the number of units in the subsequent layer, otherwise you create an information bottleneck.
- For small data sets, avoid overfitting by having a smaller number of hidden layers.
- To search for the best architecture for a given problem, start with a simple model on validation data. Iteratively increase the complexity of a model until you get diminished improvements at which point you may be overfitting.
- Add weight regularization to the hidden layers if overfitting is a concern. This constrains the weights to smaller absolute values. If you recall, we discussed regularization way back in the linear regression chapter. L1 regularization uses the L1 norm which is calculated from the absolute values of the coefficients (weights). L2 uses the L2 norm which is the square of the weights. L2 regularization is sometimes called weight decay. This regularization is only done during training.
- Another regularization technique is dropout, which only occurs in training. This randomly sets a few output weights to 0. Although this seems like an arbitrary approach, it has been shown to reduce overfitting by randomly eliminating the impact of different units that may be tuning into "noise" instead of the function you want them to learn.

24.4.2 Activation Functions

Each layer can have its own activation function. If no activation function is specified, linear activation is assumed. This is typically the choice for the output layer of regression tasks. The sigmoid activation function will output a probability between 0 and 1, so it is often chosen as the activation function for the output layer of a binary classification task. For multi-class classification, the softmax activation is often used because it outputs probabities for each class. A popular choice for intermediate layers is the relu (rectified linear unit). The relu is linear for positive values but makes negative values 0.

24.4.3 Optimization Schemes and Loss Functions

The optimizer determines how learning proceeds and is associated with a loss function that measures how well it is learning. Although there are a bewildering array of options for all these parameters, there are a few choices that are standard. For regression problems, mean squared error is the standard loss function. For 2-class classification, binary crossentropy is standard, while for multi-class classification, categorical crossentropy is typically used.

24.5   Bring Your Own Data

The previous example showed how to run Keras on some data that is included in the package. What if we want to use our own data? The following code blocks shows how to import a data set into Google Colaboratory and prepare the data for Keras. The first code block shows two lines of code that will pop up a box for you to choose a file on your local computer to upload. The data is not saved permanently, just for the run of the notebook.

Code 24.5.1 — **Google Colab.** Import Data

```
from google.colab import files
uploaded = files.upload()
```

The next code block converts the uploaded csv file to a pandas data frame.

Code 24.5.2 — **Google Colab.** Convert data to pandas

```
import io
import pandas as pd

df = pd.read_csv(io.BytesIO(uploaded['myfile.csv']))
```

24.5.1   Faster Results on Larger Data

Training in Google Colaboratory can be much faster than on many home computers. Using the default runtype is usually fine. However, if training seems to be slow, consider changing the runtime options. In the notebook, choose 'Runtime' from the menu at the top, then 'Change runtime type'. The hardware accelerator option will be 'None' by default, but can be changed to GPU or TPU. The TPU (tensor processing unit) is a special chip designed by Google for using TensorFlow machine learning. Which exact GPU or TPU is available in colab varies depending on availability of free resources. Users who want guaranteed access to specific CPU or TPU models should upgrade to Colab Pro.

24.6   Keras Regression Example

The GitHub contains a notebook created in Google Colaboratory that performs neural network regression using Keras on the Beijing PM2.5 data, downloaded from the UCI repository. The target column is the particulate matter count PM2.5, which measures parts per million of particulates in the air that are less than 2.5 micrometers wide. The other columns try to predict the pollution level and include day and time information, dew point, temperature, atmospheric pressure, combined wind direction, cumulative wind speed, snow and rain.

The data is first imported into Google Colaboratory using the method described above. The only data cleaning is to remove rows with NAs, and to convert wind direction to a categorical column. The dimensions of the data are 41,757 rows and 12 columns. In the online notebook, the first few rows are displayed.

After dividing into 80/20 train/test sets, there are about 33K rows in the training set and about 8K rows in the test set. A linear regression model is built and attained an rmse of 79.

For Keras, the data is scaled using the sklearn scaler. Then the model is built as shown in the code block below. The syntax is slightly different in this example to show different ways of using models and layers. Two hidden layers were placed in the network, with 512 and 128 nodes, respectively, as well as dropout layers. The final output layer has one node with no activation, which will default to linear.

You will notice that this code looks quite a bit different than the code in the previous example. That is because the code in the previous example used the tf.keras API and the code below uses the Keras API. In my opinion, the Keras code below is a little cleaner and easier to read, but the tf.keras API is more flexible, so it is good to be able to use both.

Code 24.6.1 — Keras Regression. Build the Network

```
from keras import models
from keras import layers
from keras.optimizers import RMSprop

batch_size = 128
epochs = 100

model = models.Sequential()
model.add(layers.Dense(512, activation='relu', input_shape=(11,)))
model.add(layers.Dropout(0.2))
model.add(layers.Dense(128, activation='relu'))
model.add(layers.Dropout(0.2))
model.add(layers.Dense(1))
```

The code block below first shows the model compile function with loss as mse, and using mae (mean absolute value error) as a validation metric. As before, we are using root mean squared error back propagation. The 100 epoch training took a couple of minutes.

Code 24.6.2 — Keras Regression. Fit the Network

```
model.compile(loss='mse',
              optimizer=RMSprop(),
              metrics=['mae'])

history = model.fit(X_train, y_train,
                    batch_size=batch_size,
                    epochs=epochs,
                    verbose=0,
                    validation_data=(X_test, y_test))
```

The online notebook shows a plot of the training which seems to indicate that better results may have been achieved with a larger number of epochs. The neural network got an rmse of around 52, which is significantly better than the rmse of 79 for the linear regression model. This is an example where complex and large data gets better results in a neural network over simpler models.

Code 24.6.3 — **Keras Regression.** Evaluation

```
score = model.evaluate(X_test, y_test, verbose=0)
print('Test rmse:', math.sqrt(score[0]))
print('Test mae:', score[1])
```

```
Test rmse: 52.44109884104499
Test mae: 34.402488708496094
```

How good is an mse of 52 on this data set? The range of PM2.5 values was up to 900, with a standard deviation of 92, so an rmse of 52 is not bad, but there is room for improvement. The mae is 34. The mae metric is more robust to outliers, which is evidenced here in having a lower value than the mse.

Exercise 24.1 — **Keras Regression.** With Boston Housing Data.
Build a Keras regression Sequential model on the Boston Housing Data. How did your results compare to linear regression?

Exercise 24.2 — **Keras Classification.** Using the Wine Data.
Build a Keras classification Sequential model on the Wine data set. How did your results compare to logistic regression?

24.7   Deep Architecture

The examples in this chapter so far have showed neural networks with 2 hidden layers similar to what we discussed in the last chapter but built with the Keras framework. Where Keras shows its power is in the varieties of architectures that you can build. Next we discuss convolutional neural networks, and recurrent neural networks.

24.7.1   Convolutional Neural Networks

Convolutional neural networks, convnets, work well with image data. The reason is the way these networks learn. A densely connected sequential layer will learn global patterns from the input data. In contrast, the convolutional layer will learn patterns in small 2D windows of the input data. This gives convnets two unique abilities. The first is that once a pattern is learned in one location it will recognize it when translated to another location. The second is that convolutional layers can learn spatial hierarchies. For example, a first convolutional layer could learn local features like edges and subsequent layers could learn how these edges and other features combine to form complex and abstract concepts like faces. This is amazingly powerful. Let's say the initial convolutional layer had an RGB channel from an image input as a 3D tensor. It could learn patterns from a subset of the input space and pass what it learned on to the next layer but now the channel will represent the filter through which it "sees" the input. To make this less abstract let's think of it in terms of the MNIST data where each sample is a single grayscale image of a handwritten digit of shape (28, 28, 1). The first convolution layer takes a small window size like 3x3 and slides this over the input image to create an output shape of (26, 26, 32) which represents a response map of the filter at different locations of the input. As the data passes through convolutional layers it is typically halved at each layer, so the 26x26 will become 13x13, and so on. This is called max pooling and its purpose is to carry forward what is important and leave the rest behind.

Figure 24.3 shows a simple visualization of the CNN process. The figure is just a screen shot of a spreadsheet filled with random numbers to represent a data matrix. The 4x4 window has already traveled over the first 4x4 elements, and has now moved one stride to the right.

0.47557	0.13031	0.26269	0.98775	0.54559	0.70388	0.41101	0.10889
0.25782	0.69232	0.53866	0.20306	0.01652	0.45732	0.49489	0.47130
0.87015	0.03241	0.00089	0.95473	0.25201	0.67926	0.66318	0.35740
0.13696	0.20884	0.20363	0.72029	0.26433	0.42732	0.87660	0.59141
0.51279	0.81518	0.50046	0.89543	0.77181	0.77192	0.45861	0.25983
0.03777	0.12560	0.54588	0.06574	0.31243	0.50573	0.60777	0.85029
0.82038	0.42600	0.16205	0.80647	0.10582	0.45355	0.59760	0.08356
0.71715	0.42875	0.85921	0.60168	0.92237	0.62636	0.71523	0.14542
0.09399	0.43249	0.84148	0.23740	0.30299	0.93350	0.03851	0.33104
0.30386	0.63560	0.72024	0.38294	0.78565	0.72367	0.52017	0.93030
0.97332	0.02479	0.31189	0.74439	0.62472	0.62113	0.13827	0.92139
0.85440	0.02045	0.41130	0.71335	0.07405	0.03085	0.43504	0.83417

Figure 24.3: Convolving

The term *convolution* refers to the mathematical process of combining two functions to create a new function. The new function will then be able to combine two sets of information. In a CNN layer, the convolution is performed on the inputs using a filter (sometimes called a kernel) to produce a feature map. The filter slides over the input and produces a feature map. This maps the input dimensional space to the output feature dimension space. The filter moves with overlap, rather than a tiled approach, which enables it to learn across the input space. The stride is the size of the filter step. The smaller the stride, the more overlap. The output feature dimensions will be smaller than the input dimensions, so padding is often used to keep the dimensions from shrinking.

A filter is basically a small numeric matrix with previously specified dimensions. Initially, the filter is filled with random numbers. The dot product of the filter matrix and the data it covers is computed and stored in a new matrix that is the output of the convolutional layer. The new output matrix is a new representation of the data. This output is passed to the next layer in the network. Multiple filters in a layer can be learning different features from the data.

Sometimes pooling layers are added between CNN layers. Pooling will reduce dimensions of the data, which will reduce the number of parameters that have to be learned, thereby shortening training time. Pooling can also reduce overfitting. One variation of pooling is max pooling, in which the maximum value a filter over a window is used for one value in the output window. For example, a 3x3 filter will take the max of the 9 values as the one output for that window. The max pooling is a new representation of the data. The intuition of the convolution followed by the max pooling is that the input data is reduced to extracted features.

The output of a convoluted layer will have smaller dimensions than the input layer. For a filter that is mxm, the input layer of nxn will be reduced to (n-m)x(n-m). Each layer will shrink the data dimensions. The filter does not convolve the edges as much as the inner portion of the data. With zero padding, border of zeros is added to the input to make the ouput the same size as the original input. The API will figure out the number of rows to add if you request zero padding. In Keras, the padding option of 'same' means the padding will be added to make the output size the same as the input size. This is zero padding. Another padding option is 'valid' padding which means no padding, that is, the output size will be smaller than the input size. The valid padding option is the default in Keras.

A notebook in the GitHub runs a CNN on the MNIST data. The CNN gets better results than the sequential model on this data set, but training does take longer. The code to set up the model is shown below:

Code 24.7.1 — **Keras.** CNN Model

```
model = tf.keras.models.Sequential([
    tf.keras.Input(shape=(28, 28, 1)),
    tf.keras.layers.Conv2D(32, kernel_size=(3, 3), activation="relu"),
    tf.keras.layers.MaxPooling2D(pool_size=(2, 2)),
    tf.keras.layers.Conv2D(64, kernel_size=(3, 3), activation="relu"),
    tf.keras.layers.MaxPooling2D(pool_size=(2, 2)),
    tf.keras.layers.Flatten(),
    tf.keras.layers.Dropout(0.5),
    tf.keras.layers.Dense(num_classes, activation="softmax"),
])
```

24.7.2 Recurrent Neural Networks

Recurrent neural networks can learn from sequential data like time-series or text. Text requires a bit of preprocessing to either one-hot vectors or word embeddings, a discussion of which is beyond our focus here. A recurrent neural network, RNN, has memory, state, which enables it to learn a sequence. The architecture of an RNN contains loops to revisit the state and learn sequences.

A problem with recurrent neural networks is the vanishing gradient problem, a problem that was identified early in the exploration of multi-layer neural networks. As you add layers, the gradient back propagated becomes smaller and smaller so that training is impossible. The Long Short-Term Memory (LSTM) algorithm is one method for avoiding vanishing gradients. The key is keeping the memory data path independent of the back propagation path and giving its own update mechanism.

Keras has three variants of the RNN: SimpleRNN, GRU, and LSTM. LSTM is the most powerful but also the most computationally expensive. GRU is a simpler alternative. In stacking RNN layers, each layer except the last should return the full sequence of outputs.

An online notebook gives an example of text classification on the IMDB movie data set. This is a sentiment analysis task. Three models are tried: a simple RNN, an LSTM, and a GRU.

24.8 Summary

The workflow for Keras involves these steps:
- Define the dimensions and characteristics of the train and test data tensors.
- Define the model.
- Compile the model with an appropriate loss function, optimizer, and metrics.
- Fit the model.
- Evalute the results.

You probably won't hit a home run the first time through these steps so changing some parameters and repeating the above steps may happen multiple times.

24.8.1 Going Further

The book to read is *Deep Learning with Python* by Francois Chollet, the chief developer of Keras. There is an R version of the book, and a Python version. The Python version is being updated to a second edition. Although you can use Keras in R, and it works well, this book only discussed the Python version, since more researchers are using Python for deep learning.

25. The Craft 7: Algorithms

In this handbook we have discussed a wide range of machine learning algorithms, but certainly not every algorithm currently being used, nor every algorithm being researched. An excellent book that will consolidate what you have learned about machine learning algorithms is Pedro Domingos' *The Master Algorithm*. The book is written for the general public to build interest in the field, but the book is interesting to machine learning researchers as well because of the way that Domingos organizes the material and provides his insight. Pedro Domingos is a researcher and professor at the University of Washington with decades of research in machine learning.

25.1 The Five Tribes

In his book (and in talks you can find on youtube), Domingos organizes all of machine learning into 5 "tribes":

- The Symbolists. Algorithm: Inverse deduction. Example: Decision Tree.
- The Connectionists. Algorithm: Gradient descent. Example: Neural Networks.
- The Evolutionaries. Algorithm: Genetic search. Example: Genetic Programming.
- The Bayesians. Algorithm: Probabilistic inference. Example: Naive Bayes.
- The Analogizers. Algorithm: Constraint optimization. Example: SVM.

There are many approaches in machine learning due to the inventiveness of researchers driven by the frustration that no algorithm performs well in all circumstances. In fact the *no free lunch* theorem[1] states that no algorithm will perform better than chance over all possible data and all possible things we seek to learn from the data. Given that bleak observation, it is

---

[1] http://www.no-free-lunch.org/coev.pdf

amazing that we can learn anything at all from data. Domingos goes on to suggest that all of these approaches could be unified in some type of master algorithm. Stay tuned, because he and others are researching this idea.

25.2 Choosing an Algorithm

Deciding which algorithm to use on a problem is not a straightforward decision. Even experienced researchers may try several algorithms on a problem before finding the one that works best with their data. The "best" algorithm depends on the nature of the problem, as well as the nature and the quantity of the data.

First, it should be straightforward to classify your problem into supervised learning if you have labeled data, unsupervised learning if your data is unlabeled and there is no way to get labels, or reinforcement learning if you want to train an autonomous agent. For unsupervised learning you are restricted to clustering algorithms so the branch of machine learning that has the most options in terms of algorithms is supervised learning.

In supervised learning, the next thing to consider is the nature of your data. Are you learning a regression or a classification task? Does your data follow linear trends or have linear decision boundaries? Then pick algorithms that "see" lines or those that search for irregular boundaries accordingly. Do you want to classify into a single class or multiple classes? Some algorithms classify multiclass labels well, for others you will have to use the one-versus-all approach. How much data do you have? Some algorithms like Naive Bayes perform well with a small amount of data but others like neural networks are unlikely to outperform simpler algorithms unless there is a lot of data and a complex problem to learn. Finally, you may try combining algorithms in an ensemble approach. Ensemble methods involve training multiple algorithms. Then, for each test example, take a majority vote of your classifiers.

VIII Part Eight: Modeling the World

Preface to Part 8

In Part 8 we look at algorithms from the field of AI that are used to model probabilistic variables, and/or environments. These methods do not fit into either the unsupervised or supervised branches of machine learning, and more properly fit into an AI course than a machine learning course.

- Bayesian Networks are graphical representations of conditional dependencies in data. Since the late 1980s they have been used in targeted domains such as medicine and economics where expert knowledge and Bayesian techniques combine for synergistic effect.
- Markov Models consists of states and transition probabilities that are linked together in a chain. In a Markov process, history has no meaning. All that matters is the current state and the transition probabilities to other states.
- A Markov Decision Process is built upon a Markov chain, but additionally has an agent that learns over time, thus changing the transition probabilities as it learns.
- Reinforcement Learning builds upon a Markov Decision Process by letting an agent learn not only the transition probabilities but learn about the states as well.

26. Bayes Nets

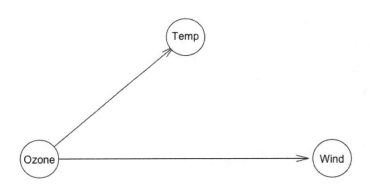

Figure 26.1: Airquality Bayesian Network

Bayesian networks, sometimes called belief networks, are unique in that they can be customized to encode not only Bayesian probabilities but also expert human knowledge. In turn, the network itself is highly interpretable. Figure 26.1 shows that Ozone is conditioned on Temp and Wind. Ozone is the parent node, Temp and Wind are child nodes. The absence of links can convey information as well. Notice there is no link between Temp and Wind. In a Bayes' network there are no target or predictor variables. Each node represents a random variable and arrows represent their probabilistic dependencies. A very important thing to keep in mind with Bayesian networks, is that the probabilistic dependencies should not be interpreted as causation. Rather, the algorithm is identifying correlations, not necessarily causations, in the data.

26.1 Bayes Nets in R

A Bayesian network is a directed acyclic graph as seen in Figure 26.1. The network was created with the code below. The bn.fit() function used below needs all the variables to be factors so first we subset the airquality data, removed rows with NAs, and converted them to binary factors with 1 meaning high and 0 meaning low. The text below the code example shows the conditional probabilities of the fit model.

Code 26.1.1 — **Bayesian Network.** Airquality data.

```
library(bnlearn)

f <- function(v){
  m <- mean(v)
  factor(ifelse(v>m,1,0))
}

df <- airquality[,c(1,3,4)]  # Ozone, Wind, Temp
df <- df[complete.cases(df),]  # omit rows with NAs

# turn quant variables into factors
df$Ozone <- f(df$Ozone)
df$Wind <- f(df$Wind)
df$Temp <- f(df$Temp)

# build the net
bn1 <- hc(df)
plot(bn1)

# find the conditional probabilities
fit_air <- bn.fit(bn1, data=df)
fit_air
```

The output is shown below:

```
Bayesian network parameters
Parameters of node Ozone (multinomial distribution)
Conditional probability table:
          0          1
0.6206897 0.3793103


Parameters of node Wind (multinomial distribution)
Conditional probability table:

   Ozone
Wind          0          1
   0 0.3611111 0.8181818
   1 0.6388889 0.1818182


Parameters of node Temp (multinomial distribution)
Conditional probability table:

   Ozone
Temp          0          1
   0 0.7222222 0.0000000
   1 0.2777778 1.0000000
```

26.1.1 Querying the Network

Once we have the conditional probabilities determined by the bn.fit() function, we can query the net. Two queries run at the console and the results are shown below.

```
> cpquery(fit_air, event=(Ozone==1), evidence=(Temp==1))
[1] 0.6833689
> cpquery(fit_air, event=(Temp==1), evidence=(Ozone==1))
[1] 1
```

The cpquery() function performs conditional probability queries on the network. Specifically, it estimates the conditional probability of an event given evidence, and returns this probability. In the first query above we wanted to know P(Ozone=1|Temp=1), in other words, what is the probability that Ozone is high given that Temp is high. The value was 0.68. The second query asked for P(Temp=1|Ozone=1) which was 1.0.

26.2 Bayesian Net Semantics

A Bayesian network is a directed acyclic graph (DAG). In order to discuss properties of the network we first review some terminology from graph theory.

26.2.1   Review of Graph Terminology

A graph is defined by $G = (V, A)$ where V is the set of nodes or vertices and A is the set if arcs, links, or edges that connect the notes. An arc $a = (u, v)$ connects nodes u and v. If the connection is undirected, the order of the vertices does not matter. If the connection (u, v) is directed, the head will be u and the tail will be v. In Bayesian networks, all of the arcs will be directed. In a directed graph, if there is a path from v_i to v_j then v_i is an ancestor of v_j, which is a descendant. The direct ancestor is called a parent. The direct descendant is a child. Graphs can be either cyclic or acylic. Bayesian networks are acyclic, they can have no cycles.

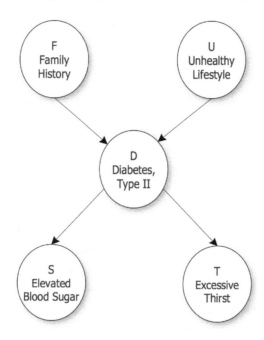

Figure 26.2: Bayesian Network

In Figure 26.2 we have a directed, acyclic graph, that provides an overly simple model of diabetes. We have 5 random variables: (1) F - a Yes/No variable for family history of diabetes, (2) U - a Yes/No variable for an unhealthy lifestyle, (3) D - Yes/No for a diagnosis of diabetes, (4) S - Yes/No for elevated blood sugar, and (5) T - Yes/No for excessive thirst.

26.2.2   Graph Structure

If two variables are independent, there will be no arc connecting them. Conditional independence is specified by the directed separation criterion (d-separation). The intuition behind d-separation can be seen in Figure 26.2. There is no direct path from F to S that does not go through D. D is said to d-separate F and S. Therefore, F is independent of S|D. This is denoted by: $F \perp\!\!\!\perp S|D$.

Directly following from the idea of d-separation is the Markov property of Bayesian networks. The Markov property for a Bayes Net states that there are no direct dependencies in the graph that are not shown explicitly. For example, the unhealthy lifestyle cannot affect frequent thirst except through diabetes. Again, keep in mind this is an oversimplified example and not necessarily consistent with medical research.

The structure of a Bayesian network implies that the value of a variable is conditioned only on its parent nodes:

$$P(x_1, x_2, ..., x_n) = \prod_i P((x_i|Parents(X_i)) \tag{26.1}$$

In the case of the sample diabetes graph, P(Thirst|Diabetes, Unhealthy) = P(Thirst|Diabetes). This indicates a conditional independence of variables.

26.2.3 Reasoning with Graphs

The DAG of the network factorizes the global probability distribution into a local probability distribution for each variable. The connections provide means of reasoning about the variables. Figure 26.2 illustrates four types of reasoning we can do with Bayesian networks:

- diagnostic - given the evidence of excessive thirst, the cause is likely diabetes; notice this traces the graph in a bottom-to-top direction
- predictive - given diabetes, it is likely that a person experiences excessive thirst; notice this traces the graph in a top-to-bottom direction
- intercausal - given a family history leading to diabetes, this may explain away an unhealthy lifestyle as a factor
- combined - given a family history leading to diabetes, this in turn predicts excessive thirst

26.3 The Algorithm

The algorithm used in the code sample above, hc(), is a hill climbing algorithm. Hill climbing has widespread application in AI. In simple hill climbing for Bayesian networks, we start with an empty graph. Each variable in the data is evaluated by a score function that quantifies how well the network with the added node would fit the data. The search through the variables is greedy, adding the variables based on the highest score. Metrics vary, including a posteriori probability, or Bayes Information Criterion (BIC). There are many variations of hill climbing in AI and machine learning.

Another algorithm available in bnlearn() is TABU search, a constraint-based greedy search. The tabu search performs hill climbing until it finds a local optimum. It then searches through the next best variables that it has not visited recently, i.e., that are not on the tabu list.

26.4 Example: Coronary Data

As another example of a Bayes' net, we look at the coronary data set in R. The data specifies risk factors for coronary thrombosis for men. The data set has 1841 observations and 6 variables, all of which are binary factors:

- Smoking - yes or no
- M. Work - yes or no for strenuous mental work
- P. Work - yes or no for strenuous physical work
- Pressure - <140 or >140 systolic blood pressure
- Proteins - <3 or >3 ratio of beta and alpha lipoproteins
- Family - neg or pos for patient's indication of family history

---

Code 26.4.1 — **Bayesian Network.** Coronary Data.

```
library(bnlearn)
bn_coronary <- hc(coronary)
plot(bn_coronary)
```

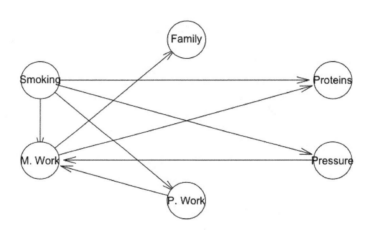

Figure 26.3: Bayesian Network for Coronary

Figure 26.3 shows the network for the coronary data. There are some links that make sense, such as Proteins being affected by smoking and mentally stressful work. There are other links that don't seem to make sense such as: Family being a child of mentally challenging work. We can list all links with "bn_coronary$arcs" at the console, and we see that the link we want to delete is the 7th one. We can remove this link as shown below.

```
bn_coronary$arcs <- bn_coronary$arcs[-c(7),]
```

Now if we replot, we see that the family node is still there but is not connected to any other node. Now we are ready to do some conditional probability queries.

```
> cpquery(fittedbn, event = (Pressure==">140"),
    evidence = ( Proteins=="<3" ) )
[1] 0.4310942
```

26.5 Summary

The term Bayesian Network was coined by Judea Pearl in 1985 to emphasize the Bayesian conditioning and the method for updating information. Judea Pearl was the 2011 winner of the ACM Turing Award.

Bayesian networks provide a graphical and highly interpretable representation of conditional probabilities in a data set. The examples in this chapter were for qualitative data but the bnlearn package can also handle quantitative data with a custom.fit() function rather than the bn.fit() function. Another package for Bayesian networks in R is DEAL, which provides several methods for using discrete or continuous variables.

26.5.1 Going Further

- Probabilistic Reasoning in Intelligent Systems: Networks of Plausible Inference. Judea Pearl. Morgan Kaufmann. 1988.
- Bayesian Networks with Examples in R. M. Scutari and J.B. Denis. Chapman & HallCRC. 2014.
- Bayesian Networks in R with Applications in System Biology. Nagarajan, M. Scutari and S. Lebre. Springer. 2013.
- Article by M. Scutari, the author of bnlearn: `https://arxiv.org/pdf/0908.3817.pdf`

27. Markov Models

27.1 Overview

A hidden Markov Model, or HMM, is a probabilistic model often used to model sequential events such as temporal patterns, predictive text, part-of-speech tagging, and much more. First we discuss the simpler case of a Markov Model where we can see all the states, then move on to discuss the hidden Markov Model for unseen states which have observable results.

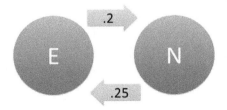

Figure 27.1: Markov Model for Two States: Exercise or Not

27.2 Markov Model

A Markov Model is a model for stochastic (random) processes. The model consists of a set of states and transition probabilities between states. The Markov assumption is that the probabilities for transition depend only on the previous state, not the entire string of preceeding states. Let's consider a simple system with 2 states modeling the likelihood that a person will exercise today, and is based on the observation a person made that if they exercised the day before they tend to exercise today, with .8 probability, but if something interferred with exercising the day before they tend to not exercise today either, with .75 probability. State E represents the exercising state and state N represents the not exercising state.

As we see in the Figure above, a person in state E stays in state E with .8 probability and moves to state N with .2 probability. Likewise a person in state N stays in state N with probability .75 and moves to state E with probability .25. Below we see some R code representing the initial state of having exercised 5 of 30 days, and the transition matrix.

```
Code 27.2.1 — Initial State. Representing Exercise or Not.

# build the transition matrix for the model
transMatrix <- matrix(c(.8, .25, .2, .75), nrow=2)
transMatrix  # output matrix
     [,1] [,2]
[1,] 0.80 0.20
[2,] 0.25 0.75
# represent the initial state in the exercise matrix
exercise <- matrix(c(5/30, 25/30), nrow=2)
          [,1]
[1,] 0.1666667
[2,] 0.8333333
```

Initially, the person had a poor exercise pattern, exercising 5 days out of 30, about 17% of the time. What happens after 6 iterations?

```
Code 27.2.2 — Markov Process. Six iterations.

for (i in 1:6){
  exercise <- transMatrix %*% exercise
  print(paste("exercise at i=", i, ":",
      format(round(exercise[1,], 2))))
}
[1] "exercise at i= 1 : 0.34"
[1] "exercise at i= 2 : 0.44"
[1] "exercise at i= 3 : 0.49"
[1] "exercise at i= 4 : 0.52"
[1] "exercise at i= 5 : 0.54"
[1] "exercise at i= 6 : 0.54"
          [,1]
[1,] 0.5447909
[2,] 0.4552091
```

We see above that E has higher and higher probability as the process iterates. This model stabilizes after only 6 iterations, so even if we iterate 5000 times we end up at about the same place: .555 and .444. It changes slightly at each iteration but stabilizes at these values.

27.3 Hidden Markov Model

The limitation of the Markov Model is that it only encodes what we know. There may be hidden, or latent, variables that influence our model. How can we discover these? Through hidden Markov models, HMMs.

Figure 27.2 shows the basics of a hidden Markov model. We only see the observed data X. We assume there is some latent variable Z that manifests X. Notice there are transitions from Z state to Z state horizontally. We do not know what the transition probabilities are, but a hidden Markov model can help us discover patterns that could have generated our data.

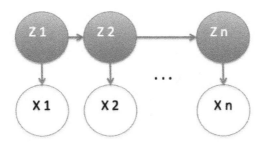

Figure 27.2: Hidden Markov Model

27.4 HMM in R

There are several packages that deal with HMM in R. We are going to look at depmixS4[1], a package by Visser and Speekenbrink. The package can generate mixture models including Markov models, hidden Markov models, and other mixture models. The documentation has several usage example. Below, we are going to continue our exercise model and see if we can detect a pattern in the data. First we load the depmixS4 package. Next we generate our observations. What we have are 7 transitions, one for each day of the week, and then we replicate that 10 times for 10 weeks. Interpreting the days in order, it seems that this person exercised (state 2) on Sunday and Saturday but not during the week.

Code 27.4.1 — HMM Fit the Model. Exercise Observations.

```
library(depmixS4)
#set of states
states <- c(2, 1) # E and NotE
n <- 140 # number of transitions (7 days, 10 weeks)
obs <-
   rep(c(c(2,2),c(2,1),c(1,1),c(1,1),c(1,1),c(1,1),c(1,2)),10)
```

Now that we have our observations, the Xs in Figure 27.2, we can let the algorithm find the transition probabilities. This is a 2-step process in this package. Step 1 creates the model

---

[1]https://cran.r-project.org/web/packages/depmixS4/vignettes/depmixS4.pdf

and Step 2 fits the model. Notice we also set a seed.

```
Code 27.4.2 — HMM Fit the Model. Exercise Observations.

# Start the HMM
set.seed(1234)
# 1. create the model
mod <- depmix(response = obs ~ 1, data=data.frame(obs), nstates=2)
# 2. fit the model
f <- fit(mod)
summary(f)
Initial state probabilties model
pr1 pr2
  1   0
Transition matrix
        toS1  toS2
fromS1 0.744 0.256
fromS2 0.100 0.900
```

We output the summary() above of the fitted model and displayed a portion of the output in the code box. Notice that the transition matrix was learned from the data. Now let's plot our results. First we extract the estimates from the fitted model. Then plot the actual observations over the estimates. Notice that the spikes of exercising (weekends) in the observations was matched by the estimates.

```
Code 27.4.3 — HMM continued. Extract Estimates and Plot.

estimates <- posterior(f)  # get the estimated state for each day
par(mfrow=c(2,1))
plot(1:n, obs, type='l', main='Observations, X')
plot(1:n, estimates[,2], type='l', main='Estimate')
```

27.5 Metrics

If we type the model name at the console we see the following:

```
> f
Convergence info: Log likelihood converged to within tol. (relative change)
'log Lik.' 4462.099 (df=7)
AIC:  -8910.198
BIC:  -8889.606
>
```

We are given information on the convergence, the log likelihood, AIC and BIC values. The AIC, Akaike information criterion, and BIC, Bayesian information criterion, are closely

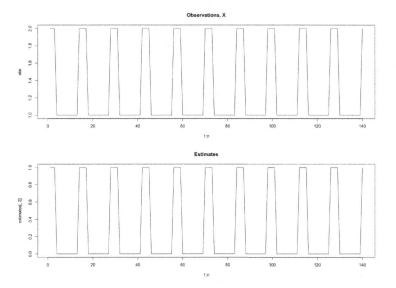

Figure 27.3: Observations and Estimates from HMM

related. AIC and BIC are typically used to select among models, here we only have one model. If we had more than one model and compared either AIC or BIC metrics, we would prefer the model with the lowest score. In, the standard formulas for AIC and BIC below, n is the number of observations, k is the number of parameters.

$$AIC = 2k - 2ln(\hat{L}) \qquad\qquad BIC = ln(n)k - 2ln(\hat{L}) \qquad\qquad (27.1)$$

27.6 The Algorithm

In the hidden Markov model, we have n observations, $X = (x_1, x_2, ..., x_n)$. We do not know the parameters, θ that generated our observations but we can estimate them. First, let us consider the likelihood of observing X given these unknown parameters.

$$p(X|\theta) = \sum_{z} p(X, Z|\theta) \qquad\qquad (27.2)$$

We can't really perform the summation directly in the above equation because we have N variables over K states. Our example above was binomial with K=2 but HMMs are often used for multinomial scenarios. We would need to calculate K^n terms, so this will grow exponentially with n. For this and other reasons, a direct solution is not feasible. Instead the EM, Expectation-Maximization algorithm is used to estimate a solution. In the application to HMM, the EM algorithm iteratively maximizes the expected joint log-likelihood of the parameters given the observations and states. That is the M step. The E step calculates expected values for the latent states given the observations and a set of initial states.

27.7 Another HMM in R

For this example we use the sp500 data set included in package depmixS4. First, let's load
the package and look at the data. The column of interest is the 6th column, logret, the log
ratio of the closing indices. For example the second row is 0.004 which can be calculated as
log(17.29/17.22) at the console. We took the ratio of the index of the previous month to
the current month, then the log. The range of this column is [-0.245, 0.15] and the mean (not
shown) is 0.0058.

Code 27.7.1 — HMM. S& P500 data

```
library(depmixS4)
data(sp500)
head(sp500)
range(sp500[,6])

> head(sp500)
            Open  High   Low Close  Volume       logret
1950-02-28 17.22 17.22 17.22 17.22 1310000   0.009921295
1950-03-31 17.29 17.29 17.29 17.29 1880000   0.004056801
1950-04-28 17.96 17.96 17.96 17.96 2190000   0.038018763
1950-05-31 18.78 18.78 18.78 18.78 1530000   0.044645411
1950-06-30 17.69 17.69 17.69 17.69 2660000  -0.059792966
1950-07-31 17.84 17.84 17.84 17.84 1590000   0.008443619
> range(sp500[,6])
[1] -0.2454280   0.1510432
```

Now that we have our data loaded and understand the data in column 6, we can run the
HMM algorithm and plot our results.

Code 27.7.2 — HMM continued. S& P500 data

```
# create the model, then fit
mod <- depmix(logret~1, nstates=2, data=sp500)
set.seed(1)
fmod <- fit(mod)

# plot
par(mfrow=c(3,1))
plot(posterior(fmod)[,1], type='l')
plot(posterior(fmod)[,2], type='l')
plot(sp500[,6], type='l')
```

The bottom graph is the actual column 6 data. The top model predicts the volatility going
down, the middle one going up. We can definitely detect volatile months in the sequence. The
sp500 data starts in February 1950 and ends in January 2012.

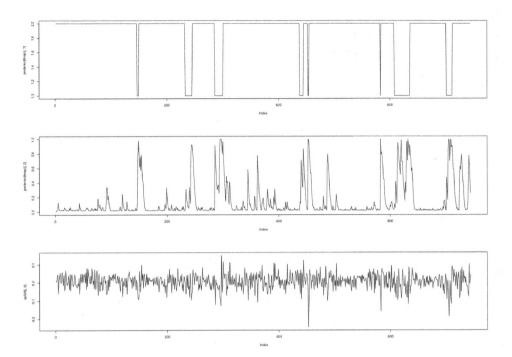

Figure 27.4: S&P 500 Data

27.8 Summary

In this chapter we explored hidden Markov models with package depmixS4. Another package worth investigating is seqHMM.[2] This package also outputs the transition probabilities in a graphical format.

The Markov of the Markov model is Andrey Markov, a Russian mathematician at the turn of the 20th Century. A Markov process assumes that future states depend only on the curent state, not states going back in time. A Markov chain describes a sequence of possible events in which the next state only depends on the current state. We saw a Markov chain in our first example of exercise or not exercise where we modeled these two states and the transition probabilities between them. HMMs are commonly used to model language, images, biological processes, virtually anything that is sequential in nature.

HMMs model hidden or latent variables that cause the observations. Variations of EM algorithms are often used to find optimal estimates for the latent variables and their transition probabilities. As we saw in the depmixS4 package, the algorithm discovers these probabilities and can output them for us.

A final thing to discuss is a Markov decision process. This is a Markov chain augmented with an action vector describing possible actions. This is often used in Reinforcement Learning, the subject of the next chapter.

---

[2]https://github.com/helske/seqHMM

27.8.1 Going Further

An excellent tutorial, *An Introduction to Hidden Markov Models and Bayesian Networks* is by Z. Ghahramani, and was published in the International Journal of Pattern Recognition and Artificial Intelligence[3].

---

[3]http://mlg.eng.cam.ac.uk/zoubin/papers/ijprai.pdf

28. Reinforcement Learning

Currently, Reinforcement Learning is a burgeoning field of AI, demonstrating success at improving self-driving cars, beating humans at the complex board game Go, optimizing data center energy usage, and much more. Reinforcement learning mimics how humans actually learn: a little trial and error, finding what works, and remembering. The reason that RL is taking off now is that it is being combined with deep learning. However in this chapter we discuss the traditional techniques of RL. OpenAI is providing a set of tools to widen participation in Deep RL. See this page: `https://spinningup.openai.com`

28.1 Overview

In previous chapters the focus was on learning from data for the purpose of either prediction or simply learning more about the data. In this chapter the focus shifts to learning how to act. We have a learner, an agent, who will learn to make decisions based on a utility function that keeps track of rewards earned for actions in different situations. The agent must learn to act under uncertainty, taking the action that most probably leads to a reward.

The core components of reinforcement learning are:
- an agent that interacts with the environment
- the environment, which is a set of predefined states, S
- a predefined set of actions, A, which the agent can take
- a set of rewards, R, that serve as reinforcement signals

The agent learns over many iterations of interaction with the environment. At each iteration, i, the agent observes the available states and selects an action. Based on the action chosen, the agent receives a numerical reward. After an action, a new set of states is available.

Learning, sometimes called Q-learning, relies upon remembering what was learned. The state-action function, $Q(s,a)$ defines the expected reward of each possible action for every state. A policy function $\pi^*(s,a)$, seeks to maximize the reward.

To jump-start learning, data in the form of sample state-action-reward sequences from which the agent learns can be fed into the learning algorithm. This *experience replay* can speed up convergence and help the agent learn faster.

28.2   The Markov Decision Process

In the last chapter we explored Markov Models which seem to have a lot in common with the reinforcement learning process described above. So what is the difference between RL and MDP? RL generally assumes there is some underlying Markov Decision Process, which it seeks to learn. In the MDP learning process, we know the states and possible actions at each time step, and the agent will receive a reward corresponding to the action chosen at the state. It is Markov in the sense that decisions consider only the current state, not previous states or actions. In Reinforcement Learning, the system may have to first learn the MDP. Another difference is that RL will try random actions in order to explore and learn new things beyond its current policy. So we can say that RL is an extension of the Markov decision process.

The Markov decision process is a 4-tuple <S, A, P, R> where S is the set of states, A is the set of actions, P() is a set of transition probabilities and $R(s, s', a)$ is the immediate reward for moving from state s to s' via action a. All of these are predefined. What we want to learn is the policy function $\pi()$ that maximizes a cumulative reward. More specifically, P() is:

$P(s, s', a) = Pr(s_{t+1} = s' | s_t = s, a_t - a)$

the probability that action a in state s at time t leads to state s' at time $t + 1$.

Learning the policy $\pi(s)$ means learning the optimal choice of action at that state in order to maximize the long-term reward. The reward is often discounted by a factor, gamma, that ranges from 0 to 1. This serves to disincentive immediate reward in favor of long term reward. The reward over the long term (possibly infinite) can be expressed as:

$$\sum_{t=0}^{\infty} \gamma \, R(s_t, s_{t+1}, \pi(s_t)) \tag{28.1}$$

How is the policy learned? It could be learned by linear or dynamic programming, more commonly the latter which we discuss here. One approach is to set up two arrays, V for rewards, and π for the policy. Both arrays are indexed by the state:

$$\pi(s) := argmax_a \sum_{s'} P_a(s, s')[R_a(s, s') + \gamma \, V(s')] \tag{28.2}$$

$$V(s) := \sum_{s'} P_{\pi(s)}(s, s')[R_{\pi(s)}(s, s') + \gamma \, V(s')] \tag{28.3}$$

These definitions above are recursively updated through algorithms such as dynamic programming.

28.3 Reinforcement Learning

Reinforcement learning is closer to how humans learn than the Markov decision process because when we learn, we have to learn everything: what actions we can take, what states we may end up in, and what rewards our actions bring. No one gives their baby walking lessons, they just figure it out, through trial and error and encouragement from those around him. RL gives a computational foundations to let an agent learn from experience. RL is automated, goal-directed learning.

As in MDP, we have a policy which specifies how the agent should act at a given state, a value function that focuses on cumulative reward over time, a reward function, and some means of encoding the environment.

28.4 The ReinforcementLearning Package

We are going to explore the ReinforcementLearning package in R, available in CRAN. The following example utilizes the tictactoe data provided in the package that consists of over 400K game states. The agent must learn the optimal actions for each state of the board. The reward is 0 for tie, +1 for win, and -1 for lose. The following code will take a few minutes to run.

```
Code 28.4.1 — Reinforcement Learning. TicTacToe

library(ReinforcementLearning)
# Load dataset
data("tictactoe")

# Define reinforcement learning parameters
control <- list(alpha = 0.2, gamma = 0.4, epsilon = 0.1)

# Perform reinforcement learning
model <- ReinforcementLearning(tictactoe, s="State", a="Action",
    r = "Reward", s_new = "NextState", iter = 1, control = control)

# Print optimal policy
head(policy(model))
```

You can dig further into the model at the console by typing model$ and pausing while the options pop up. For example, model$Reward lists the reward.

The three control parameters are for the behavior of the agent and all three range between 0 and 1 and have default values of 0.1.

- alpha - controls the learning rate; the lower the value the slower the learning; alpha=0 means nothing is learned
- gamma - discount factor determines the importance of future rewards; gamma=0 means that the agent only considers immediate rewards; gamma closer to 1 makes the agent work toward longer term rewards

- epsilon - exploration parameter, the probability that the agent will explore the environment through a random action;

There is another built-in sample experience, shown in the code block below.

Code 28.4.2 — Reinforcement Learning. Grid World

```
print(gridworldEnvironment)

# define states and actions
states <- c("s1", "s2", "s3", "s4")
actions <- c("up", "down", "left", "right")

# Generate 1000 iterations
sequences <- sampleExperience(N = 1000, env = gridworldEnvironment,
    states = states, actions = actions)

#Solve the problem
solver_rl <- ReinforcementLearning(sequences,
    s = "State", a = "Action",
    r = "Reward", s_new = "NextState")

#Getting the policy; this may be different for each run
solver_rl$Policy

#Getting the Reward; this may be different for each run
solver_rl$Reward
```

Printing the gridworldEnvironment shows the definition of the world. There are four states in a 2x2 arrangement with s1 and s2 over s2 and s3, respectively. The maximum reward is to get to s4. If you try to make a move that is not defined, you get minus 1 reward. The optimal policy, starting at s1, is to move down to s2, then right to s3, then up to s4. The policy at s4 will be different every time you run it unless you set a seed.

28.5 A Simple Python Example

Imagine a small environment seen in Figure 28.1. I credit Dr. Kathleen Swigger at The University of North Texas for the environment. The grid has dimensions 6x6. The agent has a start location and seeks to find a +1 location. Locations that are blank will have an initial reward of -0.01.

To find a path from start to the goal, initial states need to be represented:

- initialize a representation of the environment
- initialize q values based on the grid environment

Then try a number of runs:

goal ← False

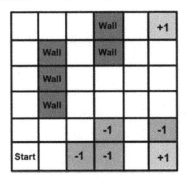

Figure 28.1: Sample Environment

while *NOT goal* **do**
    move ← pick_move
    make_move
    qvalues[*prior_location*] *← update_reward*
end while

A very simple implementation is in the GitHub and summarized below. This minimal working of example is used just to explain one way of implementing Q learning.

28.5.1 Initialization

An environment is read in from a simple text file that gives the dimensions (6x6). A Python list of lists represents the environment. All locations are initialized to a reward of -0.01. The initial [row, col] location is set.

Next, q-values are initialized. This 3D list is of size 6x6x4 because at each location, 4 moves (up, down, left, right) can be chosen. The q-values are initialized by looking at the reward in the environment for each possible move. There are two locations with +1 as the reward, and 4 with -1 as the reward. All others are -0.01.

28.5.2 Pick a move

For a number of runs, the goal is set to False. Then an iterative process picks moves, makes moves, and updates the q-values.

A function to pick moves considers the 4 possibilities: up, down, left, right. Moves that would go beyond the grid, into a wall, or back to 'start' are not considered. Then the possible moves are randomly shuffled. If there is only one possible move, that move is returned. If there are multiple possible moves, they are searched for the move that brings the highest reward. That move will be returned.

28.5.3 Make a move

A function to make a move simply updates row or col, depending on if the move was up, down, left, or right. The new [row, col] location is returned.

Machine Learning Handbook with R and Python © Karen Mazidi 2020

28.5.4 Update previous q-value

Now that a move has been made and a reward received, the previous location's q-value can be updated:

```
reward =  qvalues[oldrow][oldcol][index]
qvalues[oldrow][oldcol][index] = reward + gamma * max_next_reward
```

The gamma was set to 0.8. A lower gamma in the range [0, 1] encourages the agent to pay attention to more immediate rewards. Higher gammas make the agent more willing to find a greater delayed reward. Most implementations also include an alpha parameter for a learning rate. The alpha parameter determines to what extent new information overrides what was previously learned. Alpha ranges from [0, 1] where 0 ignores new information and 1 ignores old information.

28.5.5 Results

With this simple implementation, the agent was able to reach the goal in decreasing numbers of turns in each learning episode. Because there is some random selection, each run of the program is different but the following output is typical for parameter settings allowing up to 50 learning episodes and a maximum total number of moves of 250:

```
Goal! Reached in 20 moves.
Goal! Reached in 24 moves.
Goal! Reached in 22 moves.
Goal! Reached in 24 moves.
Goal! Reached in 17 moves.
Goal! Reached in 28 moves.
Goal! Reached in 25 moves.
Goal! Reached in 16 moves.
Goal! Reached in 21 moves.
Goal! Reached in 19 moves.
Goal! Reached in 21 moves.
Goal! Reached in 23 moves.
Goal! Reached in 19 moves.
Goal! Reached in 30 moves.
Goal! Reached in 21 moves.
Goal! Reached in 19 moves.
Goal! Reached in 16 moves.
Goal! Reached in 10 moves.
Goal! Reached in 10 moves.
```

28.6 Summary

Reinforcement Learning has deep roots in AI using Markov foundations and techniques such as dynamic or linear programming. The most exciting trend in RL is Deep Reinforcement

Learning which is allowing systems to scale to problems unimaginable with traditional approaches. An excellent surved of deep RL from an IEEE Special issue can be found here: `https://arxiv.org/pdf/1708.05866.pdf`.

Full book on dynamic programming and RL is availble here: `https://orbi.uliege.be/bitstream/2268/27963/1/book-FA-RL-DP.pdf`

28.6.1 **Going Further**

A nice survey of the field, from historic roots to current trends is provided in this MIT Technology Review article: `www.technologyreview.com`.

DeepMind is a British AI company acquired by Google in 2014. Read about innovations at DeepMind: `https://deepmind.com/blog/deep-reinforcement-learning/`.

29. Never Stop Learning

The field of machine learning is evolving rapidly and it is hard to keep up. Good sources of general information are magazines like Wired or the MIT Technology Review. These contain easy-to-digest material usually with links to the actual research. If you are interested in graduate school or in applying machine learning professionally, you need to go beyond information meant for the general public and read more academic research.

Because of the rapid pace of change in academic research, conference publications are often the best way to stay informed of current trends in machine learning research from top research institutions. There are specialized conferences for subfields such as IEEE CVPR for computer vision and pattern recognition, or ACL for natural language processing. The best conferences for a general view of the entire field in my opinion at this writing are:

- NIPS (Neural Information Processing Systems)
- ICML (International Conference on Machine Learning)
- SIGKDD (ACM Special Interest Group on Knowledge Discovery and Data Mining)
- AAAI (Association for the Advancement of Artificial Intelligence)

Reading conference papers takes time and effort. Gaining a full understanding often requires rereading and detours out to referenced papers to learn the background material. It helps to first understand that these papers generally have a common flow:

- Abstract - a brief overview of the claims of the paper.
- Introduction - a fairly short introduction to the problem being addressed and its significance to the research community.
- Prior Work - a thorough but concise summary of what has already been done by researchers.
- Proposed Work - the new work introduced in this paper along with descriptions of the

tools and data used.

- Results and Evaluations - some evaluation on how the new work presented in the paper outperforms prior work. Although negative results can be as informative as positive results, people are reluctant to publish their negative results.
- Conclusions - summary of the achievements of the research and discussion of ways it could be extended.

There is variation in the structure of academic papers but generally most will include these sections, variously worded. Papers accepted to top conferences such as those listed above have gone through a peer review process but you should still read papers with a skeptical eye. Authors presenting their research are understandably proud of their work. Sometimes the significance of the results are overstated. Other times the work is presented in such a way that it would be difficult to reproduce their results. There is a trend in conferences today of favoring papers that share code and data.

29.1 Machine Learning Trends

As an example of a machine learning paper written for a general audience, consider "Machine learning: Trends, perspectives, and prospects" by Michael Jordan of Berkeley and Tom Mitchell of CMU, which can be found here: `http://science.sciencemag.org/content/349/6245/255.full` in July of 2015. The paper presents a view from the field from two top researchers in machine learning.

The article reflects the view of machine learning that is found in Tom Mitchell's *Machine Learning* book, namely, that machine learning involves algorithms that improve performance with experience, and that a central concern in machine learning is the search for a theoretical framework that will describe how learning occurs for a given algorithm and volume of data. The article provides a high-level view of the algorithms discussed in this handbook and will consolidate your understanding of the field. Please read!

29.2 Inside the Black Box

It is often said that a neural network is a black box and it is true. Can you tell what exactly node 3 in layer 4 learned? An interesting article from MIT news (available here: `http://news.mit.edu/2017/reading-neural-network-mind-1211`) highlights some interesting research into this problem. The article also refers you to the 3 papers summarized for the article so that you can read the original research. One method of peeking into the black box is storing the output of each layer's neurons to train another neural network. In this way they can determine what each layer learned. Techniques such as this not only help researchers gain a better understanding of how neural networks learn but can enable them to modify the architecture of the networks to change what they are learning to better suit the problem.

29.3 Where to next?

In a 2019 interview with IEEE Spectrum magazine, Turing Award winner and deep learning innovator Yoshua Bengio assessed the current state of deep learning. Even with all the tremendous work in the last 20 years of deep learning, the intelligence of the systems is less than that of a two-year-old child. Elements of human intelligence that are missing include reasoning, planning, imagination, credit assignment and understanding of causality. Some critics use these limitations to criticize the deep learning field. However, Bengio believes that the tools that have been developed can take on some of these challenges. A 2017 paper by Bengio[1] entitled *The Consciousness Prior*, discusses issues related to these challenges.

---

[1]https://arxiv.org/abs/1709.08568

Part Nine: Supplementary Material

30. Big Data with R

Big data is often characterized by the 7 Vs: volume, velocity, variety, veracity, value, visualization, vulnerability. Actually, the lists such as these vary from 7 to 10 or more, but you get the idea. This section provides a brief introduction to options for dealing with big data in R, along with resources to point you towards further information.

30.1 Memory, Data and R

On Mac or *nix, R will use as much memory as it needs, given what is available. On Windows, you can check the limit with `memory.limit()` and change the size with `memory.size()`. This is important because by default, R loads all data into virtual memory. The amounts available depend not only on your hardware and operating system, but also on whether you have the 32-bit or 64-bit version installed. R uses two separate memory areas. Fixed-size objects called Ncells are stored in main memory and variable-sized objects called Vcells are stored on the heap. If you type `gc()` at the console, the garbage collection function will tell you how many cells you have of each type, with memory usage, and the garbage collection trigger threshold. In R, garbage collection is automatic but you can request it with gc() when you want, for example if you just removed a large object from memory with rm(). Here is a summary of some useful memory management console commands:

- ls() – list everything in memory
- rm(x) – remove x from memory
- rm(list=ls()) – remove everything from memory; caution!
- gc() – run the garbage collection function
- object.size(x) – find out how big x is

- memory.size() – find out how much memory you are using
- memory.limit() – find out the memory limit

Despite how you change your settings, a rule of thumb is as follows. Data up to one million rows can be handled in standard R. Data sets from one million to a billion rows can be processed in R with some effort. Data over a billion rows will need to be handled with map reduce algorithms, combining R and Hadoop or some other platform. If the data you want to work with is too large, you can try the following:

- Make the data smaller. Try working with a subset of the data until you have your code written, then expand to all the data. Hopefully from the source of the data you can get a subset, especially if you can export a portion with SQL or other software. See the next chapter about sampling.
- Get more power. Increase your RAM, get a new computer, or try cloud computing services.
- Try MapReduce with package mapReduce.
- Try BigR with Amazon AWS or RStudio in Google Cloud.

30.1.1 Limit Data Size

You can limit the amount of data you read in by limiting the number of rows or limiting the number of columns. Limiting the number of rows can be done with various subsetting techniques or random selection from the full data, then remove the full data from memory. When reading in data with functions such as read.csv() you can use the `colClasses` argument to prevent reading in columns you don't want. The format is simple:

```
df <- read.csv("biggie.csv", colClasses = c("Name","City","Zip"))
```

30.2 Subset Data Base with dplyr

Let's say you are hired as a summer data science intern. You are excited to be working with a real data scientist on some big data. One week into the internship, your data scientist mentor is called away to another project in another city and tells you as she walks out the door, "Just see what you can get done while I'm gone." Oh my.

Before panic mode sets in, take a deep breath. You are working in an R environment and last week your supervisor asked you to go through the Big R materials at `https://www.rstudio.com/resources/webinars/working-with-big-data-in-r/`. You learned that based on RStudio's discussion with clients, there are some common steps that big data exploration projects commonly go through:

- Clarify - become familiar with the data
- Develop - create a working model
- Productize - automate the work so that it can be updated and reproduced by others
- Publish - share with others

So, starting at the beginning, you want to learn more about the data. But it's really big and stored on a server. It won't fit on your computer. Why not subset it for exploration purposes, and you can scale up later? This is actually a common approach to big data.

There are many R packages that function as an API to data stores, such as dplyr, DBI, RHadoop, SparkR, and more. Typically companies use RStudio Server Pro, although there is an open source version. A nice feature of R is that you can use dyplr on the front end for data wrangling and the back in can plug into many different formats such as databases through a SQL interface. There are many functions that can be used to connect to the database such as src_postgres, src_sqlite, src_mysql, and so forth, that use the language of your data base.

The tutorial referenced above gives example code for building SQL code to select data from a remote data base, then subset by 1% to give a sufficient amount of data to build a working model. How to you eat an elephant? One bite at a time. Likewise you will slice a portion of the data to go through steps one and two to learn about the data and build a working model to impress your supervisor when she gets back to town.

30.3   The ff Package

The `ff` package provides a way to have your big data on disk while processing it a section at a time in RAM. To use the package, you must `install.packages("ffbase")` and this will install everything you need. The ff package effectively swaps pages from the disk file into RAM in the background so that it will appear to your script that the file is all in RAM. We are going to discuss a few examples below. To learn more, read the full documentation for the package, available here: `https://cran.r-project.org/web/packages/ff/ff.pdf`.

30.3.1   Read in the data

The code below shows that we have to load the ff package first, then we can read in our csv. This csv file was downloaded from Kaggle, from the PUBG video game match data. Using the arg VERBOSE=TRUE lets you know how it's progressing on the file. Otherwise you might think it hung up on a large file. This file took about 10 minutes to load, 667 seconds to be more precise, on a 2013 MacBook with 8G RAM. The file on disk is 1.74 GB on disk, yet the R environment pane tells me that d is a large ffdf object of 12 elements and size 395.8 Mb. This indicates the fact that it is working on a chunk at a time. The R notebook is not available on the github because this data set belongs to Kaggle, it is not in the public domain.

```
Code 30.3.1 — ff.  Read in data

require(ffbase)
d <- read.table.ffdf(file="kill_match_stats_final_0.csv",
   FUN="read.csv", header=TRUE, VERBOSE=TRUE, na.strings="")
```

Now that we have object d loaded, we can do a few data exploration tasks. First, we ask R what kind of object it is, and it tells us it is a "ffdf" object. The dimensions are 11,653,619 rows and 12 columns, which would definitely not fit in RAM on the computer we used. Notice that you can use the same R functions we are used to such as dim(), but in the case of str() we chose to subset it.

```
Code 30.3.2 — ff. Data Exploration

class(d)    # ffdf
dim(d)      # 11,653,619 x 12
str(d[1:10,])
```

```
'data.frame': 10 obs. of  12 variables:
 $ killed_by        : Factor w/ 57 levels "AKM","AWM","Bluezone",..
 $ killer_name      : Factor w/ 2394678 levels "#unknown","18cmGirl",..
 $ killer_placement : num  5 31 43 9 9 26 12 27 40 25
 $ killer_position_x: num  657725 93091 366921 472014 473358 ...
 $ killer_position_y: num  146275 722236 421624 313275 318340 ...
 $ map              : Factor w/ 2 levels "ERANGEL","MIRAMAR": 2 2 2
 $ match_id         : Factor w/ 128728 levels ,...
 $ time             : int  823 194 103 1018 1018 123 886 137 89 117
 $ victim_name      : Factor w/ 3924033 levels "#unknown","0219i",...
 $ victim_placement : num  5 33 46 13 13 47 15 38 47 43
 $ victim_position_x: num  657725 92239 367304 476646 473588 ...
 $ victim_position_y: num  146275 723375 421216 316758 318419 ...
```

Here are a few more data exploration examples, with the results shown in the comments. First, we asked how many rows indicate a location of MIRAMAR instead of the other location ERANGEL. Then we discovered than the range of time values was 28 to 2374. Finally, that we have about 2 million unique killers out of 11 million rows.

We can also create graphs from the full data set with a little help from the cumulative sum function.

```
Code 30.3.3 — ff. Plots

par(mfrow=c(2,1))
hist(cumsum.ff(d$victim_placement, na.rm=TRUE)[1:8], main="")
hist(cumsum.ff(d$killer_placement, na.rm=TRUE)[1:8], main="")
```

Finally, we subset the data to a smaller object so that we can run some algorithms on the smaller data before working in all the data.

```
Code 30.3.4 — ff. Subset

i <- sample(nrow(d), 1000, replace=FALSE)
small_d <- d[i,]
dim(small_d)  # 1000 x 12
head(small_d, n=2)
```

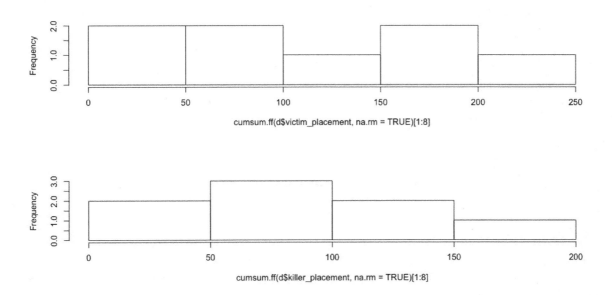

Figure 30.1: Residuals Plot for lm3

	killed_by <fctr>	killer_name <fctr>	killer_placement <dbl>	killer_position_x <dbl>	killer_position_y <dbl>	map <fctr>	▶
5312002	S1897	SkipToMyLouuu_	20	358210.1	261712.9	MIRAMAR	
7298565	Down and Out	wosaaas	39	686839.0	460346.1	ERANGEL	

2 rows | 1-7 of 12 columns

Figure 30.2: Residuals Plot for lm3

30.4 Amazon Cloud Services

If you have an Amazon account, you can go to Amazon web services `https://console.aws.amazon.com` and look at the options under Machine Learning. Not all of the tutorials are free and the costs of AWS services varies depending on what you are doing, so tread carefully.

One option for big data in the cloud in R is sparklyr, an R interface to Spark. Apache Spark is an open source platform for big data. Spark is fast and is designed to play nicely with R, SQL, Python, Java and Scala. Spark can run stand-alone or in the cloud, on Hadoop, Apache Mesos, Kubernetes and more, and can input diverse data sources. The R package `sparklyr` connects to Spark from R and provides a dplyr backend. One approach to big data with sparklyr would be to scale down big data to download on a machine for use in R. Another approach is to use Spark's distributed machine learning library if you want to keep your big data in the cloud. Amazon EMR is a big data service on AWS that provides Spark (as well as other big data applications). A tutorial for AWS Spark using R is available here: `https://aws.amazon.com/blogs/big-data/running-sparklyr-rstudios-r-interface-to-spark-on-amazon-emr/`. The code should look very familiar, there are just a few extra things to do in the AWS CLI to get set up. Before you get started you have to install the CLI on your computer so you can control your AWS from the terminal. You can find information on the CLI in Amazon.

In addition, RStudio maintains a page about Cloud Services that includes instructions for AWS: `https://tensorflow.rstudio.com/tools/cloud_server_gpu.html`

30.5 Google Cloud Services

Google calls their cloud service Google CloudML. As of this writing they are working on support for RStudio. RStudio maintains information about Google Cloud here: `https://tensorflow.rstudio.com/tools/cloudml/articles/getting_started.html`

30.6 Big Data: A Sham?

In a recent article[1], Brian Millar observes that while the big players are collecting and keeping big data, they don't actually use that much of it. He quotes ex-Googler Seth Stephens-Davidowits as saying "At Google, major decisions are based on only a tiny sampling of their data. you don't always need a ton of data to find the right insights. You need the right data." The article goes on the discuss the merits of sampling big data and running analysis on that sample, rather than forcing oceans of data through the straw. Sampling is the topic of the next chapter. The article referenced here is definitely worth reading, as is the book he mentions by Stephens-Davidowits, *Everybody Lies: Big Data, New Data, and What the Internet Can Tell Us About Who We Really Are.*

---

[1]https://www.fastcodesign.com/90168426/big-data-is-a-sham

31. Sampling Big Data

The data sets used through the book are small enough to fit into memory without using any of the special techniques described in Chapter 20. If you are tackling big data, an alternative to using the approaches described in the previous chapter is to use sampling. The technique of *sampling* is used in statistics to estimate characteristics of a large population by selecting a representative subset and determining characteristics of the subset. A thorough coverage of sampling is beyond the scope of this handbook. However, we can discuss a few key elements of sampling to give background information for those who will be working with data scientists and statisticians.

Figure 31.1: The Concept of Sampling

31.1 What is Sampling?

Sampling is a thoroughly researched topic in statistics that was used because data collection was expensive. For example, calling people for political surveys. With big data, the collection is already done, but how can we go about analyzing it? Again, sampling to the rescue. By cutting the data down to size, its analysis becomes easier. And by size we mean rows, the number of observations. There are also techniques for cutting down columns, such as dimensionality reduction techniques like PCA discussed in other chapters.

There are many, many approaches to sampling. Throughout the book, when we divided our data sets into train and test, we used random sampling. Each observation had an equal chance of being selected. Another common approach is to use stratified sampling, which involves dividing data into k buckets and making sure each bucket is represented in the sample. As a simple example, let's say we want the mean income in a data set. We can take the weighted mean of each of k buckets to estimate mean income of the population:

$$\frac{n_1 \bar{X}_1 + n_2 \bar{X}_2 + ... + n_k \bar{X}_k}{\sum_i^k N_i}$$

(31.1)

31.2 Sampling Example

An online notebook for this chapter demonstrates a sampling example using a kaggle data set on credit defaults. The data set has 30K observations and we included 11 variables. The distribution of our target column, default, has 22% of the examples with default = true. This data is not "big" by any stretch of the imagination but it demonstrates techniques that could be used on big data. We approach this data set with two primary quesions: (1) does sample size matter? and (2) does having an unbalanced data set matter?

First, we randomly divided the 30K examples into 80% train and 20% test. Running logistic regression on the full data set resulted in an accuracy of 80%. This is the "Full Data Set" row in Table 31.1, which shows accuracy, sensitivity and specificity. Recall from earlier in the book that sensitivity is the percentage of accurately classified positive examples (default=false) and that specificity is the percentage of accurately classified negative examles (default=true). For the second experiment, we randomly sampled 1000 observations from the 30,000 and divided this into an 80-20 split. This is shown in the second row of the table below. The sensitivity was about the same but there is a marked improvement in specificity and thus overall accuracy. The confusion matrix for this run shows that only 19% of the test cases were defaults compared to 23% of the test cases in the full data set example, which could partially account for the improvement in accuracy. For our third example we used the createDataPartition() function in package caret to make sure our test examples contain a percentage of default cases simlar to the entire data set. We got identical results as in the random sampling. Finally, we limited the number of default and no-default cases to 5000 each, trained the algorithm on this equally split data, and tested on the same test data as row 1. The results are a decrease in accuracy. Sensitivity dropped by 25% but specificity increased by 14%, resulting in an overall accuracy decrease of 9%.

A 2012 article by Crone and Finlay from the International Journal of Forecasting[1] can help us answer our earlier questions about sample size and balanced data. The authors note that expert opinion on sampling credit data is that 1500 instances of each class is sufficient and that biased data sets should be balanced. From our own experiment above we see that

---

[1]https://doi.org/10.1016/j.ijforecast.2011.07.006

Sample	Accuracy	Sensitivity	Specificity
Full Data Set	80%	97%	23%
1000 Data Set	84%	96%	36%
Full Stratified	80%	97%	23%
50-50	71%	74%	59%

Table 31.1: Results from Sampling Variations

the larger data did not perform better than a smaller subset and that balancing the data set resulted in decreased accuracy. The authors experimented with various sample sizes on logistic regression, discriminant analysis, decision trees and neural networks on two different data sets. The authors found that more data than the recommended 1500 per class improved accuracy, but not for logistic regression which does not required large amounts of data for optimal performance. Regarding data balancing, they found that oversampling the minority class is preferred to undersampling the majority class across all algorithms. Again, they note that logistic regression is robust to the data distribution so such sampling would not be of benefit for that algorithm.

Another examination of balancing data is found in a blog post[2] by Nina Zumel of Win-Vector LLC, a data science firm from San Francisco. Three algorithms were compared: regularized logistic regression, randomForest, and soft-margin SVM. Her results also showed that logistic regression performance was worse with a more balanced data set. SVM degraded only slightly and random forest improved but it was the lowest-performing algorithm across all samples of the data.

31.3 Current Practices

So what do data scientists and statisticians usually do with big data? A 2017 paper by Rojas et al.[3] gives insight into what data scientists are currently doing. A total of 22 data scientists working at companies like Google, Microsoft, etc. were surveyed. The survey results showed that the majority used random sampling, stratified sampling and sampling by hand. Although other sampling techniques may help data scientists gain more insight into data, they tend to not be used because the data scientists were not exposed to these ideas in their formal education and because of concerns that different sampling techniques might introduce bias. The hypothesis of the paper, confirmed by their results, was that data scientists could gain better insight into data if they used multiple sampling techniques rather than one. An experiment was conducted to probe what insights data scientists glean from 4 different sampling techniques:

- random sampling
- density sampling
- uncertainty sampling

---

[2]http://www.win-vector.com/blog/2015/02/does-balancing-classes-improve-classifier-performance/
[3]http://www.rosenthalphd.com/papers/RosenthalRojas_LDAV17.pdf

- QBC query by committee

The results of the experiment indicate that data scientists will gain additional insights by using more than one sampling technique because they each have their strengths and weaknesses. Density sampling filters out outliers to enable seeing general trends more clearly. QBC looks at features near the separating boundaries of classes, thereby highlighting features that do not indicate general trends. Uncertainty sampling focuses on outliers and the features signifying outliers. Using these techniques in addition to the current practice of random sampling gives data scientists additional insights.

Glossary

accuracy a metric to evaluate classification results; the percentage of accurately classified observations.

additive assumption in linear regression, the assumption that each predictor contributes to the model independently of the other predictors.

Akaike informaton criterion a measure based on the model fit typically used to compare models.

anova analysis of variance; often used to compare models to determine which model reduced variance in the residuals.

array multi-dimensional data structure with elements of the same type.

AUC area under the ROC curve; the closer to 1.0 the better.

bagging bootstrap aggregation; repeatedly sampling data to offset variance.

bias a tendency of an algorithm to make assumptions about the shape of the data; part of the bias-variance tradeoff.

classification supervised machine learning task in which the target is a qualitative variable.

Cohen's Kappa a measure of classification accuracy that adjusts for chance correct predictions.

conditional probability P(X|Y) is the probability of X, given Y.

confounding variables variables that correlate with both the target variable and one or more predictor variables.

correlation a measure of how changes in one variable are associated with changes in a second variable; similar to covariance but scaled to be in the range [-1, +1].

cost function a function used to measure the loss in accuracy of a model during training;

often expressed as the summed loss over all instances.

covariance a measure of how changes in one variable are associated with changes in a second variable.

CRAN Comprehensive R Archive Network, the source for R distributions, packages, documentation and more.

cross validation a technique of dividing data into subsections so that repeated train and test runs can be made.

curse of dimensionality the phenomenon of algorithms unable to perform in high dimensions.

data frame a 2-dimensional data structure in which each column can be of a different type.

discriminative classifier a classifier that directly estimates $P(Y|X)$.

dummy variables extra variables added to data by R to encode multiple values for qualitative data.

entropy a measure of how similar or diverse observations are.

error rate the percentage of misclassified observations; it is 1 - accuracy.

F-statistic a measure of the strength of the relationship between the predictors and the target variable; usually paired with a p-value.

factor an R data construct that encodes a qualitative variable internally as integer values but also as character values for human readability.

feature one attribute or predictor of data, often a column in a data set.

feature engineering modifying data to make algorithms perform better.

generative classifier a classifier that estimates parameters for $P(Y)$ and $P(X|Y)$.

Gini index a measure of node or cluster purity.

gradient descent an algorithm for finding extrema of a convex function by iteratively taking steps indicated by the gradient (slope) until the extrema is found.

hyperparameter hyperparameters are tuning parameters that are external to the model and often optimized experimentally.

information gain a measure of the reduction in entropy.

interaction effect in linear regression, the situation where predictors have some kind of influence on each other.

joint probability $P(X,Y)$ is the probabiilty of X and Y.

kernel methods methods which map data into another space by using the kernel trick of running data through a transformation.

LDA, linear discriminant analysis a dimensionality reduction technique that seeks linear cominations of predictors for each class that maximize class separation while minimizing within-class deviation.

likelihood likelihood as used in Bayes probability, is the probability of the observed data given the parameters.

linear regression an algorithm that predicts a real-valued target from quantitative and/or qualitative predictors; simple linear regression has one predictor; multiple linear regression has more than one predictor.

list an ordered collection of objects not necessarily of the same type.

log odds the log of the odds ratio.

logistic function a function with an S-shaped curve that inputs real values and outputs values in the range [0, 1].

logistic regression supervised machine learning task in which the target is a qualitative variable.

loss function a function used to measure the loss in accuracy of a model during training; often expressed as the loss on a single instance.

machine learning algorithms that discover patterns in the data.

matrix a 2-dimensional data structure with elements of the same type.

mse mean squared error a measure of closeness of fit of data points to a regression line; computed as the average of the squared residuals.

observation one data example or instance, often a row in a data set.

odds the ratio of positive outcomes to negative outcomes.

overfitting a phenomenon when training data fits the model so well that the model is not able to generalize to new data.

p-value a measure of evidence against the null hypothesis; example: p less than 0.05 is often presented as evidence against the null hypothesis.

package a set of functions and data with a particular statistical, graphical, or other focus; packages are available from CRAN.

polynomial linear regression an algorithm that predicts a real-valued target from quantitative and/or qualitative predictors in which one or more predictors are of degree higher than one.

posterior probability as used in Bayes probability, the posterior probability is the likelihood of the positive class given the data.

prior probability as used in Bayes probability, the prior probability is the probability distribution of the classes.

probability the percentage of positive observations to the entire number of observations.

qualitative data that takes on one of a finited set of values such as male or female, also called categorical data.

quantitative data that takes on any value in the real numbers.

R-squared a measure of how closely the data fits the regression line in the range [0, 1]; the closer to 1 the better the fit.

regularization constraints placed on a model during training.

reproducible research research that is well documented and verifiable by others.

residual the errors in a linear model; may be positive or negative.

ridge regression also called l2 regularization; ridge regression squares the regularization term.

rmse root mean squared error the positive square root of the mse mean squared error.

ROC Curve a visual metric which shows the true positive rate plotted agains the false positive rate.

RSS residual standard error a measure of the variance in the residuals; if the RSE=0 then the model fit the data perfectly.

RSS residual sum of squares the sum of the squared residuals.

sensitivity a measure of the true positive rate in evaluating classification results.

sigmoid function see logistic function.

specificity a measure of the true negative rate in evaluating classification results.

supervised learning machine learning scenario in which data is labeled and the task is to learn to predict labels.

SVM Support Vector Machine is an algorithm that can be used for regression or classification.

test data data used for evaluating an algorithm after training; test data is not seen by the algorithm during training.

training data data processed by the algorithm during training.

underfitting a phenomenon when training data does not fit the model well perhaps due to an overly simple model.

unsupervised learning machine learning scenario in which data is not labeled and the task is to find patterns in the data.

variance a tendency of an algorithm to vary widely with different training data; part of the bias-variance tradeoff.

vector a sequential data structure with one or more elements of the same type.

Index